FALLING UP FROM THE BOTTOM

©2023 Samantha De La Vega

Printed by Community Printers in
Santa Cruz, CA

Set in Farson Solid, Minion Pro, and Wilden

Editing, cover design and layout by
Nick Jaina

Developmental work by
Lura Frazey

www.samanthadelavega.com

FALLING UP FROM THE BOTTOM

SAMANTHA DE LA VEGA

Mama, 2004

Introduction	1
1. The Fall	3
2. Losing Mama	9
3. Farmed Out	29
4. There Be Monsters	35
5. Life with The Duchess	43
6. Beside Myself in The Big Apple	67
7. In The Weeds	97
8. Time to Go, and The Inimitable Alfonso de la Vega	117
9. From Culiacan to the Cat House	131
10. Simon's Rock	153
11. Heroin	161
12. Whitey and the Fräulein	205
13. Mexican Rehab in Two Parts	215
14. Homeward Bound	237
15. Saving Sammy	259
16. New Life	271
17. One Last Haul	281
18. Carmen's Story	285
19. Make it Stop	299
20. Keep Going	309
21. And Finally	315

Soul of the Night

The soul of the night weighs upon me
a shroud, a veil, a thick, thick blanket
the black heaves and swells around me,
nudging me like an ox on the road,
clomp clomping, fur thick with dirt
The night is an ox.
It is the breath and the scent of animal
under coarse dusty fur
a quiet companion and a fearsome ocean,
watery depths big, bigger than me
holding me up, tossing me atop its rocking surface
brushed by wind and rain
becoming bigger and stronger
and then calming once again
under the warmth of the sun.
The night is a giraffe, a docile beast,
long tongued plant eater, a lumbering beauty
It is all these things and nothing.
I lie in its heaviness, crowded in the silence,
the fears of a thousand years flickering past my eyes,
brushing through my hair.
No beginning and no end,
eternal, reborn in every moment
harsh like evolution.

—SdlV

INTRODUCTION

It was my mother who started this whole thing, so it is with my mother that I begin. I lost her at an early age, just when I needed her the most. My ideas about the world were forming, and she was my comfort. And then she was taken from me.

When I think of my mother's patience, I think of my friend Anya, who will paint a beautiful canvas with acrylic paint and, when it is nearly finished, she sprays water on it. She leaves the room, has a sandwich, goes for a walk, and then she comes back to see forms appearing in her work, the wildness overtaking her painting. She repeats and repeats this process, building out the emerging forms and letting the artwork take shape through forces outside of her. She is the catalyst, but the work creates itself. What strength it must take to let your creations potentially fall apart without your intervention.

My mother had no choice in who brought her up. She

had no choice in the stepfather that would come into her life and separate her from her own mother, and she had no choice in the society that locked women up for being inconveniently rebellious against the rules of social engagement. My mother has always done the unpopular thing by walking a line traced out by her own compass.

She paid dearly for it. She was ostracized for her incredible beauty and her deep sensitivity. She cannot tell a lie to save her life, which creates awkwardness in social situations where little fibs can help smooth things over. She knows no other way than to be true. Even her own children lose patience with the carefulness she takes in forming every word. "Get it out, Mama, just say it!"

Mothers paint the canvas, they spray water on it, and then need to have the patience to watch the forms develop. All of the wild stuff—all of the good parts—comes from their strength in stepping back and letting everything develop. Sometimes they step back too far. Sometimes they feel regret at how wild their creations have become.

None of this would have been possible without my mother.

CHAPTER 1
THE FALL

When there's an emergency at the Dakota in New York City, you don't call an ambulance. You call the front desk. That's just the way it is. In the 1960s, the front desk was managed by a kindly woman with frizzy hair named Winnie, and a small troop of on-call maintenance guys led by a fellow named Nate, who was a wiry man with a kind face and grey hair, and who did not happen to be freaked out by much, including screaming children, horrible accidents, or blood.

Between March 15th and 23rd of 1967, 15 inches of snow fell on New York City and temperatures were 15 degrees below average. My mother, sister, and I lived a simple life in apartment number 97, one of the tiny plain suites originally built for the staff of the inhabitants of the more opulent apartments below. In other words, we lived in the servants' quarters.

Mama would make us breakfast in the impossibly cramped two-foot-wide kitchen, washing dishes as she went in order to save space. Then she would set us down on the floor to play while she busied herself washing diapers in the bathroom sink, ducking in and out of the living room to check on us while tidying up our toys so no one would step on them. Our downstairs neighbors included the likes of Lauren Bacall, Jason Robards, Roberta Flack, and my grandmother, Elena Karam, a Broadway and film actress who had a flat in apartment 9 on the first floor. Later, in 1973, John Lennon and Yoko Ono moved into their Studio One apartment a few doors down the hall.

My grandmother had rented number 97 to help out my mother after a tumultuous separation from my father, who was a charismatic and explosive Mexican actor, restaurateur, and designer from a wealthy family. She had met him in Puerto Vallarta, where he danced on tables in restaurants he owned wearing clothing he had designed. One night he grabbed my mother and pulled her up there with him and she immediately fell in love. But after I was born, things had gone terribly wrong and she left him.

And so there we were, wedged into a tiny kitchen, in a living space created for the rich to stash the people they wanted to pretend were invisible.

When I grew up, I became a rock climber, and therefore I know what it's like to fall. That momentary recognition that it's too late. The gamble that didn't pay off. When you thought you could do something and your center of gravity spills over into a horrifying realization.

My first adventures in climbing were in trying to scale anything in that tiny apartment at the Dakota. When I had exhausted all the furniture, I looked up at the bars on the windows and thought it could be a new adventure.

On that unusually cold winter night in 1967 inside

the blackened medieval walls of the Dakota, I changed the course of my family's life forever. The room was warm as my sister and I played on a small blanket on the floor. Gaby was bigger than me and she had a penchant for hoarding toys. She and I argued while my mother busied herself cleaning diapers in the bathroom. And it was then that, growing weary of the battle with my sister, I set my sippy cup down and crawled across the floor, my chubby knees gathering dirt as they slid. I grabbed a wooden chair beside the table and pulled myself up to a standing position. Gaby looked to the bathroom door, as she wondered if my mother were going to come back anytime soon.

I continued on. I was on a mission to see my moon and star friends out the window. I threw my right leg up and flopped my weight onto the chair, grabbing the back and heaving myself up. Kneeling, I set my hands on the table. The moon was still waiting for me. The stars blinked. I could see Gaby now as she brushed her hair out of her face—that one strand that kept tickling her nose—and watched me with slightly concerned curiosity. I had been a frustrating and forceful baby sister since she had first met me, taking attention and grabbing at her toys. But this was different.

I grabbed the first iron bar in my fist and felt its coolness, and then it was hand-over-hand to the top. Grab, grab, step up, pull, and so on until the final move was just ahead of me. I was drunk with purpose now. I was unaware that the table was now two feet below me, and Gaby's feeling of unease had escalated to panic.

Must have moon, I thought. I braced my core and threw my right leg up once again, hooking it on the back of the bar closest to me, and heaved my body up and over the bars.

Forty-five years later, I would find myself on the edge yet again, but this time it was a much darker night, and I was running in a storm during the Cascade Crest 100-mile trail race, which boasted a rugged, remote, and craggy course in the Northern Cascades of Washington, and I had forgotten to grab a new water-resistant jacket at the aid station a few miles back. I had a blister under my big toenail, which had already been loose at the start of the race, and with each step I felt a stabbing pain. I briefly pictured my dead body being found as the rain poured down on it, the smell of my chilled sweat outliving me. I needed to get to the next checkpoint for some food. Then it would be a short five-mile push to the next one at 52 miles, where I would see my crew and get a change of clothes and a new jacket. How did I always get myself in these situations?

But in this exact moment of 1967, there I was at the top of the bars in the Dakota, hovering for a split second between home and the cold night air. It was then that my mother walked in from the other room, just in time to see me go over the bars and out the window.

I tumbled two stories, landing on the rain gutter at the base of the roof at the seventh floor, where a piece of metal pierced my lip, jutting through my nose to the right side of my face, where it finally hooked on my cheekbone and the weight of my body came to a stop.

It was quiet up there. I was bleeding. My breath made clouds in the cold around me, the street sounds seven stories below. And then I cried. Wailed, in fact.

It was then that a woman peered out of a dormered window in her apartment. She would later say that she rarely went into that room, which she used for storage, but she had needed something, perhaps a needle and thread, perhaps she was looking for an old photograph in a box. But there she was when suddenly she heard a thump and a wail and looked out the window to see a bleeding child on the roof. She dropped everything and threw open the window, reached awkwardly around her own bars to grab a hold of me, and yelled to someone in the apartment to call the front desk.

Because that's what you did at the Dakota. You called the front desk, not the police or ambulance. It was Winnie who answered the phone that night, the kind woman with frizzy brownish-red hair. Upon hearing the frantic cry for help on the other end of the phone, Winnie quickly called out to Nate. Within minutes, Nate was on his way up to the woman's apartment, and before long he was calling my mother to notify her that I had survived the terrible fall. My mother, who had been pacing around her apartment, hysterical, took a huge gasp of air and fell relieved into a chair when she heard I was alive. Gaby, who had been surprised by the flurry of activity after my abrupt absence, screamed beside her on the floor. Nate and my mother agreed to meet on the seventh floor where the woman held me wrapped in a blood-stained towel, and I was shuttled off in an ambulance, sirens howling as it careened through the dark and slushy New York City streets.

For years after, when I would return home to visit, Nate would greet me with a wide smile. He'd walk alongside Heinz, the doorman, as he opened the door to my car, then he'd grab my bags, and follow me into the front office, repeating the story of how he had helped save my life. Considering the types of people who lived at the Dakota, Nate and Winnie had seen a lot of excitement during their tenure there, but they would agree that my story was the most exciting of them all, until of course when John Lennon was murdered in 1980. They would both beam at me and tell me that I was a miracle baby destined for great things. Needless to say, my mother still relives the terror of seeing me fall, and the interminable, anguished days of sitting with me at the hospital where my hands were tied to the sides of the crib with long strings to prevent me from touching the wounds. Little did she know that years later in my twenties, I might still require such trappings to avoid making everything even worse.

CHAPTER 2
LOSING MAMA

At the time of my fall, Mama had been trying to find her way into an acting career. She was passionate about it, and it meant something to her to be able to work where she could express herself. She was beautiful, well educated, and she had soul, in spite of the fact that so many outside influences in her life, mainly familial, had tried to chastise her into submission. She was inspired and moved by depth when she saw it in people, and she felt her feelings with the courage and conviction of someone in organic disagreement with the rigid and structured society around her. It wasn't that she tried to be unique; she simply refused to hide the very uniqueness for which she was so judged. She did find work now and again, and Gaby and I even got in on the action when Grandma and Mama were both cast in Walter Ungerer's film Keeping Things Whole. Together we made a cameo appearance toward the end of the film. But Mama was young, and trying to work as an actress with two little daughters at home was rough.

The stress of it weighed on her, and she felt the pressure of my grandparents' omnipresent criticism as if it filled every empty moment like cement, dragging her down and making it hard for her to feel inspired.

My grandfather, the very powerful John Wiley Hill, was a public relations giant who founded the firm Hill & Knowlton. To this day, he is known in the industry for his work representing steel manufacturers, the oil and tobacco industries, and Richard Nixon. A stoic man who was building one of the largest PR firms in the world, Grandpa was cautious about anything that would cause embarrassment and impact his business or his clients. And as a PR executive, he had the power to make inconvenient problems go away. For many years, my mother was Grandpa's most inconvenient problem, and he increasingly pressured my grandmother to find somewhere to put her.

My grandparents met when Grandma was a single mother, working in theater herself, and waiting tables on the side. They married in 1948 when my mother, Alexandra, was seven years old.

John Hill never took his young stepdaughter into his heart. He was an assertive man who worked hard, rode horses hard, and had the grit to take on steel unions, cancer researchers spouting inconvenient truths, and the biggest names in politics. Grandpa shaped and re-shaped public opinion without sentiment, whether he was working for a client or overseeing public perception of his own family. In his world, emotional excess was a liability, and he was greatly repelled by my mother's humanity and her youthful foibles. My mother was about as different from John Hill as it was possible to be. Intelligent, introverted, and deeply sensitive, she has always been a seeker within the emotional realm. I suspect Grandpa just couldn't fathom Mama's poetic soul. He was unable to have children of his own, apparently, and had said he wanted a child, but Mama certainly wasn't the little girl he had hoped for. He was endlessly sarcastic and critical with her and was intent on creating distance between them in whatever way he could.

Because Grandpa couldn't stand her, Mama grew up isolated in the opulent silence of my grandmother's houses, as did I years later. There was Towners in New York, and the house on Somes Sound in Maine, and the beautiful, lonely lighthouse on a high cliff on Narragansett Bay in Rhode Island. Elena Karam did not allow her daughter to visit friends, have toys, or listen to "vulgar" music, by which she meant any music except classical. For the most part, life with Grandma and Grandpa was drab for Mama, and she couldn't seem to get anything right in their eyes, though there were occasions when my grandmother's character would shine through despite her relatively stern demeanor. Once when she and my mother were shopping at Bloomingdales (which my grandmother liked to refer to as *Bloomingbottles*) on 59th and Lexington, they came upon a mannequin lying naked on the floor of the store. Instead of walking by as others did, Grandma laid down on the floor near the mannequin and said, "Really, you have to pull yourself together, dear. I know it hasn't been easy, but you can't let yourself go like this." My mother was in stitches. But this was a rare occurrence.

As soon as Mama was of age, Grandma sent her to the Brearley School, an all-girls private school on the Upper East Side, but didn't provide Mama with familial support or fashionable clothes that would allow her to fit in. At home, my grandmother required children to be neither seen nor heard, unless called for.

"Disappear into the woodwork, dear," she would say, and my mother would silently slink away to become invisible.

Whatever parenting Mama received came mostly from the maid, Australia. My grandmother provided almost no emotional nurturing and never defended my mother against Grandpa's condemnation nor other children who might be abrasive to her. Once when sitting on a bench in Central Park, my grandmother had watched with curiosity as another child bullied my mother. She made no move to assist her, only eyeing the situation as if wondering how my mother would handle it. It's as if she secretly hoped my mother would start throwing hands on the other kid but was disappointed and disgusted that she hadn't.

As a teenager, Mama was not allowed to wear makeup, but she was expected to dress up and play the role of the respectable daughter at Grandpa's parties for the politicians, foreign dignitaries, titans of industry, and actors he entertained. Playing the role of a great lady was right up Grandma's alley, but Mama hated being forced into the family charades.

One night, Herbert Hoover came to visit, and Grandpa told him, "Do you know what Alexandra said when she heard you were coming? She said, 'You mean, THE Herbert Hoover?'"

Mama actually had no idea who he was, so she remained silent, sitting there in her little dress looking cute, just as expected.

These kinds of things did not endear my mother to

Grandpa.

Starved for affection, attention, and fun, Mama became enraged and rebellious as she grew older. Even teenagers with loving and supportive families can become quite sullen as they transition into adulthood, but Mama was tired of the solitude, judgment, and isolation of her childhood and she was ready to shed it with a vengeance. She quit high school to study poetry, refused to wear party dresses, and began looking for love in scandalous places. John Hill couldn't stand it. He wasn't going to be embarrassed by a bratty 16-year-old.

"I can't have this," he told my grandmother. "You have to get rid of her."

And so my grandmother did.

I doubt there was any thought of sending Mama to her biological father. He was practically a stranger, and anyway, John Hill had legally adopted my mother. Grandma had once taken Mama to a school in Switzerland, but when they arrived, my mother refused to talk and my exasperated grandmother had to turn around and take her right back home. She was too young to marry off, although Mama says Grandma was forever pushing her at men and then leaving Mama to figure out what to do with them. Mama had not been exposed to any life skills education from Grandma, and she was taken advantage of on numerous occasions, and then judged cruelly by my grandmother after the fact. Frankly, my grandparents didn't see a lot of options, so they decided to use their financial resources and do the only logical thing: have Mama committed to an asylum.

In those days, it was very easy to have someone committed to a mental institution. Women were particularly vulnerable to involuntary commitment, with no actual mental illness required. If a woman acted out or somehow didn't fulfill social expectations, she could be locked away based on the word of a respectable relative. I doubt my fancy grandparents had much trouble getting my mother committed to the psych ward at Roosevelt Hospital, and I've often wondered if my grandmother had Munchausen Syndrome. She seemed to find great reward in establishing my mother as "sick" and then playing the bereaved parent with such a terrible burden to manage. People would often sympathize with her plight in dealing with such terrible difficulties with her daughter Alexandra's illnesses.

It wasn't so easy to keep Mama locked up, though. Despite her timid appearance and refusal to speak to idiots, my mother had an unexpected determination to avoid misery. When she was there, the patients on the psych ward at Roosevelt were heavily medicated and electric shock therapy was still in regular use. Unwilling to be turned into a zombie, my mother escaped after just three months. She was soon found at a friend's house and hauled back to the psych ward in Tower 9 of Roosevelt Hospital where she received heavy doses of Thorazine. She was moved to Chestnut Lodge in Rockville, Maryland, a much more humane, private institution where she would not be medicated, shocked, or lobotomized. My mother was not the only patient there from an influential family. Chestnut Lodge was well known for its strict confidentiality, cutting-edge work in the field of psychiatry, and expensive price tag—all desirable elements when the rich and powerful are choosing a sanatorium. Mama was grateful to find that there were a few other girls in residence who were not mentally ill, and thus she had some peers with whom to commiserate. So she stayed a while and during that time developed deep empathy for people suffering from mental illness. She found them to be refreshingly less arrogant than the "sane," and more able to connect on a human level than the seemingly callous or, at a minimum, clueless wealthy aristocrats that populated her world outside of the asylum. Decades later, the compassion that grew at Chestnut Lodge would lead her to work with the mentally ill in San Francisco, but first my mother had to save herself. After nearly a year in residence, Mama came to discover that the plan was to keep her locked away indefinitely, so she ran away from Chestnut Lodge.

She hightailed it back to New York City where she moved in with friends and laid low. Then as soon as she turned 18, she entered into a very short-lived marriage to a nurse's aide from Chestnut Lodge, which sealed her independence. A girl's gotta do what a girl's gotta do. I know it took strength for her to make some of the decisions she had to make whilst trying to outsmart my grandparents at their game and also stay safe from the falsehoods they spread about her at every turn. After her marriage, there was still a little friction with my grandparents, but as long as Mama avoided embarrassing John Hill, things were relatively quiet.

That said, Mama did fall in with some unruly, jazzy friends during that period of her life. After her short-lived marriage, she fell in love with bassist Charlie Haden and lived with him for three years, hanging out with Ornette Coleman and ending up in the studio for one of his recordings. Charlie took her to Los Angeles for a year and a half some time around 1960 or 1961, where she befriended Lenny Bruce, who always made her laugh. Charlie and

Lenny had the same heroin connection in L.A., and my mother soon had her own heroin habit to contend with. It was a wild time, but eventually Mama wanted to be free from the drugs, and since Charlie wasn't ready to get clean yet, she was forced to leave him. It was heart-breaking for her, but she couldn't bear to continue with the burden of that lifestyle. She always felt a deep appreciation for him, even after many years. Charlie was a good man and had strong political convictions. Many years after they had separated, he even dedicated the song "For a Free Portugal" to the Black Peoples' Liberation Movement in Mozambique, Guinea Bissau and Angola, in Portugal, which was under a fascist dictatorship at the time, landing himself in a not-so-fun interrogation by the Portuguese secret police.

After leaving Charlie, Mama managed to convince my grandmother to send her on a vacation to Mexico, accompanied by a trusted family friend. She was 21 when she first went to Puerto Vallarta. She felt like she had arrived in heaven. It was 1962 and Vallarta was still a sleepy fishing village of 15,000 or so people with only one road out of town. There were only about 30 people from the U.S. living there and feelings were still very cordial between the Mexicans and the gringos. Mama immediately loved Mexico and felt more joy living there than she had ever felt before. The kindness of the people, the warm ocean, gorgeous weather, and the slower pace of life suited her just right. It was the perfect place for her to detox and heal.

It was on a beach in Puerto Vallarta that my mother met my father, Alfonso de la Vega. As a newcomer and a woman possessed of a radiant natural beauty, my mother stood out in the small town. And my father, a charismatic actor, restaurateur, and designer stood out too.

Daddy was a handsome, intense man from an aristocratic family in the desert city of Culiacán, Sinaloa. The de la Vega family was large and many of my father's relatives held important positions in society. The de la Vegas contributed to the city's architecture, owned land in the business center, and owned huge commercial agricultural export businesses.

Though he was known for flying into fits of rage at the slightest provocation—his eyes squinting, his face twisting furiously, and his voice booming above all else—my father's charisma and creative genius earned him many pardons. He was a rebellious man who loved being outrageous, which appealed to my mother back then.

My father was a dancer and actor, but he made his living running two restaurants: one at Playa de los Muertos and another little restaurant in town called La Escondida. In the evenings, people would have a wonderful dinner at La Escondida and then the musicians would come. Daddy knew all the musicians in Vallarta, and they loved his restaurant. It was warm and cheery with delicious food and there was a space for dancing where my parents and their friends, which included some of Hollywood's and Mexico's elite, would dance for hours every night. Sometimes, my father would have the waiters clear away the dishes and shout to the musicians, "Ok, let's go, music is for dancing!" Then he'd jump atop a table to dance, shouting to the other guests to get off their asses. When Daddy was in the room, all eyes were on him. My mother couldn't help but fall in love with him. When he asked her to marry him, she immediately said yes. And by all accounts, they danced beautifully together, sensuously in love and laughing as they moved. My mother had a lovely red wrap dress and big hoop earrings, and the most beautiful smile. Together with my father's aristocratic features and athletic build, they were gorgeous.

Once when they were having a lovely evening at the restaurant, my father bumped into a very large macho man who was slightly drunk. The man was furious, and immediately turned to face my dad, fists up. But instead of getting upset or angry, my father looked at him and, with his characteristic dramatic flair, feigned fainting into the man's arms. The man was incredulous and pushed my father back to his feet, fists up once again, but my dad fainted into the man's arms once more. He did it repeatedly as the onlookers laughed raucously, and finally the man gave up trying to fight him and walked off, flummoxed. My father had a way of being equally courageous and intelligent in his self-defense tactics and was able to diffuse unnecessary arguments in creative ways. In Culiacán many years later, when a sleazy policeman was extorting prostitutes in one of my father's restaurants, he would chase the guy off by first berating him, and then when the cop put his gun in my father's face, my father's expression twisted into a rage and he put the gun to his mouth and bellowed, "Pull the trigger, *hijo de la chingada!*" The cop did not pull the trigger, but instead ran away to get a *comandante*, who ended up arresting the cop himself at my father's behest. Daddy was not to be trifled with. He was Don Alfonso de la Vega.

Show business arrived in 1963 when *Night of the Iguana* was filmed in Puerto Vallarta. At the time, Daddy was designing beautiful clothing using natural dyes from rainforest plants and natural fabrics that were embroidered with colorful yarns. Elizabeth Taylor and Richard Burton

Playa de los Muertos, the beach in Puerto Vallarta where my mother met my father

would sometimes request custom designs from him, and my parents were close friends with Ava Gardner while the film crew was in town. Daddy always said she had wanted to sleep with him, but he had refused because he loved my mother. Whether or not Ava had her eye on my father, Mama remembers her fondly and says Ava badly wanted to be pregnant back then. She was at that age, and though her life was dedicated to her career, she had a strong desire to have a child. Once my mother was complaining to Ava that my father was violent, and Ava exclaimed, "Well, you don't need him. You're pregnant!" Ava had a spicy character and she was kind to my mother, despite the passes she made at my dad behind the scenes.

At some point during that time, my father got in a fight with a lawyer named Pedrosa. Daddy bit Pedrosa during the fight and ended up going to jail for quite some time, and that is where my grandparents met my father for the first time. What's funny is that my father was not even the slightest bit embarrassed to meet his wealthy in-laws from behind bars. Always a welcoming host, he greeted them cordially as if he were inviting them through the door of his own home. Grandma and Grandpa were shocked, but Grandma was soon won over by his charisma, wit, and erudition. Clutching the cell bars, my grandmother would exclaim dramatic sympathies to her new son-in-law. He really was quite the charmer.

My eldest sister, Gabriela, was born in Puerto Vallarta in December of 1963. The de la Vega family was growing, but so was the trouble in my parents' home. When the raucous arguments, restaurants, and parties became too much, my mother, who was pregnant again, went back to

My parents were wildly in love and spent many nights dancing at my father's restaurants

New York with Gabriela and moved into the ninth floor apartment at the Dakota. I was born September 11, 1965, and I fell out the ninth floor window about 14 months later. I was a badass climber baby with a big scar and an even bigger story after that.

Grandma and Grandpa blamed Mama for my fall and were embarrassed by the whole situation. Though Grandma also secretly blamed my big sister, Gabriela, who had been innocently present during my escapade across the room and up and over the bars. "You're sadistic," Grandma would say to Gaby when she was just six years old. "You know what you did. You were jealous of Sammy." Poor little Gaby.

She would say these things in front of me, which was quite divisive, and at my young age with such a need for attention, I capitalized on it and became my grandmother's "favorite." But you simply can't blame a kid for an accident. Even if Gaby had literally taken me, at the age of 3, and dumped my fat tuchus out the window, she simply couldn't be blamed. Besides, can you picture a toddler and a fat baby trying to manage that circus act on their own? Ridiculous. And it was years of that soul-crushing shit that drove Gaby to avoid being around my grandmother as much as possible. Early on, Mama had tried to defend Gaby to Grandma. How could a three-year-old child be responsible for an accident like that? Naturally there are sibling rivalries and petty jealousies among toddlers, but the idea that my sister had the capacity to understand the dangers of a ninth-floor window, let alone leverage them as an attempted-murder weapon, is absurd. Nevertheless, my grandmother, who was not there when I fell, refused to believe my mother. Ever after that, Gaby was the evil big sister in Grandma's eyes, demonized and blamed at every turn. It was painful to watch, and as time passed, I felt partially to blame for Gaby's suffering.

Grandpa must have taken steps to keep news of my spectacular accident out of the papers, because I've never found a single newspaper article or report about it. A baby falls out a ninth-story window in the Dakota, and nothing in the papers. *Nada.* Mama remembers Grandma trying to soothe some of the heady emotions going on, but she ultimately caved under the weight of my grandfather's disapproval and my mother ended up receiving little emotional support during my recovery from the accident. Mama was devastated. She had already been struggling with the demands of two baby girls and her fledgling acting career when my fall happened. She succumbed to using drugs again, this time to dull her pain and stress. I imagine at that time heroin was largely preferable to the Thorazine so readily employed by the mental hospitals of the day, and there really was nowhere else for my mother to go for support in the wake of such a grief-inducing traumatic event.

It was a particularly dangerous era for my mother to be involved with drugs. The U.S. was in a panic about the counterculture. Baby Boomers were turning on, tuning in, and dropping out. Soldiers were returning from Vietnam addicted to heroin in epidemic numbers. Illicit drugs were pouring into inner cities, and clouds of marijuana smoke hung over college campuses. Terrified the country had truly gone to hell, "respectable people" were freaking out. Drugs had been increasingly criminalized for decades and Richard Nixon—with Grandpa's help—was just about to become president and declare a national war on drugs. In New York state, Governor Nelson Rockefeller first tried programs he hoped would rehabilitate addicts, but when that failed, the state enacted some of the most draconian drug laws in the nation: the infamous Rockefeller laws.

During all this, my mother learned Grandma was planning to lock her up again. Rockefeller's original rehabilitation-oriented programs specified that if anyone accused a person of being addicted to drugs, the accused would have to appear in court within 72 hours and then be examined by two doctors. If it was determined that the accused was addicted, they would be sentenced to one to three years in a prison hospital. One Friday, my mother received a notice to appear in court the following Monday. Grandma had made accusations to the authorities.

During this time, Grandma had taken Gaby and me and sent us to live in the caretaker's cottage at the country house we called Towners in Brewster, NY, supposedly to keep us safe. Mama packed her things and traveled to where Gaby and I were living. We were in the care of Biddie, a mean, heavyset woman with a large wart on her nose. Biddie spent all day on a creaky wooden chair in the kitchen. She was so sedentary that it pained her to heave her body from the chair for any purpose. She'd sit with her legs spread, her large gut resting on her thighs, bracing herself with the heels of her hands on her knees, and belch out orders, breathing heavily to catch her breath between words. I was terrified of her.

Mama told Biddie she just wanted to take us out for the afternoon, but she took us straight to the airport and we all went back to Mexico. Mama quit drugs that day, kicking hard on the flight down to Mexico with her babies on her lap, the sweat pouring off her in the air-conditioned plane, and a painfully corrosive sensation in her limbs.

Back in Mexico, Mama found my dad had changed for the worse. Amid the rising din of the new Vallarta party scene, Alfonso de la Vega had been taking LSD every day and was more violent than ever. Within a few months, Mama simply couldn't take it anymore. She wanted to take us girls and leave, but Mexican law said a woman couldn't leave town with her babies without the permission of the male of the house. So, my mother went to the *commandante*—the ranking police officer—of Puerto Vallarta and asked if he would arrest my father for just one night so she could get out of town. The *commandante* knew my dad's reputation, but first needed proof my mother had just reason to make such a request. Mama was actually pretty banged up after several months living with my father, and a doctor easily confirmed she had been physically abused. Thus, my father was taken to jail, where he was kept overnight. Mama fled with Gaby and me to Guadalajara, which was as far as she had money to travel, and she began working on a divorce.

Before long, Mama ran into a friend visiting from Vallarta and she knew my father would soon figure out where she was. Concerned that he would snatch Gaby and me away from her, my mother made the mistake of asking my grandmother for help. Grandma agreed and traveled to Mexico with her butler, Jim. The plan was to have Grandma take Gaby and me back to the States while my mother secured her divorce. Afterwards, we would be reunited.

We arrived at the airport, Jim carrying me, and my mother pulling Gaby alongside her. In order to get us girls out of the country, they told the airport officials we were from the U.S. and had just been in Mexico for a visit. Meanwhile, as my grandmother would often recount later, Gaby and I were taking in all the sights of the airport and calling, *"Mira, Mama, mira!"* But Grandma never let her stage training go to waste and somehow she managed to convince the Mexican authorities to allow her to leave with two little Spanish-speaking infants she did not have legal custody of.

While waiting for her divorce, my mother met Alejandro Sela—Alex—the man who would be her next husband and our stepfather. Once she was settled in with Alex, Mama wrote Grandma saying the danger had passed and she was ready to have Gaby and me return to Mexico. But instead of her daughters, Grandma sent back a devastating letter.

My grandmother had gone to the U.S. courts claiming she didn't know where her daughter was and that no matter what, it wouldn't be safe for her granddaughters to be returned to their mother. Grandma cited my mother's previous rebellious behavior, drug use, and prior stays in mental institutions. Of course, she didn't mention it was she herself who had institutionalized Mama. God knows what else my grandmother said to the judge, but she was Elena Karam and it didn't really matter if it was true. My grandmother was a rich, elegant, well-spoken, and a trained actress. I doubt she had much trouble stealing custody from my mother in 1969, particularly when my mother wasn't even in the courtroom to plead her own case. My mother learned all these details from Grandma's letter, which also said that if Mama ever tried to come to New York, she would be arrested.

Mama's first concern was for Gaby and me. Regardless of how prosperous my grandmother was, my mother understood that Gaby and I would suffer the same emotional impoverishment she had suffered. She knew it would change us to not have her as a mother, because, despite her human failings, she would have given us attentive mothering—and that was one thing Elena Karam was ill-suited to provide.

SAMANTHA DE LA VEGA

My grandmother, Elena Karam, on stage

FALLING UP FROM THE BOTTOM

My grandfather, the powerful John Wiley Hill

*My grandmother was stylish and had character,
which intrigued my grandfather
I don't think he knew what he was getting into
when he married her*

CHAPTER 3
FARMED OUT

After Grandma took us from Mama, Gaby and I lived together for a while with Grandma and Grandpa. We missed our mother and were swaddled in sadness. The scar on my face was thick and red, and the slightest touch made it ache in a strange way. Although the only adult in the apartment during my fall had been my poor mother, my grandmother blamed Gaby for it. Gaby felt her hostility, but had no way to defend herself. She was a sitting duck. There was an ominous cloud over both of us, and we longed for the comfort of our mother. The lonely opulence of the apartments we lived in felt inhospitable, but we were so little that we innocently submitted to our situation. We didn't cry, but we stuck together, sometimes clutching each other or lying together in bed. Gaby sometimes wrapped her arms around me at night and pulled the blankets more closely around us. When Grandma would find us together, she would scold us and separate us, sending each of us to our own Louis XIV bed. She didn't mean to be cruel.

She simply thought she was creating order, but the harshness of our separation, even if it were just across a room, was unbearable. We learned to suffer quietly in our fear and soon it became as common as the wallpaper. Perhaps if we could have stayed together, things would have turned out very differently, but that grudge Grandma had against Gaby since the day of my fall blinded her and she was unable to be kind to her.

Once Gaby pinched me during some childish spat and I tattled on her. Grandma pronounced Gaby "sadistic," a now familiar word to Gaby. Grandma began to summon that word anytime she wished to target Gaby. When we were eventually farmed out to Debbie Puffer, it was a lucky break for my poor sister. I couldn't help but think she was lucky, and I envied her. It never occurred to me that it was unfair that we were treated differently; I just accepted it like everything else.

Grandma's original plan was to see if the Waldorf School in Stockbridge, MA would take Gaby and me as boarding students. This was just before I turned three years old. Gaby was four and a half. Not surprisingly, the Waldorf school didn't board toddlers, but they were willing to call Debbie Puffer to ask if she would take us in. Debbie was a kind woman, a teacher, and a Christian Scientist who cared deeply for her three boys. Her first husband, Loring, was also a teacher. Debbie loved music and played multiple instruments.

According to Debbie, when I first came to live with her and Loring, I exhibited several classic signs of childhood trauma and had persistent worries we would all be caught in a storm. Everyone would be sitting out on the lawn in the sunshine, and I would say, "Is it going to rain?

I think we should go inside because it's going to rain." No matter how Debbie tried to assure me it wouldn't rain, neither the warmth of the sun on my face nor Debbie's calm demeanor soothed me. Grandma, who was always pleased to tell horror stories about my mother, claimed Gaby and I had been left out in the rain one night in Mexico while our parents partied. In Vallarta, rain comes on suddenly, thunder booming, the wind tumbling cobblestones down the streets. Then, the storm disappears just as quickly as it came and the subtropical sun turns everything bright and steamy again. Perhaps Grandma was telling the truth. Or perhaps the very existence of these storms left an impression on my psyche, some belief that sunny days were prone to sudden eruptions of chaos. But who knows? I might have been responding to a fading memory of my own mother scanning clouds in Puerto Vallarta and insisting we go in because it looked like rain.

My own memories start one Christmas at Debbie's home in New Hampshire when Santa Claus came for a visit. I was naturally very excited. But then, the most amazing thing happened.

Santa approached Debbie and had a conversation with her. "There's Santa and he knows my new mom!" I thought. It was a Christmas miracle. The jolly old elf soon came to me and asked if I had been a good girl and what I wanted for Christmas. I badly wanted a little doll to take care of, as if somehow caring for it would make me feel safer. It's an ordinary little memory, but for me, that only makes it more special. At Grandma's, we rarely had everyday experiences that most children take for granted and I was too young to remember our time with Mama. I can only assume, too, that I was suffering from PTSD from the fall and subsequent separation from my mother and had somehow blocked out memories of her to staunch the pain. Debbie provided the first hands-on nurturing and normalcy I can recall.

At Debbie's there were other children around and I felt a certain lightness and hope for the first time. We had family dinners, baked cookies, listened to bedtime stories, and jumped into local swimming holes on warm days. My new brother Christian and I had a whole playhouse set up on the screened porch. Debbie played guitar and we all sang folks songs together. We even had a big brown dog named Kiska. On Sundays and for special events, Gaby and I got to wear dresses with pinafores that Debbie made for us. Mine was yellow gingham and the white pinafore had ruffles at the shoulder. It was my favorite dress and I felt like a real little girl in it. I'd never had anything like it before. Debbie's sons hated getting dressed up to go to Sunday School, but I relished it.

We called Debbie's parents Nana and Dada and used to visit them sometimes in Boston. Nana made incredible miniature dollhouses that had working chandeliers and running water. They were magical. I liked looking into them and imagining how the people would live. Sometimes, Nana would take us to the Boston Pops Orchestra and then we would visit Dada at his lake home. When Nana and Dada went to Austria, they brought home presents for all of us—Gaby and I were never left out. We got good Austrian books, the boys got real *lederhosen*, and the girls got authentic *dirndls*. Mine was light blue.

For a short period of time, there were hippy teenage students around because Loring had opened a private high school. The teenagers were always up to something interesting and I sought out their companionship, even though I didn't always understand what was going on. In fact, they frightened me a bit. Their cool aloofness and strange behavior made me uneasy. I didn't know what to expect from them and I worried something bad might happen when I was near them. They used to give me fireball candies and insist I could only have one if I held it in my mouth without taking it out. I would nod my head and keep my promise, sweating as the cinnamon candy burned my mouth.

I have a blurry memory of going with the Puffers to the Bob Beers Folk Festival. It was a messy, rainy day. I remember sleeping in tents and being carried around in the rain on people's shoulders. I loved the attention and care I was getting and had a great time, in spite of the filth and bad weather. The only bad moment was when Gaby got her head stepped on in the middle of the night because she had somehow rolled around in her sleep and gotten her head stuck out of the bottom of the tent. We awoke suddenly to darkness, voices, and Gaby's wails. Other than that unfortunate incident, I thought it was a grand adventure, though I was unclear on when it would end and how we would get home. I never understood what was going on back then.

I was thriving at Debbie's house and loved the Puffers. I came to think of Debbie's three sons as my brothers and of her home as our home. I didn't know that behind the scenes, Grandma was throwing her weight around. Although Debbie treated us like her children, she was regularly warned to remember that we belonged to Grandma—particularly when Grandma noticed how happy we were at Debbie's house.

Occasionally, I would ask Debbie if she would keep me forever. Unable to say yes, she would simply tell me she loved me very much. Because of it, I never felt safe, and it made my heart ache. I was keenly aware that I was different and untethered, and I always wondered when things would change. I stuck to Debbie as much as possible, and only when I was playing with my siblings or swimming in the river did I forget how alone I really was. At night when I would curl up in bed, the darkness would surround me and I'd feel a terror and a loneliness no child should feel.

Debbie ended up divorcing her husband Loring while I was still young and, a year or two later, she met Bill. She and Bill eventually married and moved into his stark Shaker home in Canterbury, not far from a boarding school he managed called Horizons Edge.

CHAPTER 4
THERE BE MONSTERS

By the time I was three, I already felt unmoored and disowned, but of course I had no idea that damage would lead to a lifetime of internal labor. There's a reason people are so repulsed by child abuse and neglect—because it damages you for a lifetime. Can you heal? Yes. Will it ever really go away? No. It's not linear. It'll come up in strange ways at odd times when you least expect it. The smell of sulfur or the way the light hits someone's face can cause an unexpected visceral reaction. Smells can take you back to places you had long forgotten. It's not that you're broken or ruined, but that the slime of cruelty becomes part of your physiology. So much so that it's a constant companion. You might as well set a seat at the table for it.

As a girl, I often navigated strange landscapes that I couldn't understand. I knew I didn't like certain things or that they made me feel icky or scared, or sad and lonely, but I had no idea what to do with those feelings or that there were even words for them. I had no idea that there were files with their names in psychiatry departments. There were behaviors that seemed odd and made me uncomfortable, but because they were cloaked in normalcy, I figured there was something wrong with me and that I needed to get used to things. I learned to ignore my intuition, and decades later a therapist would tell me that my "no" had been broken at an early age.

I've always thought it was repugnant that people would force children to hug Uncle Billy or Aunt Mary. If the child wished to protect their own person, over which they should have agency, they should be able to say no to a hug, but when I was growing up, that was out of the question. Children did what they were told or they were punished. So we hugged uncles and aunts in spite of our repulsion. And little girls learned that if boys were mean to them, that meant the boy liked them, so we learned that cruelty was normal, and we should lighten up. After a while, the pattern of denying ourselves the dignity of self-protection was such a part of our bones that we simply no longer could differentiate between what we didn't like and what was expected of us. Everything was expected and we gave it without question.

At Debbie's house, nudity had always been a regular part of life, but it was a very natural, no-big-deal thing. Nobody felt like bodies were shameful or that they had to hide when they were naked. If you were changing into your jammies, you just changed into your jammies. There was no pressure to be naked, but sometimes we went skinny-dipping or we'd see Debbie in the nude. It was just part of the culture of our home. I never thought much about it until big hairy Bill came along and made it creepy.

One night when I was about five years old, Debbie was

away on a trip, and I was having a nightmare which caused me to wake up with a sense of dread, familiar and heavy, my eyes suddenly aware of the ceiling above me as something large and shapeless surrounded me. The big brick house was quiet; eerie moonlight landed icily on the dark floor. There was a harsh chill in the air as I sat up in bed. I pushed the thin covers away from my naked body as my small feet touched the cool floor. I swept my soft blonde hair from my face and stood up timidly, considering my options. Then I stepped toward the door, my feet softly undulating over the wooden planks as I made my way across the hall.

It was even quieter and, oddly, more daunting, in the next room, but I couldn't bear to go back to the chilly solitude of my own room. The large four-poster bed stood high and in the center of the room. There was no light except what reflected from the moonlit hallway. Bill's form was motionless. I whispered his name into the cold air. The bed creaked as he sat up, his form taking multiple shapes as my eyes adjusted to the dark. He reached toward me, shape-shifting and motioning for me to approach the bedside, opening the covers for me. I grabbed the bottom sheet and pulled myself onto the bed beside him. Without warning, his large hairy arm reached across me, grabbed the sheet, and pulled it over my head, forcing my tiny body against his nakedness. He was naked too, and he wrapped his legs around me, tucking his penis between my legs. Horror and regret swallowed me and I silently retracted into myself as the repulsive warmth of his hairy stomach pressed against my cheek. I had no voice to protest and no reference point for what was happening, and it was all occurring so suddenly now. I lay there, contemplating the worsened state of my predicament and wished for the monsters back in my own little bed. I held my breath, drew deep down into myself until I could barely feel my body. The night was eternal.

I knew better than to tell. Bill had made sure of that. Whenever Debbie was gone, it seemed there was some new thing to be afraid of, and I tried to steer clear of Bill as much as I could. All of us kids avoided him like the plague, preferring to play outside, peeing outside in the bushes so as not to cross his path in the cool shadowing house. Once there was a five-year-old boy who stayed with us for a while, and one day he was playing with Gaby and me and being silly, and he kept tickling our butts. When we couldn't get him to stop, we searched around the house. We found Bill tinkering with an old shelf in disrepair and told him what was happening. Bill reached up with his thick hand and brushed a wisp of black hair from the middle of his forehead over the top of his bald spot, looked hatefully at the little boy, and told him to stop. Then he leaned into Gaby and me and said, "If he bothers you again, let me know." Our skin crawled, but we took Bill at face value. A few days later, the little kid was walking behind us and tickling our butts again, saying, "Coochie, coochie coo."

Irritated, Gaby and I told Bill. To our horror, Bill ordered the boy to strip off all his clothes and walk around the house for an hour. Gaby and I were horrified and instantly regretted asking Bill for help. We hated Bill at that moment and wanted to hug the little kid and tell him it was all ok, but it was too late. The poor kid stood there naked, covering himself with his hands, his small chest bent over his body as if the shadow of himself could consume him. Gaby and I glanced sideways at each other, not wanting to let Bill see our reactions.

Soon it was breakfast time and Bill told me to go get the little boy who by then was hiding in the basement, still naked. I went down and found him in the blue grey coolness of the cement basement. He wouldn't look at me and I looked away, feeling protective of him. I quietly whispered that Bill wanted him to come upstairs. He slowly walked up the stairs and to the table, mortified and isolated in the room full of people. I pushed back his wooden chair so he could continue to cover himself with his hands and he sat down silently, looking at his plate. All through breakfast, he barely ate. Bill told him to eat and the boy picked at his food. I hated Bill and loved that little boy with all my heart and just wanted to make it go away, to make the sunshine come out and the room heat up, to cover him with a blanket and tell him I didn't care what he did, he didn't deserve that and none of it was his fault. But instead, I looked away. We all did because we felt so bad for him.

And then breakfast was over and everyone started to rise from the table. The little boy stood up and pushed his chair out with the back of his legs and turned back to the basement, his little feet soundless on the cold wooden floor, but Bill wasn't done with him yet. He ordered the boy to the sink to wash everyone's dishes. The rest of us were all hurting so much that we could barely stand it, but we feared Bill and were terrified we would end up naked too, so we quietly carried our dishes to the counter near the sink and looked away as the sound of water and the clank of dishes filled the room.

I knew I had better not cross him or else. He showed me a lot of favoritism, as abusers do when they're grooming children, and at times the other kids resented me, but I never breathed a word about why I was so "special." I kept my mouth shut and tried to keep my clothes on. Christian, Gaby, and I would spend hours building wooden block booby traps for Bill, hoping he would get hurt and be forced to leave us all alone, but some people are untrappable.

Finally, one day on a visit to my grandparents' New York country home Towners, I told Grandma how Bill had been touching me. Grandma and I often talked in the kitchen while the butler, Jim, prepared our meals. She had a way of getting me to open up and tell her everything that was in my head. When she heard the story I had to tell that day, Grandma's face took on a stern demeanor and she interrogated me at length. Although I was uncomfortable recounting my story while Jim was in the room, I talked and talked until I had nothing left to say. I felt exhausted and sad. Then I sat looking at Grandma, shrinking atop my stool at the butcher-block kitchen table.

To my horror, Grandma asked, "Do you want me to talk to Bill about this?" In retrospect, the absurdity of a grown woman and parental figure asking a traumatized child this question disgusts me to my core. My brain began to careen through a series of unrelated vignettes: the cobblestone streets of Vallarta, festive chatter in a smoke-filled room, a thundershower on a sunny beach, cars rumbling hither and thither, my suddenly different circumstances. Over and over, these scenes repeated until the answer finally came.

"NO!" I wailed.

I stared at Grandma, my body at once retracting into itself, skin crawling, electric mortification bristling within me, my brain tearing itself loose from my consciousness again. It seemed like a knife was cutting down my spine, opening me up, a surgeon was pulling out my liver and setting it on the counter. In my mind, I thought I saw Jim look up, sadness and resignation in his face. He had always been good to me, but what could he do for me? Nothing without my grandmother's consent. In the horror show in my mind, some monstrous version of Jim picked up my liver, and with one quiet swoop flipped it into the frying pan. I could have sworn I was burning as the room filled with the aroma of me.

A blink later, Grandma, Jim and I sat down to eat dinner. Quietly.

Several days later, Jim drove me back to the cool brick house at Wentworth as he had been instructed to do. He walked up the concrete sidewalk with me, held the door open, then silently closed it behind me as Bill took my hand.

***

As usual, Gaby and I spent the next summer at Towers with Grandma. We had a routine of swimming in the afternoon and then sitting together on the couch in the screened porch, Gaby on one side of Grandma and me on the other. Grandma would have Jim bring her an evening cocktail and the three of us would talk about anything and everything that came to our minds.

One afternoon, we had just come from the pool when Grandma said, "How would you like to come live with Grandma?"

Excited by fantasies of swimming every day, and eager

to get away from Bill, of course, I replied, "I would love it! Yeah!"

Those words would haunt me later when Grandma kept me with her while she sent Gaby back to live at Debbie's. I really had to rethink my impulsivity. Gaby, on the other hand, seemed to know what was good for her. And here I was thinking I was lucking out, I had it made, I had hit the big time. A swimming pool, for crying out loud! But the whole swimming pool hook was just a ruse to make me go along quietly. And really, all this wasn't working out for me very well. Of course, the decision had already been made and her question was really just one of those manipulations that adults do when they make you think the shitty thing was your idea. But I didn't want to live apart from Gaby and, in my seven-year-old mind, it seemed like I had made a terrible mistake. I felt guilty and horrified that I had ruined everything. If only I had been able to stand Bill, I could have been with Gaby. I blamed myself for our separation and fell into a choking sadness that stayed with me for many years to come. I had messed everything up.

CHAPTER 5
LIFE WITH THE DUCHESS

Life with my grandparents could not have been more different than life at Debbie's home. It was as if the two places existed on separate planets.

Grandma's friends called her Duchess. I never knew the origins of that nickname, but I suspect it had something to do with the refined way Grandma carried herself.

Elena Karam was born in St Louis, Missouri. Her father was a Lebanese immigrant, Basil Karam, who came to the U.S. as a stowaway when he was still a child. I imagined him, my age, a little boy, running away on a big ship where people spoke a foreign language, and worst of all, didn't care about him and would just as soon throw him overboard. I felt like I understood him. Grandma's mother was a farm girl named Nellie Rankin who was a remarkably gifted seamstress but didn't have much else going for her. And as is the case with so many artists, they are underappreciated and certainly underpaid, as was Nelly. When Grandma was five years old, her family moved to 114th Street in Harlem. Not long after their move, Great-Grandfather Basil abandoned his little family for another more aristocratic woman. Nellie was left to support my grandmother and her older son, Alfred, with what she could earn cleaning hotels at night. My grandmother would sometimes tell me the story of how Nellie would come back to the apartment during her meal break in the middle of the night with food she had gotten at the hotel. Nellie would wake her children and they would have their dinner of whatever Nellie had been able to procure. Nellie sometimes wrote to Basil explaining they had nothing and begging for five dollars so she could meet the rent. There were many lean years and my grandmother told stories of eating a slice of bread with ketchup on it, describing it as a "feast." My heart ached for my grandmother when she'd tell me these stories, and I was so thankful she was safe here with me, where I could take care of her.

Grandma had no intention of spending the rest of her life in that kind of abject poverty and somehow she found the means to attend the University of Michigan, graduating with the class of 1931. She studied speech and got her Masters in Journalism, while working as a waitress on the side. At one point she wrote a humor page for the first incarnation of *Life Magazine*. Long before she was in the movie *America, America*, the story of Elia Kazan's life, Grandma was a stage actress, and by 1933 she had made it to Broadway. In 1938, she was also in the Federal Theater production of *Haiti* with Canada Lee and Rex Ingram, two prominent black actors of the day. *Haiti* was a play about the Haitian revolution in which black Haitians delivered themselves from slavery. Grandma played a character named Odette who believed in the revolution and supported it.

Comparing how Grandma expressed herself to letters written by Nellie and Uncle Alfred, it's easy to see how Grandma had elevated herself from her humble beginnings. But, when compared to her new peers who had grown up in elite circles, Grandma came off as eccentric. When upset or trying to make a point, Grandma would suddenly begin emoting in the Mid-Atlantic accent used by actors of the '30s and '40s. She abhorred the idea of being considered common or vulgar—and she had a long list of things she considered common or vulgar—yet she was forever putting people off with her in-your-face devotion to interests like food faddist Adele Davis, Jungian psychology, and animal welfare. Grandma just didn't quite fit in. Frankly, people thought she was a little nutty, although they would never say so to her face. Nowadays she would be considered progressive. She was certainly born of humble means, but she was also a stage and screen actress married to public relations titan John W. Hill. So, I think the nickname Duchess was meant as a subtle hint. Grandma never seemed to pick up on it.

Grandma's closest friend was an old Victorian woman we called Tanty, although her real name was Frances Williams. She had once been an excellent stage actress herself and she had a great deal of influence over my grandmother. In fact, Tanty had been instrumental in having my mother locked up, and later, taking Gaby and me away from Mama.

Grandma and Tanty were deeply concerned about making sure I didn't turn out common or vulgar and spent a great deal of time coaching me on how to appear as special as they assured me I was. Grandma was forever stepping up behind me and straightening my shoulders so I would develop good posture. Tanty oversaw elocution. If I asked, "Are we going all the way there?" pronouncing "all" as "aahl" like a normal person, Tanty would reply, "It's awl, dear." If I listened to popular music, Grandma would say, "That's common. And vulgar." After a while, I began to think of everything outside our beautiful but insular world as something I was supposed to avoid. I remember once going to somebody's mansion and thinking of them as "poor." Not in a snobbish way; just in a simple, childish way. Their home looked humbler than our digs at the Dakota and Park Avenue, so I interpreted the situation as I was being taught to at Grandma's house. In my defense, I didn't realize yet that Grandma's tastes were notably opulent.

She loved the Spanish designer Mariano Fortuny and never missed an opportunity to drape something in his divine fabrics. She had gray and blue silk Fortuny curtains that soared 12-feet up to the ceiling and a set of Louis the XIV settees that were upholstered with Fortuny fabric in the Dakota apartment. She also indulged in purchasing a collection of Fortuny dresses, known for their crinkly silk fabric, which she tied into knots and stored in boxes on the floor of her closets. These dresses were eventually shown in all their glory at the Museum of Modern Art in New York City. The splendor of my grandparents' apartments comforted me and, not knowing any different, I believed everyone lived in the same conditions. Years later when I would visit smaller homes in the country, I recall innocently thinking the owners must not have been doing very well.

The confusing thing for me was that these other people were generally kind and affectionate toward me. For sure they were more interesting than the lavish silence in our house. I yearned for the life of "them" out there where people were lively, children were allowed to speak at the table, and a little harmless mischief was laughed off. And I was curious about their "vulgar" pop music and "common" tastes, no matter what Grandma said.

Still, there was a steadiness and routine at the Dakota that was reassuring. People paid attention to the details of life there. The people who worked in the building were always warmhearted toward me and became very important to me over time. Even Grandma seemed to be at her best when we were at the Dakota. She cherished her home there because it was hers and hers alone. It was where she spent the most time when she was getting in character for a new role. She was happy there and in her element.

Every day she would prepare my breakfast of "a perfect egg," which is what she called her slightly soft four-minute boiled eggs. The flat was originally a smaller artist flat, as she described it, and the kitchen was unusually small, so I would sit on the stairs right next to the kitchen and she would give me a gold-colored tray that held the perfect egg in a small egg cup with butter and salt and a glass of orange juice. After breakfast, I would leave our apartment and go down the long hall to the office to sit with Winnie at the front desk, or I might go outside and stand in the heated guard's shack with Heinz, a large German man who worked as one of the doormen. Then Walter Cronkite's grandson would come down and wait with me. Next, a shiny black car would show up and drive us to our schools.

In the afternoon, Mrs. Collins would bring me home

to our Park Avenue address around the corner from school, which we called "800" since it was at 800 Park Avenue, then Jim would drive me to the Dakota later on. Sometimes we'd see John Lennon coming up the Dakota hallway on our way from the office to our apartment and Mrs. Collins would say, "Oh, there goes that boy from The Monkees." This never failed to pique my interest because I had a huge crush on Davy from The Monkees, but I lost all interest when I found out it was actually just John Lennon from The Beatles; a band I had no exposure to since radios were prohibited in my world.

Unfortunately, a nutritious breakfast was about the extent of Grandma's knowledge about what children needed. She made no arrangements for me to have other children to play with and most of the time required me to stay quiet and out of sight. Like her "perfect egg," I appeared to be okay on the outside, but I was soft in the middle and it hurt my feelings when she'd shoo me away to silence. I spent a lot of time in my bedroom at 800, reading *Eloise in Paris* or sitting in the window looking down at the humans on Park Avenue as if I were watching television, which was not allowed very often at Grandma's houses. Very quickly, I read through the limited collection of children's books we owned, and there were few toys or age-appropriate activities for me at Grandma's house. My bedrooms were basically guest rooms outfitted with expensive adult furniture and imported wallpaper from France, with nothing to welcome a child in and little to occupy my young mind.

I don't think Grandma thought of me as an individual in my own right with emotional or developmental needs. I was more like a pet cat to her—ignored and expected to not be a bother while she was going about her life. At times, she would call me out to provide her with companionship when she sat down at the end of the day and found herself lonely. On occasion, we'd sit on the porch in Towners, listening to the katydids chirping and smelling the humidity in the air, and we'd talk about Grandma's childhood and how her mother hadn't loved her, or Grandma would tell stories about movie sets she'd worked on or old lovers who were appalled by her flat chest. My own loneliness was thick and suffocating, and it grew around me like quicksand, becoming a familiar prison I no longer resisted. My attachment to Grandma became anxious and had a desperation to it that made me feel dirty. When I would see my schoolmates with their parents after school or at plays and such, I'd envy the ease and joy with which they communicated. I didn't sense that neediness in them, and it made me feel even more alienated from the world around me. I simply cared too much, and everything hurt much of the time. Even the most quotidian of moments.

To be fair, when she wanted our company, Grandma could be a lot of fun. She had a knack for telling stories and, after years in theater, was skilled at slapstick. One night when Gaby was with us, Grandma came into our bathroom wearing her white cotton "tent" nightgown. The tent was long and white with tucks at the empire waist. Somehow, we landed on the subject of shaving armpits and we asked Grandma why she shaved hers. She started to tell us a story of a hairdresser she knew who had smelly armpits. She acted out how the woman would lean over, inadvertently putting her armpit in Grandma's face. Pulling her hair up in all directions, Grandma made faces of exaggerated disgust and feigned passing out while Gaby and I roared with laughter. Lighthearted moments like that made me love Grandma and want to be like her. I too enjoyed acting out stories and getting a reaction from an audience, so I never got tired of her stories of the theater.

She'd be heating up her evening tea with a spiral heating coil in the attic at Towners and start to talk about acting in the Group Theater in the 1930s and of times like when she was upstaged by a then-unknown Barbara Streisand.

"It was always lots of fun in the theater, and that Barbara Streisand, she was a pip!"

"She was, Grandma?"

I'd sit on the toilet and watch her moving around slowly in her tent nightgown.

"Oh my, yes! She had a way about her that commanded attention, no matter what was happening. Even when I had the stage, Barbara would be dithering about in the background with her feather duster. I'd be acting out a serious scene and the audience would be in an uproar! It was very confusing."

Then Grandma would roll her eyes to the side as if to be looking over her shoulder at Barbara, her smile curling up into a quirky sideways grin and her eyes sparkling a bit with the humor of it all.

"And there Barbara would be, poised on her tiptoes, one leg bent upward behind her, like a princess about to be kissed, as she dusted the face of a statue or the books on the bookshelf. And the audience would laugh again. It was really quite infuriating! The nerve!"

Grandma would laugh and stir her tea, and I could see she had been happy once.

I used to tuck those stories into my memory bank like gold bars, taking them out now and again, turning them over in my mind. They were warm thoughts to put me to sleep at night. I knew Grandma was good, deep down, despite her strange ideals, and I knew she loved me in her way. I was her favorite, she made no bones about it, perhaps because I was strong and willful like her and asked so many questions about her life and listened with such intent. I think she was also fascinated by my powerful engagement and belief in life, even when it hurt me. But Grandma was also in her own world much of the time and even I had trouble entering it unless she momentarily looked up and invited me in. So, I hovered about, lying on my balcony bed, or sitting in the window seat looking out at the humans of Central Park bustling through their daily lives.

***

My grandfather John W. Hill was born in the late 1800s and grew up on a farm in Shelbyville, Indiana. He tried starting a couple of small newspaper ventures before starting the first iteration of his company, Hill & Knowlton, in Cleveland. By the time I lived with him, Hill & Knowlton was one of the largest, most prestigious PR firms in the world. He was generally away on business somewhere and didn't really involve himself in my day-to-day life.

Grandpa was often embarrassed by Grandma's theatrics. She would send my sister and me around in his fancy Park Avenue public relations parties to ask Russian attachés and Saudi Arabian diplomats to sign Friends of Animals petitions to save the whales and Grandpa would be infuriated. On weeknights at home at 800, his sprawling apartment that took up the entire third floor of 800 Park

Avenue, Grandma spent most of her time in her room and Grandpa in his, though he had a secret door that went from his large walk-in closet into the den, where he would sometimes watch television. They weren't too friendly, due to Grandpa's extra-marital affairs, so Grandpa lived at 800 and Grandma lived at the Dakota, though years later I would find out from my mother that they both had had regular affairs. And then I would stumble on clues, like a photo of Grandma laughing with a certain Count Mountabatten, with whom she had had a romantic interlude. My grandparents had dinner together on Sunday nights for appearance's sake. I spent most of my time in the bedroom that had been assigned to me trying to "disappear into the woodwork, Dear," as Grandma so often instructed.

Grandpa was a reserved person who went about his life quietly and tastefully. From what I could tell, he never got up to a shenanigan even once in his whole long life and he didn't plan to start just because there was a young child in his house. Though my mother would tell me stories years later of his and Grandma's many arguments about lovers they had taken. She had found their letters in Grandma's file cabinets after her death. Apparently, Grandma would travel somewhere on a ship, have a torrid affair with Count Mountbatten or someone else, Grandpa would find out and scold her, dramatically claiming how unfair it was. Then he would turn around and do the same. They were always finding out about each other's betrayals, but they stayed together, albeit in separate rooms, which was actually quite common in those days. I was fascinated by Grandpa and was forever hanging around trying to entice him to pay attention to me. Now and again, he'd pat me on the head and smile, or even chuckle when I said something particularly precocious. "Grandpa, do you like to ride horses?" I would ask, when he'd come downstairs in his jodhpurs, his shiny leather boots reaching his knees. "Yes, I do, Sammy," he would say, his big smile reaching from ear to ear. We didn't talk much, but I loved him and I liked the stabilizing force he provided whenever he was around. I sensed that people respected him and there was a special type of order when he was home.

He used to sit at the dining room table near the bay window at Towners reading the morning paper and drinking his coffee. He'd be already dressed for the day. One day, I spent probably a half hour crawling inch-by-inch slowly across the floor so I could come up under the newspaper between his legs and shout, "Boo!"

I scared the shit out of him. The distinguished John W. Hill lost his cool and probably spilled his coffee. "Don't do that!" he shouted and went off on me. Mortified, I ran down to the basement where I sat on the really dark stairs full of spiders. I was there for an interminable stretch of time, unwilling to come out even after I got hungry and needed to pee, before the door at the top of the stairs opened. It was Mrs. Collins, Grandma's maid.

"Sammy! There you are! We've been looking for you!"

We never spoke of the incident again, but I was careful about trying to play with Grandpa after that. Over and over, the message my grandparents sent was that I was to be quiet, stay in my place, and make no demands of them. They would attend to me when they felt like it and the rest of the time I was to be neither seen nor heard. I don't think it's that they didn't love me. I think that's how their love worked.

The Christmas I was in second grade, Grandpa arrived

at Towners in high spirits with a load of gifts. Christmas morning, my sister and I hurried down the long winding staircase, yelling for Grandma to hurry up. Gaby and I opened the door to the living room and there was a sparkling tree and colorful pile of presents. The most memorable was a long skinny stuffed dog that looked like it was lying down. I was disappointed with it because Gaby got a giant Snoopy and I always preferred whatever Gaby had to anything I had. I cried so hard over that giant Snoopy that Grandpa, apparently still in the Christmas spirit, went out and got me a big Snoopy too. I took this as a sign that Grandpa loved me dearly, but he was like Grandma. His worldview simply didn't take the needs of little girls into consideration.

Also, like Grandma, Grandpa was very health conscious, which was pretty ironic considering he and his company spent decades helping the tobacco industry convince the public they shouldn't worry too much about how cigarettes cause cancer. But he didn't fuss at me constantly the way she did. In fact, he barely talked to me at all.

I tried not to be a bother, but I was a child. Like all children, I sometimes needed adult help and comfort.

One night, Grandma and Grandpa went out for the evening, and they left me at home at 800 all by myself. Jim and Mrs. Collins must have both had the evening off. I was watching TV in the den when the phone rang. Only nine years old, I was unaccustomed to answering the phone. I picked up the receiver on the rotary dial desk phone cautiously.

A strange voice came over the line. "Is your refrigerator running?"

I had no idea; I'd never thought about it. "Let me go

see," I said. I sat the heavy receiver down next to the phone and ran all the way down the long hall to the kitchen. Indeed, the refrigerator was running. So, I ran all the way up the long hall back to the den and picked up the receiver to report, "Yes, it is."

"Then you better go catch it!" the caller said and hung up.

I literally didn't understand. Whatever did they mean? And who the hell was telling me what to do? How'd they know something was up with my refrigerator? Baffled and anxious, I made my way out of the apartment and down the elevator, a journey I never took alone. At the front door, I found the doorman and told him I was scared. He said I could stay with him.

Shortly after that, Grandma and Grandpa arrived home, dressed to the nines, and found me with the doorman.

"Sammy, Darling, what are you doing here?" Grandma asked. She seemed put out by me.

Usually, when I asked for help, she said I had betrayed or embarrassed her. This time, she only said, "Well, we're here now," and then hurried me away, but I couldn't shake the feeling I had done something wrong.

***

My grandfather's butler Jim and his maid Mrs. Collins both lived with us in rooms near the kitchens at both 800 and Towners.

Jim was a tall African American man who kept his hair cut short and his face clean-shaven. He was the butler and chauffeur, cooked, did the shopping, and took care of

Grandpa's room and riding boots. He was somewhat large and had big hands and a kind face. His big smile would light up a room. He laughed readily and loved to joke with me. His favorite nickname for me was "Mess-around." He'd say, "Mess-around, get up in here and wash them hands before you eat," or "Mess-around, come get this beer for your grandpa." I knew he was being funny, but it kind of hurt my feelings because I wanted to be taken seriously, at least sometimes. I needed that, but I was far too young to understand all the many complicated reasons Jim would have had for being careful about how he treated me.

My best chance of getting some attention on any given day was Grandma's maid, Mrs. Collins, a rotund light-skinned black woman with lots of moles on her face and neck. She had rebellious frizzy hair, which she pulled back in a bun as best she could. She wore blue polyester uniform dresses, and her thighs, clad in tan nylons, made a swish-swish sound when she walked.

My grandmother called her Evane Collins, because that's what Grandma thought Mrs. Collins' handwriting said. Years later, Grandma—who was always nitpicking on details—paid for a copy of Mrs. Collins' birth certificate and learned her name was really Ruth Ann. I guess Grandma didn't know how to fix the situation, so Ruth Ann was Evane Collins forever to Grandma.

I called Mrs. Collins "Biggolliniba," because I was silly, and eventually shortened it to "Biggollin," because I loved to mess with her anytime she'd let me. She put up with a ridiculous amount of shit from me, but I always made her laugh, too. She took care of many duties my own mother would have normally handled and helped to reduce my isolation at Grandma's house.

Sometimes I would toy with Mrs. Collins, inching out of my bedroom in our Connecticut house, and down the staircase in a sleeping bag until I made my way into the kitchen where she stood at the stove. I would wrap my sleeping bag hands around her ankles and she would say, "Girl, Ima git my switch!" Mrs. Collins had a switch she had pulled off a tree, which she kept in the closet in the foyer at the other country house in New Milford, Connecticut. She never used it, but she liked to say she would if she ever needed to. She would chase me out of the kitchen, hitting the sleeping bag with the switch while I laughed hysterically, ooching out of the kitchen and through the house with Mrs. Collins right behind me.

Once in a while, Mrs. Collins' husband, the Reverend Collins, would call on the phone from Mississippi and I'd get to talk to him. He'd always ask, "You bein' a good girl?"

"Yes," I'd reply.

Mrs. Collins would pipe right up. "She ain't bein' no good girl!" Which was totally fair.

I loved Jim and Mrs. Collins and I believe they loved me some too, even though I was just the granddaughter of their employer and only a mixed-up, self-centered little human stray at that. And I liked being around them because they talked about things and joked and laughed and paid attention to me, even if it was just to tell me to get out of the kitchen.

***

Weekends and summers were spent at Towners and time there was endless. Not in an I-wish-this-would-never-end way, but in a long-slow-boring way. Grandma would wake up in her bedroom, which we referred to as "the brown room" since it had brown flowered wallpaper, and her coffee would be delivered to her by Jim or Mrs. Collins. Then, Grandma would sit in bed and read The Times in her cotton tent nightgown. Her pillows would be propped up behind her, one horizontally and one vertically to support her back. Her bed was a large Chinese wooden table with ornate carved legs and a custom mattress she'd had made. Grandma liked a firm bed for her back.

On weekends, Grandpa would be in residence. He would be up early, impeccably dressed in jodhpurs and knee-high black leather boots that Jim had just shined. Sometimes Jim let me help shine Grandpa's boots or buff them out with a brush. When I was little, the boots came to well over my shoulder. I'd shove my hand down to where the foot curved, hold onto it as tightly as I could with my small hand, and brush that thing till I could see myself in it. Grandpa would have a simple breakfast and then leave for O'Riordan Stables. He was a strong horseman and riding was his favorite pastime. Grandpa's horse was also named Jim, a gentle giant who stood 17 hands high. When Grandpa would come home from riding, he always had a look of fatigued confidence, and I was thrilled. His tall riding boots shone through a dusty coating, and he looked quite dapper and strong. I wanted to ride with him, but I was told that I would have to wait until I was older. I made it my goal to get older so I could ride with him. I knew I'd be just like him.

My bedroom at the Towners house was next door to Grandma's. It had two beds in it, one for me and one for Gaby, but Gaby was rarely there. Her empty bed made me lonely. My Uncle Wiley had once lived in that room. One summer, Gaby and I were picking through the messy closet and found his stash of Playboy magazines. They must have been discovered and tossed eventually, but while they were there, Gaby and I made a study of them. There was one story in which a woman referred to her vagina as her "cunny," and I found that particularly disturbing and stupid, even though I hadn't yet been exposed to the word "cunt." The magazines were still there long after Gaby was gone, but I didn't look at them when she was away because it made me feel even lonelier. Every now and again I'd stand on the pile of bent pages to get at something on the top shelf of the closet, the faces of vapid women with sexy 1970s-style expressions looking up at me. Because of them, I knew there was a world out there, but where the heck was it when I needed it?

I usually had one or two cats in my room with me. They were my only companions through the long summers and I grew quite close to them. Grandma gave me cardboard boxes for them to sleep in and I would stack them at the foot of my bed, cover them with blankets, and line them with towels to create a kitty shanty town. Naturally, the cats preferred my bed at night, which was great with me. I would squeeze into the bed around them, careful not to move all night so they would stay put and keep me company. Years later, I'd get pissed at cats that disturbed my sleep because they reminded me of the quiet Towners nights with cats piled up around me. Funny how one day something can comfort you and the same thing can torment you later on.

In the morning, I'd wake to the deep, cool silence of the house and pad across the hall to the little pink tiled bathroom for my morning ablutions. Then I'd head down the long hall and winding staircase, running my fingers along the ornate wallpaper, walk through the dark green wallpapered den, and push open the swinging doors to a short hallway near the phone room and kitchen area. The kitchen, with its wooden cabinets and large butcher block table, was where I would find Jim or Mrs. Collins doing the morning prep for my grandparents. I'd sit at the table and they'd cook me up some breakfast on the large chef's stove, and then pour one serving of milk and one serving of orange juice into rounded blue glasses. My grandmother insisted I have a whole breakfast with both juice and milk and generally eggs, toast, and bacon. A copy of Adele Davis's *Let's Eat Right to Stay Fit* stood close by on the counter beneath the vitamin cabinet, a testament to Grandma's nutritional alliances. My grandmother was ahead of the curve in that way, because during my childhood, being concerned with healthy nutrition was more a thing for hippies than grandmothers.

After I finished my breakfast, I would start to get up from the breakfast table and Jim or Mrs. Collins would chastise me, saying, "What you think it is, your birthday?" and I would go back and take my dishes to the sink for them to wash.

Then Jim would say, "Now go on, get up on outta here, Mess-around," and that's what I would do. I'd get up out of there.

During the day, I usually roamed the property, bored and directionless. There was no schedule or structure and very little input about how to spend my days. It was just breakfast, then nothing to do until dinner, and then nothing to do after dinner. If I passed by Jim, he would say to me with a smile, "What you doin', Mess-around?" I was never doing anything, which I felt kind of guilty about, as if it were my fault I wasn't doing something more.

Most summer days, I'd go down to the big boulder located between the house, the swimming pool, and a little cottage that was sometimes used for guests like Mai and Raouf Zarouk, an artist couple from Tunisia that my grandmother sponsored for a while.

The boulder was one of my favorite spots because I felt a sense of adventure there. The boulder presented what rock climbers call a one-move problem. To climb it, I had to reach up, grab a tiny nubbin on the rock face, then pull myself up while spreading my feet on the grippy surface, and finally heave my way up with a mantle move to get atop it.

Not too far from the boulder was the forsythia bush where my grandmother buried all her dead animals. She had intimated that her father was also buried beneath that bush and I would often visit it, sitting on the coolness of a mossy stone bench and feeling the spirits. Just behind it was a wooden fence with a gate that closed off the property from the woods behind it, and further on was the freeway. I'd re-read Bartholomew and the Oobleck to the sound of distant trucks braking in the distance. It was lonely, despite the ghosts of the cats and my dead ancestor.

Sometimes I would hang around Bobby Johnson, the caretaker at Towners. I liked Bobby. He was kind to me and walked around finger-poppin' happy most days. He whistled a lot and was fit and energetic. He was in love and I suppose that had something to do with his smile. He had recently asked his girlfriend to marry him so he was finally going to have another mama for his eight boys. I liked that idea. Plus, Bobby taught me to whistle using two fingers from each hand placed strategically and awkwardly under my tongue. It was a sad betrayal the day Bobby whipped me with his belt under Grandma's orders.

I can't even recall what I had done wrong, I just remember Grandma calling Bobby up to the Brown Room and saying, "Bobby, take Sammy downstairs and give her a good lashing." Then Bobby took me firmly by one arm, walked me rapidly down the winding staircase, pulled his belt with the shiny buckle out of his belt loops, and whipped me with it as I flailed around, screaming dramatically in the wide hallway near the kitchen. He only lashed me about three times, but my faith in him was permanently marred. He must have realized that, because he apologized to me, but I never saw him the same way again.

As with anyone who was kind to me, I had felt a special bond with Bobby until the day he whipped me. After that, I kind of realized he was just another person under my grandmother's control and there was no real safety for me with anyone. It was yet another crushing blow and a re-affirmation of my solitude. I was only about eight years old or so that day, but it wasn't childish self-pity that made me think that way. Truthfully, Grandma had control over everyone in her circle, at least to some degree, and especially when it came to me. Even if she couldn't dictate another person's behavior outright, she had her ways of making sure she kept me othered and separate from the rest of the world. If I shared an emotion or a thought with an adult that led them to ask more penetrating questions, they would learn I was unhappy. Then they'd talk to Grandma and I would be in trouble for "betraying her and turning people against her." Grandma would scold me and tell me to stop being dramatic. "Never act off stage," she would say. I believed I must be faking it and that there was something wrong with me. I figured I was different from anyone in the world, but I couldn't figure out why. If she felt sufficiently threatened, she would separate me from the person I had confided in and I would never see them again. Grandma only condoned superficial interactions between me and the small group of people she permitted in my life.

Occasionally, Grandma's friends would come to visit and I'd get some surprise attention. The sound of gravel crunching beneath the tires of their shiny new cars would herald their arrival and they would step out into the sun smelling like perfume and smiling as Jim handed them a welcome cocktail. I was usually allowed to greet the guests and then Grandma would wait with feigned patience as they questioned me about my dress and school or offered me a bit of chocolate fudge they had brought. Their cleanliness and the crispness of their new clothes filled me with a sense of security and I'd stay in the oasis of their kindness for as long as I could. They would laugh and chat, their conviviality filling the air as they lounged on the lawn before descending to the pool for a swim. Then they would shower in the Pine Room across from the house and be gone soon after dinner. I was always sad to see them leave, and I watched from my upstairs room to catch a last glimpse of their brightly colored clothes and big hats as they happily entered their cars. Then they would drive away, the sound of their car engines drifting off into the distance, merging with the sounds of trucks braking on Highway 164 below and the days would go back to dragging slowly on. For a few days after their visits, I would wander the Towners property daydreaming about what they did at their own homes. I figured they laughed all the time and ate dinners around the table, and maybe they slept in matching pajamas.

In the early evening, Grandpa would retire to his chair by the fireplace in the living room at the back of the house and ask me to fetch his Triscuits and cheese—always cheddar—and a bottle of Miller beer, which Jim would have ready in the kitchen. On the way back, I would always take a sip of the beer, just to test it, and when I arrived back at Grandpa's chair, I would be rewarded with a smile and a pat on the head. I liked to sit there with my grandfather while he ate his snack. Occasionally, his German Shepard Rex would stand up to get a treat, then lay back down after receiving his portion and his own pat on the head. I loved bringing Grandpa his crackers and cheese. My snack deliveries at Towners were a major part of my relationship with him.

On hot summer evenings, my grandmother would take a cocktail to the back porch. There was a green couch there with cushions and I used to sit there with her, listening to classical music and watching the fireflies blink on to welcome the night. On the green couch, Grandma had attention to give. We would have long talks there as the darkness deepened around us. Sometimes Grandma would tell stories about her mother or our mother. Sometimes Gaby would be with us and Grandma would ask how things were at Debbie's and Bill's. Many times, I poured out my heart to my grandmother on the green couch.

I needed a playmate, and one year Grandma brought home a dog. Skippy arrived one early spring day. Bobby Johnson had just taken the winter vestibule off the kitchen door, letting the smell of spring into the house. As Bobby was finishing up, Jim pulled up in the brand-new VW van Grandma had bought on a whim, and out jumped a little Shepherd mix. I was sitting in the wooden arms of my favorite climbing tree—a beautiful Japanese maple—but when I saw Skippy wagging her tail and bending backward in a c-shape of pleasure as Jim petted her, I climbed right down and ran over, my blue sneakers crunching on the gravel and anticipation rising within me. Finally, a companion to share the long, silent summer days! I imagined exploring the property with Skippy, strolling side-by-side, and sitting together under the Forsythia bush. I would teach her tricks. She would be my best friend. It was going to be great.

    I led Skippy to the lawn and found a stick to throw. "There you go, fetch!" I directed. Skippy stared at the stick, panting and smiling, but didn't move.

    "Ok, let's try it again," I said agreeably. After all, it was her first day with me. Skippy didn't know yet how much fun we were going to have. I retrieved the stick and threw it again calling, "Fetch, girl!" Skippy wagged her tail, grinned, and lay down. This went on all afternoon. To demonstrate how thrilling sticks were, I leapt about waving the stick, tossing it, running over to it, picking it up, and then waiving it again, all the while calling to Skippy in a high-pitched voice calculated to enthuse.

    Skippy couldn't have cared less.

    I didn't know what to do. I really, really wanted Skippy to be my friend, but she seemed to have no idea what I was on about. She was amiable enough, but didn't respond to my invitations to play. Millions and millions of stray dogs in the world and my grandma had brought home one that just sat there. It boggled my mind, but no one else seemed to notice there was a problem. No one bothered to help me work with Skippy or taught me anything about dogs or training them.

I gave up and Skippy spent most of her time in the dog run with Grandma's Egyptian Saluki, who was skittish and bitey. Sometimes Skippy would be allowed out, but over time she grew fatter and even less prone to play. In my mind, she became just another one of us hapless "saved" creatures in my grandmother's care.

CHAPTER 6
BESIDE MYSELF IN THE BIG APPLE

Periodically, Grandma would write to Mama and hint that perhaps it was time she was reunited with her eldest daughters. Mama had married Alex Sela under the condition that trying to get custody of Gaby and me was part of the deal and Alex had agreed. Whenever Grandma wrote giving Mama even the slightest hope that she could start seeing us or live with us again, Alex and Mama would pack up and travel from Mexico to wherever we were. Each time, they thought Grandma might finally let them have us. The anguish of years without us and the persistent message from my grandmother that whatever she would become was not enough, peppered with this type of intermittent reinforcement, was an excruciating emotional roller-coaster for my mother. And yet she held out hope, as any mother would.

In 1971, Grandma wrote that she had purchased a house in Applebachsville, Pennsylvania that she was willing to let Mama and Alex use. They made a long journey in an old beat-up truck all the way from Mexico to Pennsylvania and just before my sixth birthday, Mama and a parrot named Harry came to visit us at Grandma's house.

I was fascinated by my mother and her parrot, and I felt a strong pull to be by her side the minute she walked in the room. She smelled of earth and patchouli and she had a gentle and comforting voice, unlike Grandma's, which was always harried and tired. Her smile shone like sunshine on me. Mama had been a mythical creature in my mind, somewhere far away, and now she was here by my side. Grandma had always told me my mother was sick and couldn't be with me. Seeing Mama standing there in front of me looking quite well was confusing to me, but I rarely questioned Grandma because it didn't get me anywhere. In the past, a couple of letters had arrived containing pictures of babies. I remember when I first saw the picture of Ayin, I thought, "Oh, what about me?" I couldn't understand why Mama had that little baby but she didn't have me. So, when Mama arrived to see us, I wanted her all to myself. I longed to spend all my days sitting in her lap while she read me books and all my nights sleeping next to her. Mama was young and beautiful, and I was sure she did all the exciting things young people did that Grandma definitely did not do, though I didn't know what any of those things might be. It was a magical day, but Mama was only here for a short visit to discuss the Applebachsville house plans, and my heart ached when she had to leave me again a few hours later. Before she left, she knelt down in front of me and brushed my hair out of my face. Her gentle voice reassured me she'd see me again soon, and a warm hug made me yearn to go with her. All the little cells in my body floated into the limbs that touched her, like anemones yearning for the freedom of the ocean. After she was gone, the loneliness of Grandma's house closed in around me and the night felt scary again.

Another day, Grandma took us to Applebachsville to visit Mama at her new house, which was really an old one-room schoolhouse. As we eased up slowly in one of Grandpa's cars, my mother and Alex came out of the front steps, smiling. Mama was overjoyed. Alex was calm and collected. Gaby and I were thrilled, pressing our noses against the windows of the car. Jim came around and opened our doors and we went straight to our mother and reveled in her affection. That afternoon, she drew pictures of flowers and butterflies with colored chalk on the old chalkboard of the schoolhouse. Then we did yoga with her and Alex. For a little while, Gaby and I were in seventh heaven, but the grownups were at odds.

Mama had wanted to cook lunch for us, but Grandma had wanted to bring lunch. Alex, annoyed with the disagreement over something so petty, and sick of Grandma's domineering attitude, snarled in her direction, "Oh Elena must get what she wants at all times!"

My Grandmother looked up, astonished, and said in a theatrically pained tone, "Now really, Alex, was that necessary? I simply won't be spoken to in this way." Then she turned her face to my mother with a pleading expression. She was a wounded bird.

This further irritated Alex, who was just getting started.

"Mustn't inconvenience the Dutchess," he went on, gathering steam.

He picked up a cup on the counter and looked at Grandma. "Is this your cup?" Then he pointed to the blackboard on the wall, and started walking toward it. "Your blackboard?" He found a piece of chalk and slowly started to draw lines on the board, walking up and down along the blackboard, his hand with the chalk dragging behind him as the chalk scraped a white line over the beautiful butterfly Mama had drawn for us just a short while ago.

Grandma looked at him, her cheeks red as her blood pressure soared. Her hair was coming out of her hair pins and she looked tired. "Now Alex, I won't have this."

Alex was on a roll now, and he stormed around a bit throwing out jabs, "You won't have it? You won't have it? What else won't you have? Do we need to march like soldiers for you? Left right, left right," as he marched around, legs and arms stiffly moving back and forth. It was getting ridiculous.

I found it quite interesting. I had no idea what was going to happen, and this was more entertainment than I had seen in a very long time. I was enthralled by this strangely human behavior.

Mama, on the other hand, was beginning to look deeply upset. She knew that if things got too out of hand, Grandma would simply leave and would most likely take us with her.

"Alex, STOP IT. This is really not okay. What are you thinking? STOP! Go outside and cool down so I can talk to my mother!"

Finally, as if suddenly snapping out of a fever, he looked briefly at Mama, threw up his hands and stormed out of the house. My mother, relieved that the chaos was quieted, took the opportunity to slam the door and lock him out. But within minutes, Alex was pounding on the door, saying sarcastically, "Let me in! I won't be locked out of MY new house!" And when the door remained closed, Alex grabbed a hatchet from somewhere outside and started hacking at the door.

There were six sturdy bangs—THUD, THUD, THUD, THUD, THUD, THUD—and then his fists banging on the door. I could see small slits in the wood when the hatchet made its way all the way through the door and little splinters of light shone through.

I had never seen someone break down a door with a hatchet, nor had I seen anything like this fit of rage, and I was frozen, not quite sure how to react. I tried to look normal. I figured if I were casual about it all, Grandma wouldn't think I couldn't handle it, and she'd let me stay. I breathed slowly and looked okay.

And that was the end of our happy day. Only two hours after we arrived, Grandma shuffled Gaby and I back out the door and into the car. The ride home to New York was long and quiet and the car smelled of leather. I felt sick.

I guess Mama and Alex left Applebachsville soon after that, because I didn't see my mother again for a long time. I was baffled and sad, but I was already so accustomed to disappointment that I just rode it out. There was nothing I could do, and bothering Grandma for details was met with hostility, so I tucked my longing for my beautiful mother deep inside me and pretended to shrug it all off. The loneliness of Towners was even more unbearable in the days after her disappearance, but it soon faded into a blur of the mundane with the same books and the same cats to keep me company.

***

As miserable as I was during the long, silent hours at my grandparents' homes, you'd think school would be a welcome relief, but PS6 in Manhattan terrified me. It was one of the top elementary schools in the city, but the whole place was teeming with backpack-laden kids, colors, chatter, long hallways lined with slamming metal lockers, and—for me at least— social issues.

There was another girl in my class named Samantha. The other Samantha was a chunky girl with braids and colored ribbons in her hair and for some reason she had it in for me. She must've sensed my sensitivity and woundedness, and there's nothing a mean middle-schooler likes more than to capitalize on that. She sat on the opposite side of the room where I assume she spent the day dreaming up new ways to torment me. We had loud yelling matches during class. I met her threat for threat, but secretly counted on Mrs. Ostier to break it up so nothing would actually happen. Truthfully, I had no beef with Other Samantha; I was just afraid of her and didn't know any other way to handle the situation. Like the iguanas in Mexico, I tried to appear bigger and tougher than I was, hoping I could hiss and lash my way through the situation without anyone figuring out that PS6 freaked me out.

I tried with all my might to fit in at school, but I had no idea how and I was having more and more trouble staying present within myself. Recess was in a big cement courtyard, which was surrounded by a high cyclone fence. Outside the fence, the city was unknown and jam-packed with bustling people, sidewalks leading to who-knows-where, and buses roaring by with faces staring out the misty windows. Inside the fence was Other Samantha, echoing voices, shoes clicking on hard floors, and hundreds of students who all seemed to know how PS6 worked. My surroundings came to feel continuously blurry. Life was just a series of happenings: people, perfect eggs, raucous colors, noise, the long hallways of 800 Park Avenue, the scuffed floors of PS6, the clean white carpet, plus and minus signs crisscrossing papers, starched sheets, heavy books with worn corners, and the swish-swish of Mrs. Collins' nylons rubbing together as she walked. I faded in and out of myself so often I didn't know where the world ended and I began. Grandma put me in therapy with a nice man named Dr. Gerald Dabbs. Grandma loved therapy. She had attended lectures with Carl Jung in Zurich many years before, and spent years in Jungian analysis in New York.

Going to Dr. Dabbs' office meant taking public transportation once a week, something I would normally never be allowed to do. Mrs. Collins would come find me in my room, help me get my jacket on, and hustle me out the door and down the elevator. The doorman would open the heavy golden doors and we would stride through. Momentarily, I would feel like a princess and be warmed by his kind smile.

Mrs. Collins and I would head down Madison Avenue to catch the bus in front of Gristedes supermarket. There were few times when I would actually participate in mundane tasks such as riding the bus, and I never set foot in stores. It was simply not permitted. I remember the feeling I got the first time I handled money. The bill was wrinkled up and looked dirty, as if the tannish background and the dirty green print might wash off on my hand. The notion that it was there to exchange for something was alien to me. Until then, Jim and Mrs. Collins had done the shopping for my grandparents, and I had never set foot in a store myself, though I do recall once waiting outside in the car while Jim ran into the A&P in Patterson, NY. What's funny is that I didn't know it at the time, but only in retrospect did I realize that it was unusual that I hadn't seen or handled money before the age of 14.

Except for the one time when Mrs. Collins gave me a nickel to run into Gristedes Market on 5th Ave to get a Chocolite candy bar. I was just feet away from her as she stood in the bus stop waiting to escort me to my psychiatrist appointment. And it was that candy bar's fault when I spelled the word "chocolate" incorrectly on a spelling test later on. The store was dark and cluttered with narrow aisles stuffed with candy and other goods, and there was an old man behind the counter. He was somewhat heavyset with a larger nose, like my Uncle Al, and he looked Lebanese or Greek or something. He had a scruffy white beard, as though he hadn't shaved for a few days. He sold me the candy bar and I ran back out to Mrs. Collins to wait for the bus with her.

The circumstances of the purchase are irrelevant as I think back to that moment, and yet the memory of that dirty bill has stuck in my head all these years. The person's outstretched hand, reaching toward me, the bill seeming like a forbidden fruit, yet somewhat more vulgar. Me staring at it, paralyzed, and considering backing away gently, and covering my face or looking down at my feet. *Who, me?* It is not permitted. What a betrayal to my grandmother to carry out such a brazen act of self-validation by engaging the world of the many by handling money, lifting the spell, and capably walking into the world, or in this case, a store.

And when the world seemed distant and alien to me,

when I got anxiety getting on buses in my later teens, and when common human behaviors, like going to the movies with friends, were entirely incomprehensible to me, like someone speaking a different language, I could see that these things were equidistant to me. In my 30's when I would finally learn how to handle money responsibly by studying the Dave Ramsey method and employing a friend to teach me how to use a spreadsheet to track expenditures and income, I would find out that it was the parents' duty to teach children to manage money. That was actually a thing parents thought of. Dave Ramsey stated it was the father who should teach such things, but I'm a feminist so I scoff at that notion, but it became clear to me in these small ways that there were things I should have learned that I wasn't taught. Very basic things like you brush your teeth before bed and when you wake up, you wear pajamas instead of sleeping in your clothes; you can save money and buy things with it; and money doesn't grow on trees, you have to work hard for it and then you can decide what matters to you and budget for it. I found these lessons to be treasure troves of knowledge that freed me from the impossible and complex maze of life. My brain would at once burst with joy at the thought that I had some control and I knew the steps to maneuver such things, and at the same time, I'd experience moments of tremendous cognitive dissonance and grief that my very well-educated and wealthy family had simply abandoned me to my own devices, no one making the slightest effort to guide me into a life of self-care and to find my greatest potential.

And I tell you with all humility that I had untapped potential in spades. I had spent years berating myself for not knowing how to behave, watching others do it, whatever it was, and being baffled by what would seem to be simple tasks. Those around me probably assumed I was willfully lazy or just plain stupid. When really, I see now that I was stunted by lack of exposure to even the simplest of quotidian human behaviors. So, years later when I made the decision to lean into the darkness and shoot heroin, it wasn't because I was myself willfully dark or evil, but because I simply saw nothing else available to me, and that drug seemed quite available in the moment—a single act of rebellion to lean into something completely my own and entirely prohibited, to cut the ties to my painful family origins and find something. . . different. And I tell you this not out of self-pity, though I have had my moments, I assure you, but out of the plain and simple awareness that this actually happened to me. It might seem like a simple thing to walk in the world, but how could I know that women clacking in their high heels down Park Avenue had money in their purses, and they had places to be and watches to tell the time, and note pads with phone numbers and people's names? How could I know that the stores opened during regular business hours and that people went to work to earn the money to then earn the privilege of entering the stores? And that clothes either fit or they didn't, and if they didn't, you got a different size? You didn't order a whole pile and have them fitted to you at home. And that you bought tokens for the bus and they came in a small roll which you kept in the small zipper pocket of your purse, and that you put your purse on the same hook every time you walked in the door, so it'd be there the next time you needed to ride a bus or go to a store. And since it was prohibited for me to walk in the world or talk out of turn, I couldn't even ask you. So yes, it seems simple, I'm sure, to many. Seems like I was a willful child, or a petulant teenager indulging in heroin, when really I was trying to find my way home on a bus I had no money for.

***

Dr. Dabbs' office was on 5th Avenue on the first floor of a tall building. The wide lobby had an ornate carpet and tall ceilings. The halls were lit with warm sconce lighting. Just inside the door was a small waiting room. When Mrs. Collins and I arrived, there was usually another child and her mother there. Wishing I was there with my mother, I'd look away until Dr. Dabbs came for me.

During our sessions, Dr. Dabbs asked me a lot of questions in a gentle voice. We often played games together. I liked that I could play whatever I wanted and at times I was bossy with him. He didn't seem to mind and always let me have my own way. I really didn't understand what we were doing, but I liked getting out of the apartment.

Back at PS6, I was doing my best to fit in and mostly failing, but I managed to make a friend named Stephanie. She was allowed to go home for lunch and one day she took me with her. She lived a regular family life in a regular New York City apartment, which made her poor and common, based on what Grandma had taught me, but I was totally willing to overlook that because I was starved for adventure. I was figuring out there was a whole world in New York City with interesting things happening in it and I was keen to be exposed to it.

When we got back to PS6 after lunch, we discovered the place was in an uproar. There had been a panic when they realized John Hill's granddaughter was gone because they imagined me kidnapped and held for ransom, or at best, lost. That was the end of PS6. Grandma transferred me to the oppressively perfect Hewitt School, a private all-girls K-12 academy that knew how to keep track of a girl who might be taken hostage.

Therapy with Dr. Dabbs didn't last much longer either. Grandma seemed disgruntled about how it was going. "I'm paying for this," she'd complain. "And the next thing you know, everybody hates me."

The day I got lost on the way to Dr. Dabbs' office apparently gave Grandma the excuse she had been looking for to pull me out of therapy. I used to walk ahead of Mrs. Collins on our way to the bus, listening for the sound of her shoes on the sidewalk to tell me she was still back there. I was ashamed to be with her instead of a real parent, and I didn't want anyone to associate us with each other. One day I thought it was Mrs. Collins' shoes I could hear, but it turned out to be someone else's. It was very scary, but somehow I found my way to the doctor's office and went inside. Mrs. Collins was already there and she was freaking out. We never went again, but for years afterward, whenever the subject of child therapy came up, Grandma would say, "Oh yes, therapists always blame the parent and make you the villain and I was tired of being the villain." Decades later, I spoke with Dr. Dabbs and all he would say was, "Your Grandma was a force to be reckoned with."

***

During the summer of 1973, Mama arrived at Towners

and stayed with us for several months. She looked tired, but she was always warm with us. I thought she was beautiful. She would kneel down and look at both Gaby and me in the face, smiling warmly, then gather us up in her arms, and gently hug us for a really long time, talking to us and saying how much she had missed us and how good it was to see her sweet little girls. She was having some trouble with Alex, so it was only Mama and my little sisters: Ayin, Sky, and Lhasa. Grandma lodged them in an apartment above the "Pine Room" at Towners. The Pine Room was across the lawn from the main house, attached to the back of the garage. It was a large building with a stone back deck overlooking the part of the property that stretched down to the pool at the bottom of a grassy hill. It typically stood empty, but was sometimes used for hosting parties, since it had a fully stocked bar, or for housing guests in the upstairs apartment. As its name suggests, it was completely made of pine.

Grandma didn't like kids much, as they required attention, which she demanded for herself, so she told my mother that Ayin, Sky, and Lhasa were to remain closeted in the apartment above the Pine Room, and they were not to come to the main house. Ayin and Sky were about four and three respectively, and Lhasa was just about to turn one year old. She spent most of the time crying loudly in a crib that had been put there for her, tears running down her fat, red baby face. One day, Grandma sent Gaby and me over to watch the girls while she talked to Mama on the large screened-in porch at the back of the main house. The katydids chirped loudly in the warm summer air and we tried to entertain ourselves for what felt like hours. At one point, Gaby and I convinced Ayin to get into a suitcase, and then zipped it up around her. She didn't like it, so we reluctantly let her out. We felt slightly mean, but we couldn't help ourselves. They had, after all, taken our mother from us. Or at least that is the way we saw it back then. We stayed for hours, biding our time with the girls in the Pine Room apartment, but finally we could take it no more. We gathered ourselves into a little group and the four of us were going to leave Lhasa crying in the crib and go get Mama. We reached up and grabbed the handle of the apartment door and as the door squeaked open, our eyes caught sight of a giant spider in a tree near the banister at the top of the stairs. Our horror of the spider beat us back into the apartment and we huddled together crying, somehow allies once again. We were back and forth like that all summer.

My relationship with the girls was always complicated by my desire to have my mother in my life as they did. It was intense to be near my mother. Every minute I wanted to crawl into her lap and snuggle up into her arms. Every part of my being felt it only made sense to be with her, but I knew Grandma wouldn't allow that. I didn't understand the girls and didn't want to like them, but they were now a part of Mama, and the girls looked up to Gaby and me because we were older. My eight-year-old mind just couldn't sort it all out.

One way or another, summer came to an end, so I had to put on my clumpy Buster Brown Oxfords and go back to New York City to attend fourth grade at Hewitt School. Gaby went back to Debbie's and sometime that winter, Mama and the girls rejoined Alex in Mexico.

***

Academics came easily to me, and The Hewitt School provided a very good education starting in third grade. I studied French, Latin, and Greek Mythology, wrote long compositions, and out-read most of my classmates. Socially, I was still the odd girl out. Of course, Grandma had explained to the staff in serious tones how "Poor Sammy" was broken and not like other children, which meant I would be treated differently in subtle ways that the other children would pick up on. She was always doing that and ruining my chances for a fresh start.

Whenever I started a new school or was going to stay somewhere new, I secretly hoped for adventures with children my own age. I would envision myself playing outside, doing cannonballs in a river or playing kick-the-can, because I had done all that back when I had lived with Debbie. Unfortunately, I never arrived anywhere new without Grandma. Then there would be a hushed conversation. Grandma would explain her expectations for my care in serious tones punctuated by comments like, "Poor dear" or "No late bedtimes." Of course, she would tell stories about how she had nobly taken up the burden of caring for her daughter's troubled children and naturally needed the other adults in my life to assist her in her quest to rescue me from all that had gone before. I'm sure most people took her at face value, at least initially. Why would they not? It was true our mother was not in our life at that time and it was true Mama had struggled with addiction while Grandma lived a "respectable" life. Knowing only the bare framework of our story, it's easy to see how well-meaning people must have jumped at the chance to be a hero to a "poor" child in need of intervention. In truth, it was one more way Grandma kept me separate, alien to others, and set apart from human society.

After one of Grandma's talks, there would be a slight shift in the atmosphere and I would suddenly be the other, the outsider, the one who needed special care. It was all a self-fulfilling prophecy. Because of those conversations, I was treated, and ultimately transformed, into the broken child she made me out to be. Headmistresses, pseudo foster homes, family friends, and dormitory resident directors would all receive the same introduction to "Poor Sammy" and I, helpless to defend myself, fell into the role, unaware there was another option.

In addition, since Grandma didn't allow television, I wasn't familiar with any of the current fads or popular TV shows. To top it all off, I looked completely out of place. All my classmates came from wealthy families and dressed like the stylish prep-school girls they were, in fancy captain's coats and penny loafers. Thankfully, we wore uniforms at school, because Grandma selected and purchased all my clothes.

Once a year she would go to B. Altman's and shop for an hour or so, picking and choosing what she wanted for me without my input. When she was finished, Jim would bring the car around, hold the door open for Grandma, and then load all the bags into the trunk. On a day Grandma wasn't too busy, she'd dump all the new clothes into a pile on the floor, and then have me try them on, one-by-one, so her seamstress could determine what needed to be taken up or in. The clothes were so bad that any reasonable person would have assumed they had been purchased for desperate middle-aged refugees who needed to find office employment in the manufacturing sector. Twice Grandma brought home items of clothing I could wear with my head held high, feeling like a young woman of the times. One was a little black plaid dress with giant holes in the sides that were connected by a metal ring just over my belly button. The other was a pair of denim bell bottoms. Everything else in the clothes pile was an affliction to my young soul, right down to the size EE wide Buster Brown Oxford shoes Grandma insisted on purchasing for me.

"They're good for your feet," she'd say.

"They're fat kid shoes," I'd protest. "Everybody else at Hewitt wears penny loafers."

"They support your arches," she'd reply.

Wanting to fit in, I begged Grandma for penny loafers, but she refused to budge. She'd top off this train wreck of a wardrobe with two coats. I suppose all that padding around my core helped balance out the double-wide Oxfords on my feet.

So, I clomped through the hallowed halls of my elite academy feeling stupid and trying to shrink into myself as much as possible to avoid detection.

At the end of the school day, the other girls would be picked up by their wealthy, well-dressed, good-looking parents. Mrs. Collins always arrived to collect me wearing her polyester uniform dress, her hair looking all crazy and her moles sticking out on her face, very obviously not my parent. Embarrassed that my family didn't come for me, I would walk far ahead of Mrs. Collins, hoping no one would realize we were together. One time my grandmother gave into my wheedling and came to pick me up at school, but as I probably should have expected by then, Grandma simply couldn't pull her shit together for me, ever. The car pulled up, Jim opened the door for her, and she stepped out of the car looking messy and wearing blue jeans rolled up high on her legs, some clumpy shoes, and a loose jacket she sometimes wore up in the country.

"Wait a minute, Grandma!" I called, not wanting my classmates to get a better view of her. Grandma could tell I was ashamed of her and never came again.

***

The summer after fourth grade, my mother and stepdad made yet another attempt to reunite with Gaby and me. My grandmother relegated Tanty's house in New Milford, Connecticut to this endeavor, and even offered up her Chinese bed from the Brown Room, so it seemed like it was really going to happen, finally. I buzzed about the house, unable to contain my excitement. The boredom of Towners was more boring.

Mama and her family arrived in a classic blue-green 1956 Ford pickup that they had purchased in Brownsville, Texas. Alex's cousin, who owned an auto shop, had painted and re-upholstered it. The truck creaked and grumbled like an achy old man as it pulled into the driveway, tires grinding on the gravel, heralding their arrival. All their belongings—including a cage containing a small parrot and a big green macaw, Chavinda and Maclovio—were heaped in the truck bed. The girls were kind of piled up on each other between Mama and Alex on the bench seat in the cab. There was literally no room for anyone to move and they all had an air of exhausted endurance. The girls looked dusty and their hair fell in their faces. I wasn't too thrilled about the girls. They were really just a hurdle to get to my mother. Alex was incidental. I was still baffled that my mother had other children. It didn't really make sense to me because Gaby and I were her daughters and, well, where did these other girls come from?

Bobby Johnson, the long-time caretaker from Towners, was working with a guy named Ken, a creepy new guy who smelled of garlic and had greasy hair. They were to transport the Chinese bed from Towners to the house in New Milford in a small orange Chevy truck used for property maintenance. A heavy Chinese table straddled the truck bed and a mattress rested on top of the table. None of it had been tied down. I guess Bobby sat atop the pile to keep the mattress from sliding off. Ken was driving and I was squeezed into the front seat between him and Mrs. Collins, whose hands were folded over her large breasts.

All of a sudden, Ken started to pull out of the driveway and suddenly Mrs. Collins exclaimed, "Ooooo, something done fell off the back of the truck!" Ken stopped the vehicle and the two of them got out to see what had fallen. I could hear Mrs. Collins' voice getting higher and higher as she exclaimed, and curious, I jumped out of the truck and hustled over to see what all the commotion was about.

Bobby and the mattress were on the ground. Bobby had hit his head in the fall, and a thick red pool of blood was gathering beneath his head as he lay in the ditch, his head impossibly tilted in the grass. The look on his face was shock and sadness, like he knew something was really wrong. Bobby was only 35 years old. He was the father of eight young boys and was just about to get remarried. He had taught me how to whistle and he had apologized to me after that time Grandma made him whip me with his belt. I knelt down on the ground next to him and gently held his hand, holding it as his grip tightened. I knew he was banged up but I assumed he would just get up in a few minutes. But after a few minutes, Bobby made a strange moaning sound and his hand went limp. Mrs. Collins nudged me with her foot and said, "C'mon girl. Let's get you in the house." I walked away looking back over my shoulder as Ken knelt over Bobby, and I never saw him again.

After a while, Ken came into the kitchen and said mechanically that Bobby was going to be in a better place. I turned away from him and looked at the counter and felt the kitchen light dim around us. This felt too final. Like there had to be another chance. But it was done and there was nothing any of us could do. I later found out that Bobby had suffered a brain injury and died. I had always thought Ken didn't like Bobby, and now Bobby was dead because of his carelessness. My heart ached and I felt a strange yearning for things to be different, like an unbearable swelling inside my whole body that had to be released. But I didn't release it.

Days later, men came to the house in New Milford and interviewed me. Sitting in the grayness of the kitchen, enjoying adult attention and completely freaked out over Bobby's death, I made sure to emphasize how Ken had never liked Bobby and had smiled when he said Bobby was going to be in a better place. Ken was dismissed and I was glad to see his greasy, garlic-smelling self gone.

It was a horrifying beginning to what would end as another failure to rebuild our family, and the emptiness left in Bobby's place was a new type of emptiness. Until then, I was keenly aware that people could disappear on a dime, but I had a feeling they were there, somewhere, in the ethers of the universe, lying on beaches or sipping drinks in chatty restaurants. But Bobby was gone gone.

Never coming back. On top of it, the life my mother, stepdad, and sisters lived was alien to Gaby and me. We didn't have a clue how to behave or get along and, in some ways, we didn't want to. There was a familiar lack of structure, and their family cohesion felt like a wedge between us. Gaby and I simply didn't know what to do.

My mother and the girls and Alex had come from Mexico and it appeared that Alex was a hippy. Our half-sisters, whom we all referred to as "the girls," adored Gaby and me and were fascinated by us because we were older and had grown up "rich" at Grandma's house. But Gaby and I perceived the girls as my mother's replacement children and were so eaten up with jealousy and hurt that we couldn't return their adoration.

Grandma was no help. Actually, she was worse than no help. Grandma was divisive and fueled the fires of our discontent. Deep in my heart, I wished everybody would just disappear so I could have my mother all to myself forever, but Mama didn't know what to do with her eldest daughters' difficult behavior either and I don't think she liked us very much. Wounded, I would watch her curled up on the bed with one of the girls, talking quietly in the glow of a lamp, and wish it were me she was talking to.

I was too young then to understand the impossible situation my mother and step-father were in. On the word of my grandmother, they had dropped everything to make their way from Mexico to the east coast in the hopes of having Mama's family all together again. And not for the first time. Still, they had come for us again, arriving with hardly any money. At the remote house in New Milford, without a dependable vehicle, Alex couldn't get a job.

Once, in an attempt to hustle up some cash, Alex

made homemade yogurt and tried to sell it to the people in town. At the gas station, while buying 25-cents worth of gas, he tried to sell yogurt to the attendant. I was mortified and sank down in my seat. I thought he was stupid and goofy. Another time, Alex dropped me off at my friend Mary's house and tried to sell Mary's mother some yogurt. Even though she was my only friend in New Milford, I never went back to her house again because I was too embarrassed.

Once again, Grandma had intended or pretended to help, but had actually set up an impossible situation. She had given us a fancy house, but no logistical support for us to succeed. It was like giving a starving person a golden bowl and a chicken, but no stove. It was a shit show until one February day when Grandma took back her fancy house and rickety old Peugeot and two eldest granddaughters, leaving my mother and her family unhoused in the middle of winter in Connecticut.

I learned later they survived by contacting my mother's friend Alfie who knew Susan Hennessy, the granddaughter of Dorothy Day who, along with Peter Maurin, was one of the founders of the Catholic Worker Movement. Susan contacted her grandmother and asked if there was a Catholic Worker house with room for Mama's family. Fortunately, Dorothy said yes. They ended up staying for a couple of years and Miriam was eventually born at the Catholic Worker Farm in June 1977, right there on the Hudson River. They were only an hour or two away, depending on whether we were living at the Dakota or at Towners for the summer, and somehow there was no way to bridge that distance. Back in New York, I resigned myself to being friends with the statue of Kwan Yin that stood behind the swinging door in the dining room at 800. Kwan Yin was a good listener and always up for some make-believe games, but she never bothered to come up with new games. It was like she just put up with me. Still, I had no problem making out with her now and again to keep myself entertained.

***

There were two places where I didn't feel like the weird kid: dance class and on the back of a horse.

For a while, I studied under Anita Zahn, a well-known teacher of Duncan dance, in an ornate ballroom with very high ceilings. When I danced, I was full of confidence and a sense of freedom. I performed with emotion and complete abandon. Anita was thrilled with my unabashed expression and eventually told my grandmother that I was one of her favorites, commenting on how powerful I was on the dance floor. That did it. Grandma put an end to it. She removed me from Ms. Zahn's class and never put me in dance lessons again.

And as you might imagine, the same thing happened with riding lessons. I learned to ride at the O'Riordan Stables where my grandfather kept his horse, Jim, a gentle giant who stood 18 hands high. I had to stand on stairs to mount Jim, but I was super proud when I graduated from the two ponies, Nip and Tuck. I rode around the ring, posting, and then cantering, and couldn't wait until Grandma would buy me some jodhpurs. I already had a riding helmet, which I was proud of because it made me feel official. Then one day my teacher, Florence Anne, told Grandma what a good rider I was, exclaiming that I rode like Grandpa: fearless and strong. Soon after, Grandma pulled me out of riding lessons. Clearly, I was not disappearing into the woodwork well enough to suit her.

Expressing myself in any way was a huge no-no, but expressing emotions like sadness and fear were particularly taboo because Grandma said that was an embarrassing betrayal. She would accuse me of "just trying to get attention," with a tone that made it clear children getting attention was a bad thing. Even if my struggles seeped out accidentally, for instance, in the form of a bad grade or another adult expressing concern about me, Grandma would take it as a betrayal. She began punishing me by canceling my birthdays and Christmas. I just couldn't get things right.

The bright spot of third grade was making a friend: Glenn Evans. Grandma let me go to her house sometimes. The Evans family had a fancy two-floor apartment and a happy family life. Glenn's mom cooked meals and they all sat at the dinner table together, laughing and talking. One day, her brother didn't want to eat his vegetables, so he wrapped them in his napkin and stuffed them into his sock. When his mom figured out where the vegetables had gone, he didn't get in trouble, she just told him to go throw them in the garbage. I soaked it all in because I was starving for normal, spontaneous family dinner conversation. At Grandma's and Grandpa's house, children were not allowed to talk at the table.

Once, when I was sleeping over at Glenn's, I got scared. I wasn't used to sleeping at other people's homes. I wasn't sure of how things were done in that house and I didn't know where the adults were sleeping. Glenn's room was red, which started to work on my imagination. My restlessness woke Glenn and I told her an elaborate tale about how I had seen the devil. After that, we were both wide awake and scared late into the night. Her mom must have heard us because she came into the room, but instead of being angry with us, Glenn's mom comforted us. She didn't seem to think we were an embarrassing problem at all.

One day, I walked into Hewitt School and realized something was very wrong. There was a weird tension in the air and I could hear people around me saying, "Should we tell her? Should we tell her?" But no one told me anything because I wasn't part of any inner circle; I was just the weird kid with bad clothes. I looked for Glenn, hoping she would know what was going on, but couldn't find her. I was supposed to spend the previous night at her house, but Grandma had refused to let me go, so probably everybody except me knew what was going on.

It wasn't until we were all upstairs that I was pulled aside and finally learned the terrible thing that had happened. There had been a fire at Glenn's house. Glenn and her mother and father all died the night before when I was supposed to be there for a sleepover. Glenn's brother was the only survivor and they didn't know what condition he was in.

Girls gathered around me and the teacher was there, all eyes on me. My head reeled and I felt the pressure of their gazes. Grandma had taught me to never make a scene and I didn't want to get into trouble for embarrassing her, so I looked down at my feet and held in my tears. I was speechless and, absent a way to let my feelings out, I felt paralyzed and helpless. I didn't move, and soon I felt my teacher's hand on my arm, pulling me toward the door.

I could hear the hushed murmurs of my classmates, as I was led out of the building.

I was sent home early that day. I only had to cross the street to 800 and Mrs. Collins was there waiting just outside the doors. She took me upstairs and hung up my jacket for me. I went to my bedroom, sat on my bed, and cried quietly. Grandma was in her room. I'm sure she knew what had happened because the school would have called her to tell her they were sending me home. She came to my room much later when I was just sitting on the bed, listening to the sound of traffic, images of my friend and her kind family burning to death as her brother was dragged out a window by a fireman on a ladder. I envisioned the smoke

Mama and Alex with Ayin, Sky, and Lhasa, before Miriam and Mischa were born

billowing out of the windows and their charred bodies. *It must have hurt so much,* I thought. Poor Glenn.

"This is why Grandma doesn't let you go places," she said.

After that, it was harder than ever to get permission to spend time at a friend's house. And Glenn wasn't coming back, so that was the end of my one friendship. More and more, I felt separated from the world. Everybody else was out there living, and I wanted to be out there living too, but it wasn't allowed. I could not walk down the street by myself or go to a friend's house or even accompany the adults shopping. When I had the opportunity to engage in anything new, I threw myself into it, tasting its sweetness until my body vibrated with the feeling of living and belonging. But as soon as Grandma caught me enjoying some perfectly normal little thing, she would put a stop to it, ostensibly for my own good.

One summer, Jim gave me a little Army-green transistor radio. I finally had something to do and was ecstatic. I spent a brief few days ambling around the Towners property with the plastic radio pressed to my ear, hot on my cheek, feeling the vibration of the radio announcer's words on my skin. It excited me to know there was a strange bustling world out there, even though I couldn't relate to much of what he said because I wasn't allowed to watch television or go out into the world except to attend school. My delight with this curious electronic companion was short-lived, however, because when Grandma discovered I had it, she took it away.

"This is not appropriate for you, Dah-ling," she said, in an overly concerned, intense voice and a theatrical mid-Atlantic accent.

I was devastated, but I sunk quickly into the familiar feeling of disappointment, tinged with a sense of guilt for wanting something so common as entertainment.

In 1972, Grandma eventually tired of dealing with me and sent me back to live with Debbie and Bill on Atwell Hill Road in Wentworth. They had moved there, renting a place of Grandma's that had space enough for their children and Gaby and me. We drove a long way in Grandpa's blue Chrysler New Yorker—five or six hours, which seemed eternal to me. Jim drove and Grandma and I sat in the back together. Finally, we went up, up, up a dusty road and arrived at a small white house at the top of a steep driveway. It was a hot summer day and insects buzzed lazily around us as we climbed out of the car, snack wrappers and blankets falling about us in disarray. Debbie came out of the house, stepping lightly across a stone pathway.

"You made it!" she called with a broad smile.

I was instantly glad to be there. The boredom of the car and Grandma dissolved as I followed Debbie toward the house, admiring her vertically striped multi-colored boot-cut pants. Grandma and Jim didn't stay long. As the sound of the car grinding over the dirt road slipped down the hill, I hoped I could stay at Debbie's forever. Life at Debbie's was always more fun. There were bedtime books and instructions on when and how to brush our teeth, sit down dinners with everyone talking, and chores for each of us kids. There was an hour of TV now and again and long days playing out in the fields or picking blueberries for the old woman who lived up the road in a ramshackle old house with no paint on it. We played flashlight tag with the Ports kids up the road and I hung out with my best friend Tara or went swimming with Gaby, Christian, and Matthew at Paige's swimming hole in town. I still liked to get dressed up for church on Sundays, although the services annoyed me, and Debbie began teaching me guitar. Occasionally, her musician friends would all come up to the house and sit around the wood stove playing music. There were banjos and Limberjacks, dulcimers, and autoharps. I'd try to play along now and again and we all sang and laughed and ate treats. Except for when Bill hugged me and shoved both his hands down my shorts to grab my ass, I was very happy.

The next spring, just before Wentworth Elementary School broke for the summer, there was a school dance. Christian and I got dressed to go and then swung by Brad's room for a visit under the A-frame of the eaves. Brad was in his early teens and we thought he was super cool. He was smoking pot and we wanted to try some. You know, to look cool, too. Christian and I each took a big hit or two of the joint and then got in the car with Brad to head to the school dance. By the time we arrived, the weed was hitting me. As I got out of the car, I heard a voice, very far away. Suddenly, a mélange of bizarre noises and visuals surrounded me. It seemed like people's hands were floating through my head. Eventually, I had a massive panic attack and ran outside into the field behind the school. Mr. Vaughan, the principal, was notified, and came out to talk to me, but I simply couldn't be near him. He appeared large and looming, eerie and threatening, his voice echoing from far away. It was all too much; I disassociated. Debbie was called, Brad was in deep doo-doo, and I was soon on my way home to a very displeased Grandma.

I spent the summer at Towners, dissociating and trying to hang on for dear life to my tenuous sanity. Something had broken loose inside me. I was terrified and free falling with no one to guide me. Grandma tried, holding me in her arms as I cried and begged her to keep me from "going away" again, but then I would end up disconnected from myself, swimming in an eerie fog of ambient anxiety again.

The Towners house

CHAPTER 7
IN THE WEEDS

Anxious attachment wasn't natural to me, but I came by it honestly. Children are born peaceful, until they are dangled by their feet and smacked in the cold earthly air. We are taught by the world to cry out to advocate for ourselves. Our bodies know that if we are silent, we might starve. It is only when we are uncomfortable that we get attention, like baby birds in a nest squealing for the worm and flapping their wings for balance and positional superiority. Weakness breeds contempt and is reviled like the plague. It often results in death in the natural world. So, we learn quickly that the violence of discomfort precedes anything good, and that to survive we have to fight. But to succeed in battle one must have a strategy or know how to retreat. We simply can't fight effectively if we don't understand the battlefield. If we are entirely lost, we stumble about until we are injured or find solace in some happenstance haven.

Early on, my mother, my sister, and my father were

taken from me, and it became difficult for me to feel a secure attachment to anyone. I grew up in the large, lonely houses of my grandparents, punctuated with a few months to a year here and there with Debbie or a friend's family. And during these years of unpredictability and loneliness, Grandma would periodically go away on trips with Grandpa. There was a trip to Saudi Arabia to visit King Faisal, and a couple of trips to Hawaii to visit her friend, the playwright Aldith Morris. There were others peppered in now and again, and each time, she would leave me at 800 with Jim and Mrs. Collins. Except for one trip she made to film *F.I.S.T.* with Sylvester Stallone in Dubuque, Iowa, and a brief stint in LA where she stayed at the Chateau Marmont and I stayed with her brother, Uncle Al in Towners.

But generally, when they were away, I'd be in the city with Jim and Mrs. Collins. Jim would attend to business around the flat by day, then he would go back to his home in Brooklyn, and Mrs. Collins would stay with me at night. I'd go to school during the week, and Mrs. Collins would pick me up and walk me home across the street, then I'd bumble around the house until it was time for dinner. After that, I'd make my way down the long hall, sometimes trailing my fingertips along the fine wallpaper, bumping over door frames, my feet padding lightly on the soft carpet, until I reached the swinging door of the kitchen. Mrs. Collins would hear me come in and she'd say something like, "C'mon girl, get up here on one of them stools and get you some dinner." I'd eat and chat cheerfully with her, happy to be talking to someone, then she'd take my plate and send me back down the hall. The loneliness of the great hallway would swallow me up as I trudged back to my room.

I'd often sit in the window seat in my bedroom looking down at Park Avenue, watching the yellow cabs go by and doormen opening doors for fancy women in their fur coats and heels. They chatted loudly and their laughter would punctuate the night air, floating up to me like the sounds of a Lautrec cabaret painting coming to life. The nighttime gave me a slight sense of dread, as the darkness would creep in, crawling up the walls and making hollow noises as if ghosts knew my name. Some nights before bed, Mrs. Collins would come down the long hallway to help me bathe, her nylon-clad thighs announcing her approach with a *swish swish* sound, but then she'd be off to her end of the house to watch *Sanford & Son* in the maids' quarters. I might then make my way to the dark den with the cracked green leather couch to watch TV; something I wasn't allowed to do if Grandma were home. This made me feel even lonelier, but it gave me something to do for a while. When it was late enough, I'd head back to my room, wishing it were tomorrow, and climb into the cream-colored Louis XIV bed and toss and turn until I fell asleep. If I were too afraid and couldn't sleep, I'd tiptoe down to Mrs. Collins' room and ask her if I could sleep with her.

"Get in here," she'd say, "but hush up child, 'cuz I'm watching my picture." Mrs. Collins always called movies "pictures" and it confused me. I'd snuggle in next to her big, warm body and proceed to tease and mess with her.

"Girl, now leave me alone," she'd say, but I knew she didn't mean it like Grandma and Grandpa meant it, because Mrs. Collins would play back. Her bark was bigger than her bite, and we both knew it.

The starkness of her room and the strangeness of her

TV shows made me sad, but it was what I had, so I used it for comfort. Everything was so unfamiliar and strange, and yet it seemed so mundane that I was sure there was something I was missing about it all. It hurt my head.

When Grandma and Grandpa would eventually come home, they'd sweep into the foyer, Jim carting their luggage behind them, my grandmother looking elegant in her high heels and red lipstick, her hair pulled back into a tight bun, and her white TWA bag in hand. Grandpa always had small gifts for me, even if it was just a piece of candy or a touristy silver spoon from his travels. I'd follow Grandma to her room and watch her unpack beautiful textiles and gowns, jewelry boxes, and the like that had been given to her by princes and presidents' wives. Grandpa would head to his room to shower and relax for the rest of the night.

The pain of those solitary times was harsh, but I resigned myself, accepting my fate until Grandma would come home and I'd experience a sense of relief. It was so much bigger than me that I had no fight. But when I knew Grandma was going to be leaving and I still had a chance to protest, that was a terrible time. The fear would strangle me, and I'd feel a sense of impossible desperation engulfing me.

I would ask Grandma, "What's going to happen to me when you die?" or "Are you coming back soon?" "Can I go with you?" "Why can't I go too?" And she would answer and that would be that. I'd watch her walking down the hall with Grandpa, with that white TWA bag once again, then the quiet of the hallway would set upon me again, like a heavy cougar draped over me, its fangs sinking into me, the deafening silence of the flat ringing in my ears as cars honked outside in a distant world.

The hardest part of it all was that it never got better, though I kept thinking it would. The grind went on for years.

We spent a lot of time at 800, as I was attending Hewitt, and Grandpa's place was very close to my school. My room at 800 was scary to me. It had an odd mix of furniture. The two Louis XIV beds and the hand-painted wallpaper imported from Paris were stark reminders that I was a guest, as they reflected nothing of my own personality, nor did they offer any child-friendly comforts. Near the bathroom door stood a dark Japanese Tonsu dresser that was always filled with Grandma's ballgowns and a set of Greek skirts she had purchased while on the set of *America America*, the story of Elia Kazan's uncle's life and his very difficult journey to America, filmed in Greece. It was a large room and I felt small in it. Nightmares visited me frequently when I slept there. One I had repeatedly was of a procession of people in masquerade costumes. Surreal in their excessive mirth, they paraded toward me with an evil human-sized stinging bee at the back of the line, which walked on two legs and aimed to kill me. I would wake from my nightmares in that big, dark room and then tiptoe down the hallway to my grandmother's room where I would lie on the floor in my nightgown, smelling the cool air blowing from under the door. She would wake to find me there, cold and curled up in a ball. For a time, she kept a small mattress on the floor of her bedroom for me to sleep on, but if I moved around too much, she would tell me to settle down and then I'd try to lie as still as I could, uncomfortable and wishing I could move. Still, it was better than being afraid in my room. I loved the smell of Grandma's room and I liked her delicate gauzy nightshirts from India. She was my world. I'd be like her one day.

One morning when I was ready for school and went to say my customary goodbyes to Grandma, my coat snagged on her coffee pot filled with boiling water next to her bed and I pulled it down onto my leg, scalding my calf. Grandma put butter and a bandage on the wound and sent me to school. When I came home, it had blistered terribly and I had to stay home in bed the next day. My grandmother would not take me to the doctor, however, opting to always care for me herself. She bathed my legs in cool water and sent me back to school as soon as possible. This was typical. Grandma never took us to the doctor. I think it was a behavior remnant from her childhood. If I were sick, she would bundle me in itchy wool with Vicks VapoRub or feed me chips of ice while I vomited uncontrollably, nursing me ever so slowly back to health, but there was little emotional warmth in Grandma's homemade ministrations. Being sick, when I was already so lonely, was miserable, but there was nothing to do but weather it.

Once in a while I would rebel, although it only resulted in greater isolation. One night Grandma had gotten angry with me about something and shut me in my bedroom at 800. I was furious and sad so I lay on the bed kicking the Louis XIV headboard. Grandpa's room was next to mine and the next thing I knew, John W. Hill was at my doorway. He never said anything, but I saw his arm reach for the door and *BAM*, he closed it. I was crushed to know he was angry with me but also felt betrayed that no one came to comfort me in the depths of my distress. I fell asleep on top of the covers, my head still at the foot of the bed, the sounds of cars on the street below, and lights flashing against the red, white, and blue striped French wallpaper.

My grandmother, Elena Karam, on the set of America America, *the story of Director Elia Kazan's life*

Although I was in school, it was not acceptable for me to have people over to the house, so I spent all my time in isolation. Grandma was always in her room and Grandpa was at the office, so I made up ways to occupy my time as best I could. When I couldn't keep myself entertained, I followed Grandma around or bugged Jim and Mrs. Collins in the kitchen for a few minutes until they told me to "get up on outta here, Messaround."

I often stood in Grandma's bathroom doorway and talked to her while she got ready for bed. I remember her clearly one night standing in front of the mirror in her tent nightgown, her dyed black hair hanging thinly down her back, a picture of old age and fatigue.

"Your Uncle Al was my mother's favorite," she said. "Al could do no wrong in our mother's eyes." Then Grandma told me about a long-ago night when she was late getting home, and worried Nellie would be angry with her. She had taken a shortcut that required her to jump a tall fence. It was dark and as she grabbed the top of the fence to pull herself up, she felt a stabbing pain in her hand where a rusty barbed wire had dug into her palm, making a large gash. She bled profusely, but somehow managed to hide it from her mother. Nellie was tired and poor and prone to fits of rage if the kids were too troublesome, even though she loved them in her own way, and Grandma did everything possible to avoid her wrath. Over the course of the next few weeks, Grandma managed her infected hand all on her own and her mother never found out. My grandmother was eight when that happened. She showed me her palm. Her hand still bore a thick, jagged scar all those years later.

"Why didn't your mother love you?" I asked.

"I never knew," she replied.

I leaned into her slight body, feeling her warmth through the cotton nightgown, and hugged her.

"I love you, Grandma," I told her. "I'm sorry."

That night I went to bed feeling closer to my grandmother. Somehow, I felt like my love for her would keep us both safe, and besides, the threats were in the past. We were allies, and even though I was another of her unfortunate rescues, I sure as hell didn't know it at the time. Like the stray cats that she saved, I lived within the long quiet halls of 800 and the various country houses they would buy but barely inhabit. All my basic needs were met—I had a warm bed and food—but the long years were eternal. Lamentably, I was possessed of the inconvenient vitality of a normal, growing child, and in time, this would separate me, even from Grandma.

***

The summer after my third grade year, Uncle Wiley stayed with us at Towners. Handsome and cool, he annoyed my grandparents. I thought he was awesome. Wiley lit up the quiet, cool hallways of Towners, as if a halo of hotness hovered around him, his long hippy hair cascading rebelliously over his shoulders and down his chest. His smile belied a secret, and I knew there was more to him than my grandparents wanted there to be. Although by adoption Wiley was her son, he really was my grandmother's grand-nephew. Grandma had a niece who had gotten pregnant out of wedlock and since in those days it was a huge no-no, to spare the family any scandal, my grandparents adopted him and named him after Grandpa's middle name.

Wiley was going through a lot when I knew him, though I didn't fully understand the extent of it. I found him exciting. He wore bell bottoms, listened to Cat Stevens, and liked *Playboy* magazine, which made him a little scary. The forbidden is always intimidating, but it pulls you toward it like the cliff's edge. He slept in the maid's quarters just off the kitchen, and the wall between Wiley's bedroom and the living room where my grandfather took his evening beer was made of thin sheetrock, so privacy was a bit of a sham.

Wiley was home from the Stockbridge School, where he had reportedly developed a horrible speed habit. He passed the long hours at Towners smoking pot out of a multi-tubed blue pipe while he worked on a large model ship. I liked the smell of weed that wafted up from the crack at the bottom of the door as I stood in the hallway outside trying to think of an excuse to hang out with him. After pausing there for a few moments, I finally summoned the courage to knock on his door. Wiley was happy to see me when he opened the door and invited me in, stepping back and waving his arm grandly. He quickly sat back down on his bed, took a big hit of weed from his pipe, and went back to working on the model ship, dousing it in a big cloud of smoke that looked temporarily like an ocean fog. A minute later he popped another bud in the pipe and slid it toward me, raising his eyebrows and smiling. He put his forefinger to his lips and whispered, "Shhhhh" as he nodded his head toward the sheetrock wall.

I picked up the pipe and he helped me hold it as I pulled in the smoke. I let out the first hit and he held the pipe in front of my face again, so I grabbed it and repeated the ritual. We both laughed and I knew something was different. I was different. I had broken some unspoken rule and had temporarily escaped the slow, grinding clutch of my mundane life at Towners.

Unfortunately, on the other side of that thin wall, Grandma and Grandpa must have heard or smelled something suspicious and I heard Grandma call out:

"Sammy, come here,"

"Be right there."

I looked at Wiley apologetically, tore myself away from the comfort of his room, and slunk away, a bit stoned.

Wiley was promptly expelled from the house for giving dope to poor me, but our bond was sealed. From that day on, Wiley and I were close in our own weirdly inappropriate way, kind of an honor-among-thieves type of bond. He would later die of alcoholism, alone in a shitty Florida double-wide in his mid-thirties, but we'd get a few more laughs in before he did.

***

In 1975, Grandpa sold his 800 Park Avenue apartment and moved to The Carlyle. Soon after, he was diagnosed with a brain tumor, and any large social gatherings in his home abruptly ceased. The new apartment had regal red carpeting in the foyer and impossible white carpeting in the living room where the baby grand piano stood. There were white window shades on all the windows. I thought The Carlyle was kind of a bummer because compared to Grandpa's sprawling third floor apartment at 800, the new apartment seemed dinky. The one good thing about the Carlyle was a friend from school lived across the street so we would shout loudly out the windows or send flashlight signals to each other across the wide boulevard, high above the clamor of relentless city traffic.

Not long after we moved to The Carlyle, Mrs. Collins traveled to Mississippi with her husband, so my grandparents hired a German nanny to watch over me. *Blech.* I hated Hedi with her thin, flat rear and her Prince Valiant bowl cut. She didn't allow me to slather myself with baby powder after baths and couldn't understand why I wouldn't eat my peas. She had a large wart on her chin and didn't appreciate my gerbils, which had reproduced at a somewhat unacceptable rate. Eventually, the gerbils got so fat that two of them died trying to crawl out of a hole in the mesh cage. They were stuck wriggling in the wire until they suffocated. I blamed Hedi.

We were living at The Carlyle the day Mrs. Maytag— of Maytag washers and dryers—dropped a long cigarette ash onto the white carpet. I happened to be standing at just the right angle to see it happen and hurried to tattle to Grandma who frowned and said something about the nouveau riche, as if Grandma wasn't nouveau riche herself. It was a topic of discussion for years afterward. I felt proud of myself for feeling territorial about the condition of our home, even though I resented that white carpet because, as I saw it, the Carlyle apartment wasn't Grandpa's real home.

As Grandpa's illness progressed, I must have seemed too much of a burden again, because Grandma sent me to Connecticut to live with Sally and Charlie Lowe. They were a youngish couple that looked after Tanty's old property for Grandma, but lived in a small apartment in New Milford.

It was during that stay with the Lowes that Grandma sent me a pair of penny loafers, which I had begged and begged for back in the days when I was going to The Hewitt School in New York City. But I wasn't an eight-year-old attending an exclusive all-girls private school anymore. I finally got the damned loafers only when I was eleven years old, my grandpa was dying, and I was attending Schaghticoke Middle School where my new shoes inspired no end of derisive laughter.

I'm sure Grandma was trying to do something nice, but I was beginning to understand she was hopeless at taking care of growing girls. I didn't need footwear. I needed someone to guide me through my sadness and fear. I felt like I was about to lose the one person who ensured we weren't going to go completely to shit. All the structure I had in my life was because of Grandpa. When he was in the house, there was order and stability. Everybody did what they were supposed to do, meals were on time, the house was clean, and there weren't too many cats. Everything was dialed in and I felt safe. I was about to lose that and I felt a permeating sense of dread.

It was around that time when my science teacher, Mr. Sacca, showed my class a black-and-white reel of the Hiroshima bombing. In the movie, bodies of little children were melted into the ground and sand had turned to glass. I had nightmares about that movie for a long time, but there was nobody to tell, nobody to help me deal with my fears. My family was far away and the Lowes had their own problems. Money was always tight for them and Charlie was an alcoholic who we later learned was gay, so I'm guessing there were marital issues too. I was just the granddaughter of their wealthy employer. They fed me and gave me a bed to sleep in, as they were being paid to do, but didn't concern themselves with me any further than that and I felt a slight hint of resentment from them.

On a March day in 1977, Jim arrived to get me. He drove me back to The Carlyle. Grandma took me to Grandpa's room where he was laying in the hospital bed with both arms under the covers. A nurse was in attendance. Grandma said my grandfather had been comatose for days.

"John, Sammy's here," Grandma said quietly. Then she prompted me: "Say goodbye to Grandpa."

I put my hand on his bed and just looked at him. As I stood there, my grandfather opened his eyes weakly, took the trouble to pull his hands out from under the covers, took hold of my hand and kissed it, and then he smiled. My grandmother was flabbergasted. For the rest of her life she would tell the story of how Grandpa awoke to see me and say goodbye, even when he wouldn't talk to anyone else. It has become part of the family mythology that I was Grandpa's favorite. I have no idea if that was true; I only know I always gravitated toward my Grandpa because he felt stable. My grandmother's life was an enigma to me, but Grandpa had a life I could see and make sense of. He had a business and business friends and people who respected him. He was a horseback rider and a man of tremendous personal discipline. Though I barely knew him, Grandpa was solid and I loved him. After Grandpa died, I just didn't know what was going to happen anymore.

***

Grandma had to sell Towners, which sucked because it

had been one of the constants in my life and we had already lost Grandpa. Other things slipped more insidiously. Jim and Mrs. Collins no longer bothered to wear their uniforms, meals were any time instead of on a predictable schedule, and suddenly I was allowed to watch TV as often and as long as I wanted. It was nothing that was going to kill anybody, but it messed with my sense of security, which had always been elusive anyway. Grandma did end up getting Towners back, but everything else just kept slipping more and more. And almost immediately, there was the problem of what to do with me.

Grandma wanted to work and got a small part in a movie called *F.I.S.T.* with Sylvester Stallone. She was to play his girlfriend's mother, Mrs. Zerinkas. It was a family affair. I was assigned to find her lines in the script and underline them for her. When it came time for her to go to Dubuque, Iowa and Hollywood to film, my grandmother's younger brother Alfred was to care for me. This was novel. Usually, when it was inconvenient for Grandma to have me with her, she sent me to live with one or another of the caretakers who looked after her various properties. It was unpleasant at best.

Uncle Al lived in Florida and was from the other side of the tracks. He had not pursued an education like my grandmother and remained a working man who was a Florida Coast Guard, and also worked for a while at Cape Canaveral, where they launched rockets into space. He wasn't around much; I got the feeling Grandpa didn't have much use for Uncle Al. I thought he was fascinating. He had a blue Maverick with a dashboard filled with all kinds of police and HAM radios and scanners, and he had a shiny black revolver he kept in a desk drawer in the kitchen when he visited us at Towners.

Uncle Al asked my grandmother before she left for Hollywood if he could teach me how to shoot the revolver, which endeared him to me despite Grandma's prompt "no." Uncle Al and I careened our way through that summer free from Grandma's rules and judgment. We even took a road trip to Florida in his Maverick, staying overnight in a motel and saying "Breaker 1-9" into the CB as we tailed 18-wheelers using cruise control to avoid getting speeding tickets. We stopped at diners along the way and I chatted with him, asking all sorts of questions as we watched trucks come and go in the parking lot. Uncle Al always answered my questions in his deep voice and, now and again, would pat my head and smile.

***

In 1979, we moved to New Milford, Connecticut. Grandma had purchased Tanty's property there years before to keep it "in the family." The large square 1800s home was immaculate and Tanty had lived there forever, but she had finally grown too old to care for it and moved to a fancy duplex apartment in an elder community. Grandma's intention was to preserve the house for Tanty, should she ever wish to come back, which Tanty thought was absurd. Tanty urged my grandmother to redecorate, but Grandma insisted on keeping it like Tanty had always had it, though she moved our furniture in. It looked strange to me, except for my room, which was the same as it had always been when I visited Tanty: pink rose wallpaper, a white sleigh bed, a Victorian roll-top desk, a beautiful mahogany dresser, and a little table with a mirror where I could attend to my appearance before school. As usual, I was not allowed to put anything up on the walls because of the wallpaper.

Grandma had always been a lot laxer with her appearance when we were in the country, but after we moved to New Milford, she really let herself go. When Grandpa was alive, he had provided structure and kept our daily lives in line. After he was gone, Grandma fell apart. She no longer employed Jim—I assume she couldn't afford to—so Grandma took to eating out of cans while standing at the kitchen counter, her blue jeans rolled up sloppily, her hair pulled into a messy bun with three hairpins. At night she would take her favorite cats out of the cages and retire to her bed with them. Worse, Grandma retreated from the world, which meant she once again withdrew me from the world.

Thankfully, she decided Gaby and I would attend Canterbury Prep School in New Milford that year. We were to board at the school and I was excited at the prospect of living full-time with people my age, but as usual, I struggled to relate to my peers.

The other students arrived in dark cars with shiny windows. Well-dressed mothers and fathers fretted over them in the dorm rooms as they settled in. I, on the other hand, had been dropped off by Grandma with a couple of suitcases and found my way up to my dorm room myself. Because there was a dress code at the school, Grandma had been forced to shop with me. She purchased a brown blazer that matched only a few things I wore, a pair of bright red corduroy pants, and some other dorky, ill-fitting clothes. I hadn't yet figured out style and looked out of place, but I was there. In spite of a pervasive feeling of aloneness and fear of the unknown, I was interested to see what would happen next.

One of the first people I met was a classically beautiful blonde girl named Christina who lived immediately above me on the third floor. She was somewhat naive, so we got along well. The other kids, who were dressed fashionably in prep school clothes and happily well-adjusted, buzzed about their lives, going to classes, doing well in school, and smoking cigarettes in front of one of the boys' dorms. Having been taught how to succeed in the world, they walked with confidence and played lacrosse. Meanwhile, I had very few life skills and no idea how to manage my schedule or myself. So, I just plodded along, trying to find my tribe. Christine was the first. Angelique from Puerto Rico was the second.

Angelique boarded at Canterbury, just as I did, and we used to climb out onto the roof of her room to listen to Pink Floyd's *The Wall* and smoke cigarettes. Angelique had permission to smoke on campus, but I certainly did not, so I had to resign myself to snagging drags off other people's cigarettes and hoping Grandma never heard about it. Angelique was so confident and self-assured; however, I wasn't afraid we would get caught on the roof. She seemed to know what she was doing and I felt at ease with her. She even wore her braces shamelessly and had fiery dyed red hair that looked like a thick, wiry helmet. Once her family took me with them to New York City and we got our hair done, which was a first for me. I got mine cut and straightened and couldn't believe how good it looked and how relevant and human I suddenly felt.

I enjoyed the relief of my first drunk when I was at Canterbury, too. I drank a quarter pint of Bacardi 151 straight, all by myself, and *oh the warmth*. I felt so good, so free, like I just didn't hurt anymore at all and no longer gave a shit about my inhibitions or what others thought of me. My self-doubt, malaise, and pathetic yearning for love and even the most basic sense of well-being all faded away in the warmth of the firewater. Of course, the day ended terribly. We were found super drunk in a barn on someone's private property and the cops were called. We were taken to the police station where we had to wait for someone from school to come get us, and of course they informed my grandmother and suspended me for a few days and then prohibited me from leaving campus when I returned to school.

Gaby was also getting shitfaced and smoking weed at

My dear Uncle Al

Canterbury and eventually we both received a letter politely informing us we were not welcome back the next year. It was a blow. Underneath our bingeing on alcohol and misfit behavior, we desperately wanted to fit in. Grandma was not impressed. She decided it was time we became our parents' problem after all.

CHAPTER 8
TIME TO GO, AND THE INIMITABLE ALFONSO DE LA VEGA

One day, near the end of the school year, Grandma walked into the living room at the New Milford house and asked Gaby and me if we'd like to go to Mexico and meet our father. Just like that. Until that moment, I had no idea that my father was even alive. I had a dad! "Yes!" I said. I couldn't wait. For once, I wasn't going to the house of someone else's "great dad," I was going to visit my own great dad. I could hardly contain myself. I honestly believed that, finally, I was going to be rescued by my long-lost father like in the movie *The Little Princess*.

Mama was planning to go back to Mexico, so Grandma made arrangements to send Gaby and me to Mama, who would deliver us to our father. The first leg of our journey took us to the Catholic Worker Farm in Tivoli, New York, where Mama and Alex and the girls had been living since the cold February day when Grandma kicked them off her Connecticut place. By that time, it had become a pattern for Grandma to hint that perhaps Mama could have us back if she lived nearer. In case it would finally work out, Mama and Alex would pack up the girls and move to some house Grandma offered to let them use. It never worked out for long, leaving Mama and Alex to figure out what on Earth to do next, and the Connecticut attempt was no exception.

The Catholic Worker Farm was supposed to be a communal utopia where people from all walks of life lived together and looked after each other. Maybe the place lived up to Catholic Worker ideals when it was first started in 1964, but by the time Gaby and I arrived, it was obviously going to seed. Most of the people who lived there were very poor and broken in one way or another. Very few of them helped with the work. There was a lot of drunkenness and gross behavior there that scared me.

I recall one time sitting in the kitchen chatting happily with our family friend Betsy while she kneaded bread dough. We were complaining a bit about the Catholic Worker and Betsy said she liked it with the exception of one thing. Then, without missing a beat, she flipped the dough over and picked out a number of wriggly little cockroaches. We just stared. Only one meal was served each day and Gaby and I were always famished by dinner time. To eat the bread or not to eat the bread? That was the question, but there was no good answer.

Mama and Alex had a two-room place at Catholic Worker where paint was chipping off the walls and the beds were on the floor. At night, Mama would tuck the little girls into bed and lay down with them. The light would be on and I could watch her talk to them, mothering them like she would have mothered Gaby and me if we hadn't been taken from her. But we were too late to the show. Teenaged girls don't get tucked in by their mothers. Watching Mama with my little sisters, my heart would ache and it made me short-tempered with the girls, which was unfair, but I couldn't help myself. Gaby and I felt kind of left out and we resented the girls for having our mom in a way we never had. At the same time, we liked how the girls looked up to us because we were teenagers.

Gaby and I didn't have chores or any structure to our day—Mama didn't believe in schedules, even when she home-schooled the girls--so we were at loose ends. We spent that hot summer lazing around the historic buildings with their cool walls, tall ceilings, and artistic chipping paint, watching the Hudson River flow by, waiting to go to Mexico.

In preparation for our trip, Alex and my mother bought a full-sized school bus and set about fixing it up to be livable. Alex painted it yellow with green stripes and removed the accordion-like front door, replacing it with a round wooden one. By the time we were ready to roll, the bus was outfitted with wooden shelves from front to back on either side, laden with books and hanging potted plants, and sported a different color curtain in each window. My mother's antique Spanish table stood in the front. A large bed covered the entire back part of the bus and Alex had even installed a fully functioning porcelain toilet. We took our leave from the Catholic Worker farm and drove in the heavy bus to my grandmother's house where we stayed in the caretaker's cottage for a while. My parent's crazy-but-brilliant friend Alfie stayed in the bus, which was parked on one side of the house.

Alfie was a tall man with a large belly, a booming voice, and a black shock of tousled hair that he habitually ruffled with his hands before bursting into loud opera librettos that he had composed. At all times, a heavy green bottle of Rhine wine dangled thickly from his large hands. He mostly wore loose-fitting overalls that made him look even bigger and more insane, but on occasion he would come in wearing his tighty-whities and all us girls would grimace and shrink back into our beds, whispering to each other about Alfie being at it again. We found him quite entertaining and loved him, but we also found him quite shocking and loved to hate him.

When it finally came time to leave New York, we were all excited to get going. I divided my time on the road wisely: sometimes sitting in a folding chair next to Alex as he drove and saying "Step on it!" when he looked back at me, and sometimes loafing in the back of the bus in my denim short shorts, flirting with truck drivers behind us.

After a few weeks of driving, with periodic stops in places like Ogallala, Nebraska, and Salt Lake City, we arrived in California. We roamed around Mendocino to L.A. until we were so broke that our parents had to resort to dumpster diving for food at times. Grandma must have been told about our destitution because she flew Gaby and me back to her for the school year. The rest of the family had to tough it out as best they could.

***

The next summer when I was about 14, Gaby and I rejoined Mama, Alex and the girls in Castroville, California, where Marilyn Monroe got her start by being crowned the first Artichoke Queen. From there, we headed down the 101 south to Mexico via La Rumorosa, the legendary mountain pass in Baja, California. As our creaky school bus climbed the steep grades and lurched heavily around hairpin turns, we looked through the multi-colored curtains blowing in the hot air and could see straight down, in the ravines below us, the twisted metal of jackknifed trucks and piles of rusted cars that had never made it to their intended destinations. We envisioned our own bus heaving over the cliffs, colliding loudly with the rocks, the metal cutting into us, and were suddenly scared religious. Gathered on the bed, we learned to say the rosary, praying aloud in unison to find comfort, hoping our words would prevent our imminent death in the Sierra de Juarez Mountains.

We survived the cliffs of Federal Highway 2D only to find ourselves driving endlessly through the thick desert air, gliding heavily past cow carcasses with vultures atop them. My youngest sister Miriam was a baby then and had become more dehydrated than the rest of us, so we took turns feeding her ice cubes, purposely letting the melting water drip down her chin and onto her chubby tummy to cool her down.

A week or so later, we were happy to find ourselves at a fancy camper-trailer park in Ciudad Granja. Alex began teaching English at the Centro Cultural in Guadalajara, leaving my mother to care for all six of us girls. The trailer park was populated with travelers in RVs and happy families. While parents took care of campsite business, kids joyfully swam in the outdoor pool all day. Upon our arrival, Gaby and I immediately threw on some short shorts and went hunting for boys. On our first night there, we found some new friends and drank copious amounts of tequila. We were soon in the back of the bus throwing up in a bucket under the tired eyes of my mother and stepfather. The girls were enthralled by our behavior. They peered at us as we took turns leaning over the five-gallon bucket, each of us holding the other's hair out of her face. We were scarcely done when we high-tailed it outside to our tent, which we had hastily thrown up the night before, screeching as giant flying cucarachas landed on us, digging their sticklike insect claws into our skin and grabbing hold of our hair. I imagine my mother thought that was just what we deserved.

A few days later, Gaby and I found ourselves with my mother's friend Napoleon, bumbling along in his white VW bug on our way to Puerto Vallarta.

I was excited to meet my dad and was quite curious what he would be like. My sense of adventure was high and I felt a new strength in my freedom from my grandmother. The simple fact was that the greater the distance from her, the happier I was. It didn't matter that we had no money or that I had no idea where the hell I was going. It didn't matter that Napoleon was a stranger, chattering on happily to us as if anything he said mattered. It didn't matter that I had no center or ties that bound me to something greater than the immediacy of the moment. I was free, and I was curious. And after all the years of living in the unknown and unexpected, living in the moment was no stranger to me. In fact, I had found a home in it.

The smell of the dust and the old creaking Volkswagen with the hard plastic seats permeated the air and created a different aura that I had never experienced before. Gaby, on the other hand, shrunk back from Napoleon, sullen and annoyed. She had wanted to stay and hang out with her friends after the close of school but was torn away from them with no hope of returning. I'm sure that in her wish to remain there in Connecticut she had not thoroughly considered what it would have actually been like had she stayed there isolated with Grandma. She would have had no transportation and, most likely, Grandma would have forbidden her to go out. I briefly envisioned Gaby tying sheets together and dropping down from her bedroom window to the cool ground under the shroud of night. But nonetheless, she was furious to be in Mexico against her will.

As we drove along toward Vallarta, I pondered my grandmother's decision to send us all this way. In spite of the Socratic fashion in which my grandmother had posed the question to us, the choice had already been made and the conversation to gauge our interest was a mere formality. It was typical for things to just happen to us, and we would float down the river of experience with no understanding of the logistics or overall dynamics that we would be dealing with. Often, it didn't work out so well for us. Years later as an adult, I would think to myself that the conversation could have gone like this: "Hey girls, you're going to meet your dad who is gay and lives with his lover, whose name is Inomar. They live in the jungle with no running water and no electricity, but they are very close to Puerto Vallarta—a mere 30-minute hike down a windy path above the Rio Cuale—and if you need anything, you can call us using the public phones in Puerto Vallarta. We will be checking on you periodically to make sure you're ok." But nope, there was none of that. There was simply, "What do you think of meeting your father?" And even the "meeting your father" was disingenuous, because the intention was to have us live with him. Years later I would ponder what had possessed my grandmother to even consider such a thing. 12 years earlier, my mother had asked the *commandante* to lock up my enraged father for a night while she escaped with us to Guadalajara, and now here we were on our way to live with him without a clue about how he lived, how he planned to take care of us, if he were competent to do so, or if it were safe.

And so it was that we found ourselves in Napoleon's car on a sunny day in Mexico, heading to meet our very creative, fiery, unconventional father.

In Puerto Vallarta, we bumped along cobblestone streets, past fine stucco and tile apartments high on a hill, and shady little houses with ceiling fans rattling in the cool dark, to the back of town where the roads were dirt and poor people lived. We stopped in a cloud of yellowish-brown dust, climbed stiffly out of the small vehicle and stood curiously in the street with our belongings. Napoleon was a pleasant fellow who had been kind to take us all that way and we felt a certain liking for him, coupled with a slightly desperate and familiar feeling of hope that he wouldn't leave us alone in this strange place. He chatted cheerfully, questioning the air around us: "Where are they? They must be coming soon."

It wasn't long before my father and Inomar emerged from a narrow pathway at a snappy clip, towing an impudent donkey, which Inomar periodically swatted with a switch he had torn off a bush somewhere. A streak of blood dripped down the donkey's face, and I felt a familiar twinge of pity for him, but I stood still saying nothing, trying to look okay. Inomar was handsome and tan, a muscular Indio man with long brown hair, which he brushed out of his face periodically with his thick, strong hands.

He was ripped, and I was immediately attracted to him.

My father, on the other hand, was slender with pale white skin, sparkling green eyes, and an aristocratic nose. He wore a poncho-like blue-and-white-striped shirt, red bikini underwear (as opposed to an actual bathing suit), and flip-flops, which snapped against his heels as he walked briskly toward us, smiling widely and saying in a loud, deep voice, *"Mis hijas!"*

As my father embraced us, Gaby cringed, bristling with silent outrage. I leaned into him, thrilled that this man was my father and he was smiling and looking directly at me. He smelled dusty and natural and I liked him immediately. I had spent so many years watching other kids greet their parents on the sprawling lawns of Canterbury, in tiny New Hampshire towns, or in the bustling streets of New York City, shiny black cars swooping in smoothly, doors flipping open, chauffeurs in attendance, as the children always smiled and joyfully submitted to the glorious moments of inclusion and love. Now it was my turn. I reveled in it. Napoleon was relieved to have completed his task and, saying a quick good-bye, spun on his heels, lurched heavily into the tiny, dust-covered bug, and was off before we knew it, leaving a cloud of dust in his wake. We never saw him again. Years later we would find out he died in a car accident on the road from Guadalajara to Mexico City, just a year after his younger brother died in a car accident on the same road.

My dad told us he had prepared a space for us in his humble home as Inomar made quick business of piling our luggage onto the stubborn donkey, whose face—to our horror—continued to bleed from the switch. Then we lumbered slowly up the path toward El Remance, where my father lived among the poor. Up we went, weaving around corners, looking down at the river below us, until we finally reached our destination: a small two-room house with a tin roof, a porch with a hammock my father didn't allow anyone else to use, and no running water or electricity, just a well in the back, and an outhouse. I felt cheated. I finally had the dad, but the situation was certainly unattractive and made me feel lonely again. As we entered the house, unceremoniously placing our bags on the green cement floor, we studied the room, and I instantaneously shifted into hoping for the best; something I had become quite adept at.

My father was from a good family who lived in Culiacán, Sinaloa for generations. Family legend was that Pancho Villa had stolen land from us way back when. Daddy was an actor in Bellas Artes in Mexico City—his name first on the marquee. In the 1960s, he did Sartre's *No Exit* in the nude and was known for his outrageous, avant-garde performances. He designed clothes for movie stars, including Liz Taylor and Richard Burton while they were filming *Night of the Iguana* in Vallarta, and even had a store to sell his designs on Michigan Avenue in Chicago. It hadn't occurred to me that we'd find him living in a cement box without a shitter.

It turned out my father had been dropping acid, which he got by mail order from a lab in England. He lived for years in Oaxaca where he took copious amounts of LSD and subsequently came to believe he was the third coming of the Messiah. Naturally, he'd renounced all his wealth and started a "spiritual group" that featured frequent orgies. He actually had quite a following of people, some of whom would fly down to Mexico on their private jets. He slept with many of his followers, justifying it as a "spiritual journey" to each of them. Alas, he would accept no gifts from any of them, in keeping with his vow of poverty.

While I regretted not arriving in time to enjoy him while he was still in favor of wealth and fame, I was quite curious about my father, who now led us into the house, taking us through the first room and into the second room where he placed our luggage on the bed that stood in the middle of the floor. In the jungle, all beds are in the middle to keep insects from crawling up the walls and into them. Daddy explained all sheets and blankets had to be stripped from the beds daily and placed in a sealed wardrobe to prevent bugs from making nests in them during the day. Once we forgot to take the bottom sheet off and came home to a wriggling mass of large black ants underneath it. We were impressed and never forgot again.

During our first days there, my dad took us around, slappety-slapping through the streets of Vallarta in his flip-flops, introducing us to everyone with a large smile on his face. Everyone would wave from their stores and homes, greeting us with big smiles and then, given the opportunity, they would furtively pull us aside to say, "If you ever need anything, let us know."

Daddy took us to a store called Sucesos where some of his designs were still sold, and let us pick out a number of outfits. Overjoyed, I went for the skimpiest purple string bikini bathing suit with beads on the sides and the sexiest jumpsuit I could find.

We spent a few months living up in El Remance with my dad and Inomar. Gaby and I tore up and down the dusty trail alongside the rushing, muddy Rio Cuale into Vallarta to spend our days lying on the sand at Playa de los Muertos, right in front of the El Dorado restaurant, which was owned by an acquaintance of our dad's. In the evenings we'd change into our gauzy 1970s jumpsuits and hit the nightclubs, bumping to "Funky Town" and flashing lights in the discos, Capriccio and Sundance. It wasn't that I liked to party per se; I just liked the people and the music, the laughter and the conviviality. I rarely drank, as the only drink I knew the name of was the Whiskey Sour, which I really didn't like. Instead, I learned to play backgammon with my new friend Arturo and to dance happily. We'd stay out all night until around 5 a.m. I'd bounce back and forth from the dance floor to the dark corners in the back where I played backgammon and smoked cigarettes with Arturo while Gaby did her own thing.

I met Arturo on the beach in front of El Dorado. He was the son of a Guadalajara architect and although he was 27 and I was 15, we became fast friends. He was always quite a gentleman, and was very kind to me, even after he met my father, who was a bit of an embarrassment due to his intense character and direct way of speaking to people. Together, we traveled around Mexico, ate at fine restaurants, snorted pink Peruvian flake that he carried around in fancy flasks, and sipped cold drinks in the hot sun. Arturo was never my boyfriend but was a constant companion during my years in Mexico, and I'm still in touch with him to this day.

Arturo threw fun parties where there would be instruments lying about on the floor or on shelves and tables. People would pick them up and play them, grab a little cocaine from a bowl on the table, or pull off some pot from a bail sitting on the floor. Once at his parent's chalet at Lake Chapala, we were playing backgammon on the bed and I lazily hung my head over the edge. Beneath the bed was a giant bale of pot. After a while, though, I got sick of doing cocaine all the time and started chastising Arturo if he would offer it to me. Many years later, he would do eight years in prison in Guadalajara for trafficking or something of the like. He later found God and changed his ways.

It was an exciting time. Gaby and I had no money, but it wasn't a problem because all around us were people who were willing to pay our way. I was a free spirit supported by people around me who did my dad the honor of watching out for us, and I felt cared for and sustained to some degree by everyone, no matter where we went.

I remember one day sitting by a well in the Mexican jungle, surrounded by the lush green forest, a sense of peace washing over me, and a certain awareness of myself and a force burning bright inside me. The two-room house of my father and Inomar, the spiders and their thick webs, the fireflies, and the rushing river—they all somehow fed my soul, and my sense of freedom grew. I felt wild and brave. I was tan with long dirty blonde hair and I lived in a purple cotton bikini and was always barefoot. Each new thing was an experience unfettered by Grandma's fears and neuroses. I grew into a fierce lion child.

FALLING UP FROM THE BOTTOM

CHAPTER 9
FROM CULIACÁN TO THE CAT HOUSE

Sometime around August of 1980, we packed our things and moved to Culiacán, Sinaloa, where my dad had been born and his family had lived for generations. When we arrived, my father was given his parents' old house near the *mercado* in the center of the dusty desert city. We entered a rickety yellow double-door that opened up from the street into a foyer. Beyond that was a large ballroom with pillars and very high ceilings. Our voices echoed throughout the place. The floor was covered in a foot of dust, tree limbs, and other detritus piled in disarray, but upon further inspection, we found the ballroom floor was a beautiful mosaic that my father later told us had been imported from Spain by his parents. One side of the house was a series of rooms lining a hallway, each with rickety double doors, 15-foot-high ceilings, and bars on the tall windows. Across from those rooms was a garden patio area. At the end of the hall was the kitchen, which was indoors, but opened up into a covered patio and other smaller uncovered patios.

The first thing we set about doing was to clean out a couple of bedrooms, and a third room, where Daddy and Inomar put a *petate* made of palm fronds down on the floor with overstuffed pillows with a TV. This became their smoking and TV room. They'd smoke weed and drink tequila throughout the day, and watch TV shows; my dad flipping through the channels, constantly watching two or three shows at the same time and changing the channel during commercials. It was soon after we moved in that I was standing in the TV room talking to them, when a news report came on telling us that John Lennon had been killed at the Dakota, where I had lived with my grandmother in New York City. John and Yoko lived across the hall from apartment #9 where we lived. As a girl, I had seen them on occasion coming up the hall or sitting in the front office with Winnie while we waited for our respective cars. I remembered Yoko having a warm smile as she looked down at me sitting beside her one day. I had often waited with Heinz, the doorman, a kindly German fellow, in the entryway to the Dakota, sitting with him at times in the little warming hut, or standing by the door to the front office. It seemed strange that John Lennon had just been shot and killed there, yet standing here in this dusty desert city in my family's house, it seemed so far off, and I quickly forgot about it.

Because of the state of the house, Gaby and I went to stay with our uncle Jesus and his family while my father and Inomar worked diligently to clean things up. Tío Jesus and Tía Berta had a house in Chapultepec, one of the nicer neighborhoods in Culiacán, where the streets were clean and there was a fancy *campestre*, or country club, where we could all go to swim and flirt with boys. Berta was fun and would let us listen to music and smoke cigarettes in the recording studio in her house, plus the place had an indoor toilet, so that was a step up.

My cousin, Delia, was my age, loved Hello Kitty, and was very flirtatious. She was clearly very light-hearted and had a large group of giggly friends who all wore makeup, fun clothing, and ponytails. "Silly," I thought to myself, but I also wished I had parents who would take care of me so well that I could also be secure, comfortable, and innocent.

We had arrived in Culiacán shortly before my fifteenth birthday. Berta and Delia were excited to throw me a *quinceanera*, the customary big celebration for girls turning fifteen in Mexico. Picturing myself in one of the big puffy dresses with petticoats I had seen in the Mexican movies, I was not so sure. Fortunately, Tía Berta didn't expect me to wear a gigantic ball gown, so the party was scheduled and everyone was invited to Berta's house. Gaby and I dressed up in Daddy's snazzy Vallarta designs and all eyes were upon us as we pulled into the driveway and stepped out of my cousin's car. I was excited to see people my age and there was plenty of booze and good music. Berta had made the playlist herself in her studio, which is where Gaby and I mostly hung out, smoking cigarettes and flirting with cute fellas while Delia coached me on things to say in Spanish.

Before long, Daddy found us there and insisted we get out into the main house and dance. I tried, but it felt forced and unnatural to me and I simply couldn't do it. Daddy flew into one of his rages. He grabbed me by the arm, yelling that it was time to go, and dragged me out of my own *quinceanera* early, humiliated, and in tears. Back at our house, Gaby and I sat on the bed, crying and lamenting Daddy's temper while Daddy and Inomar watched TV, drinking tequila and smoking pot. It didn't seem to bother Daddy that he had ruined my special night. That was the way he'd always been. If things weren't going his way, he would shut everything down and humiliate whoever crossed him. The longer we were in Culiacán, the more we saw the problems with Daddy.

I was fascinated by my father and felt a strong kinship toward him, if for no other reason than he was mine, and I did manage to earn his admiration for how quickly I learned Spanish. Occasionally, he would play word tricks on me, like the time he sent me to the grocery store for eggs and instructed me to say, *"Tienen huevos?"* to the store clerks. *Huevos* means eggs, but it is also slang for testicles, and given the way the question was posited, the store clerks bust out laughing and shouting to each other as I stood there looking baffled and blushing in the old dusty store in the center of the city. I returned home to find my father and Ino in stitches. I had a good sense of humor and rolled with it, which made my dad like me more, but I also quickly learned to call eggs *blanquillos*.

I longed for a father who would see me, love me, and guide me, but in time, I came to realize my father had trouble seeing past himself.

He didn't have conversations with us. Daddy pontificated and the rest of us listened. After meals, we would retire to the tearoom where Daddy's couch was elevated above little pillbox seats placed on the floor for the rest of us. We would look up at him and he would tell stories about his heyday, remarking in his thick Mexican accent, "Ava Gardner was beautiful and she was fun, but I loved your mother and I wasn't going to betray her." Then he'd tell another one about the days when Liz Taylor and Richard Burton and their famous friends would dance the night away in his restaurants. People laughed and carried on when my father was around, because he was impossible to resist.

"Why do I always arrive after the good times are over?" I used to wonder while my father's stories drifted away in the thick heat of Culiacán. I envisioned my father in the 1960s, smiling and laughing, handsome, holding Ava Gardner in his arms, or better yet, my beautiful mother. I pictured her wearing large silver hooped earrings and a red dress. She had the most amazing smile and their chemistry was electric, the air on fire. People went home and made love after seeing my mom and dad dancing.

He had once been a fine arts actor whose name was at the top of the marquees in Mexico City, but by the time I got there, he was just an aging cult leader repeating stories about himself and smoking strong weed, flanked by his minions, Ino and Jaime. By that time all three of them wore only white and shaved their heads and eyebrows. Ino always walked, stood, or sat to my Dad's left, and Jamie was always at his right.

My father expressed adoration toward us, but he didn't know how to care for teenage girls. Gaby and I could have used some parenting, or at least some instruction on how to spot Culiacán's brand of trouble and stay out of it before we were out of our depth. We expected life in Sinaloa to be the same as in Puerto Vallarta where the townspeople had watched out for us and we could be free-spirited, innocent girls. In Culiacán, where narco-traffickers ruled and jaded cowboys in pointy boots leered at us, we sometimes found ourselves in dangerous situations we didn't understand. Dad's attitude was, "I guess they'll learn on their own."

The clothing he had designed in Vallarta was beautiful and sexy and he would allow us to select and wear outfits that were way too provocative for our age. When he let us, in our naiveté, wear those clothes in Culiacán, it called undue attention to us in a city rife with drug traffickers and mobsters as well as rogue cowboy types who didn't give two shits about us being minors. On more than one occasion, Gaby and I ran into trouble and Dad would just wave his finger at us and say, "You see? You don't listen." Listen to what? He never told us anything about navigating life safely in Culiacán. He expected us to fall in line, but he never showed us the lines. Instead, he let us stumble over them and then blamed us for the outcome.

Once, Gaby and I went with an acquaintance Ricardo and his friend Manuel to visit his family's beach house. Ricardo was about 35 years old and was from a wealthy family in Culiacán, but it was unclear how they made their money. When we arrived at Altata, a sort of solitary beach with a row of fancy modern houses built along the shore, it was close to nighttime and we were hungry and a bit tired. Ricardo quickly ushered us into the house, and we stood taking in the structure, shocked by the emptiness. There was no furniture in the house and the kitchen was empty except for a small tray with bottles of alcohol on the counter. Ricardo pulled out some shot glasses, and, sliding the tray over and grabbing a bottle, he served up a number of shots. "C'mon girls, lessgo," he said. Gaby and I didn't want to seem disagreeable, but we were kind of regretting our decision to accompany them. The night wasn't looking so good now and we were starting to wonder where we would sleep.

My stomach was empty, and I felt the shot burning all the way down. Gaby and I looked sideways at each other, still trying to go along with things, not wanting them to know we were uncomfortable. We were a little embarrassed that we didn't like the situation, but we knew we were too far from home to ask to go back, so we continued to go along with things, albeit somewhat reluctantly.

It was now awkward, because we really didn't have much to say, and the descending darkness outside was making us nervous. Ricardo ushered us all out on the beach in front of the house where he quickly made a fire, and brought out some blankets. He poured a few more shots and, since there was no dinner, Gaby and I went along. There really wasn't anything else to do. We all talked quietly on the beach by the fire, and I felt a sense of dread welling up in me. I realized I was scared of Ricardo, and he was grabbing Gaby's hand and taking her inside. I was left alone on the beach with Manuel, and it was getting cold outside, so he told me to come get under the blankets with him. An image of Bill Meeh pawing me in his bed popped into my head. I knew I just had to be invisible and it'd all be okay. Within minutes, Manuel, who was a good 20 years older than me, was leaning into me, his heavy hands touching me, and his mustache scratching my face. I withdrew into myself as he raped me, while he spoke to me as if we were friends, as if he cared. "I won't cum inside you," he said every time I said, "No, no, no…"

Gaby's experience with Ricardo was much the same as mine, and the next morning as we got ready to head home, we looked at each other sorrowfully, understanding that we'd talk about it later. When we went for a last quick trip to the bathroom before the long ride home, I whispered to Gaby, "I'm not a virgin anymore." "Me neither," she said. We hurried and went downstairs, trying to act normal.

Before heading back to Culiacán, Ricardo unloaded a number of guns from his truck and we had a surreal target shooting session, aiming at bottles and beer cans down the beach. Gaby was terrible at it, and shrunk away, sitting down in the sand beside the truck, tired and annoyed. I, however, was surprisingly good at it and hit a number of the targets spot on. My rapist praised me, slapping me on the back with a big smile, as he gathered the weapons, putting them into cases in the back of the king cab.

15 wasn't my best year, but fortunately, Manuel did break both his legs in an accident soon after our little get together, and I got to picture him sitting in a wheelchair with his stupid pointy boots and his shiny belt buckle.

After the terrible incident at the beach house, Daddy knew what had happened, because of course that's what had happened. "Well, I guess you learned your lessons," he said, and accused us of being unruly. His lessons were like spider bites. You didn't see them coming and they stung for a long time.

Dad had this idea that he was sort of a dashing Pygmalion and the rest of us were his to sculpt. During his barefoot, LSD-soaked years in Oaxaca, he had taken to renaming his followers. Inomar had been Ramon prior to taking up with my father. One day, I asked Daddy what he would rename me.

"Don't ask if you don't want me to call you that from now on," he replied.

I was so curious, I insisted. From that day on, he called

me Temandía because he said I was like a diamond—*diamante* in Spanish—that needed to be polished. The implication was that he would do the cutting and polishing to suit himself. Meanwhile, what I needed as a girl coming-of-age was beside the point.

Things got a little better after we met a short, stout lesbian named Lourdes who whistled her esses. It was kind of a love-hate thing because Lourdes had the hots for Gaby, which irritated Gaby to no end, but Lourdes was safer than the cartel dudes and we liked having someone to hang out with other than my dad and Inomar. Besides, Lourdes had a dusty dark blue Datsun and was willing to give us rides. She even tried to teach us to drive, bumping along the uneven narrow streets of the city, dodging teenage market kids with makeshift soccer balls made out of wads of garbage wrapped and wrapped repeatedly with twine.

Home life was very different in Culiacán as well. There was little escape from the drudgery of my dad's "renounced" life or his frequent angry outbursts. My father had tons of rules and everything was on a timeline. Breakfast had to be served at a specific time, the tortillas brought fresh from the marketplace by me. I'd wake up and rush to the *mercado* to stand in line as the heavy metal machine churned out the warm corn tortillas and muscular market boys hurried by carrying sides of beef, blood caking in their hair at the base of their necks and dripping down their white aprons. If breakfast was late, my father would fly into a rage, grabbing the cast iron skillet and dumping the food out on the floor. Gaby and I would have to clean it up and go hungry until dinner.

One day, my father caught me roller-skating on the

mosaic floor in the ballroom at the front of our house. He snarled at me and told me I was grounded and to stay in the house. Then he stormed out. Before long, I realized I had my period and needed tampons. Lourdes offered to give me a quick ride to the store. As we pulled away from the house in her car, I saw my dad rapidly flip-flopping down the street toward home. I leaned out the window to tell him where I was going, but when Dad saw me, he rushed toward me, grabbed me by my hair, and pulled me out the car window into the busy street. He held me out in front of him by my hair, kicking me in the ass all the way home. Boys from the marketplace stared. Many of these boys had flirted with me when I had shopped at their stands. Sometimes they would even pull a newspaper clipping out of their wallet to show me one of my pictures from the society section. I was utterly humiliated to have them see me being abused in the streets. I went to my room and lay in bed, thinking of these boys. They'd been enthralled with the sexy American girls and their unusual gay dad. They'd seen the paper in the *mercado* and cut my photo out, wishing they could know me, and thinking I had it good. Then they had this amazing moment of cognitive dissonance when I was being degraded in front of them, and they were, in fact, the happier of the two. I cringed and put my head under my pillow. I never had it truly good.

On occasion, friends of my dad's would come to visit us in Culiacán and we'd get a bit of respite from the daily dose of volatility and ire. Mahabra, another of my father's previous followers, came to visit one day, sweeping in gently, his delicate voice a novelty in our home. Mahabra, originally Abraham, but renamed by my father, was kind and funny and winked at us sweetly behind Dad's back. I had never really questioned why Mahabra—and everyone else—had let my dad rename him. I had just assumed that they knew my dad was amazing and that they were shedding their old selves to be reborn through his inspiration. *Ta daaaa!!* Mahabra had seen my dad's fits of rage before and had known what we were in for when we left Vallarta. During that visit, he saw it firsthand. One day, as my father raged on about cold food and the kitchen being too messy, Mahabra leaned over and whispered in my ear, "You can count on me if you ever decide to leave." I kept that message in my heart. I had already tried to leave on a few occasions, but Gaby had always made up with our dad and convinced me to stay. Still, I knew I wouldn't be able to bear life with my father forever.

It wasn't that long after Mahabra's visit that a particularly violent outburst out of Daddy made up my mind for me. I told Gaby I was leaving. She could stay or come, but I was going and this time she wouldn't be able to talk me out of it. Gaby agreed and Aunt Olga gave us some money to escape. We left carrying our clothes in milk crates. I had my white Maltese dog under my arm.

During our time living on Calle Hidalgo, I had become friends with two brothers who were pantomime artists and I had taken up the art myself. We'd perform at a variety of small gigs around town, in schools and in town squares where groups of chattering kids would ask us lots of questions after our shows. The brothers, Guillermo and Raymundo, were kind and funny so it was to them I went to for help to escape my father. Guillermo helped us to the bus station where we caught the *burraso* bus to Vallarta. The *burraso* stopped frequently as it crossed the desert from Culiacán to Mazatlan, Guadalajara, Tepic, and then Vallarta. Chickens and goats got on with people throughout the night, so by the time we reached Vallarta, my white pants were covered in dirt and our dog had peed on the floor at our feet multiple times. My head ached and I was hungry and thirsty, but relieved to be back in Vallarta. We immediately began to look for old friends of my father's who had previously promised to help and ended up staying with a woman named Aurora in her small home in downtown Vallarta.

Aurora had worked for my dad in some capacity years before. Maybe she had been a designer or worked in his art gallery, I didn't know, but she was kind enough to give us beds to sleep in. Suddenly out from under our father's rules and temper, Gaby and I got out of hand quickly. We'd go to Carlos O'Brien's and have drinks, and then head to Capriccio near Mismaloya Beach to dance until the wee hours of the morning. Gaby got involved with a guy named Gino who worked as a bartender at Carlos O'Brien's and we started crashing at the apartment he shared with his friend, Saul. Coincidently, the apartment was owned by our godfather, a well-known Vallarta artist named Manuel Lepe Macedo, who was known for his colorful Art Naif paintings of Mexico. Gaby and I stayed with Gino and Saul for a couple of months. Saul and I bummed around town by day and met up with Gaby and Gino in the evenings. Gino turned out to be an asshole and Gaby didn't have such a great time of it. Saul, on the other hand, was a pretty decent friend and I enjoyed hanging out with him. Somewhere along the way, Gaby and I must have called Grandma, who called my mother in San Jose del Cabo. My grandmother sent one of the caretakers who looked after a property in Connecticut to accompany my mom to Vallarta and they both arrived one day, kicking sand with their feet as they walked up the beach toward us. Gaby and I were lying in the sun in front of the El Dorado restaurant. When I saw my mother, everything that had happened suddenly washed over me. I stood up and ran to her, throwing my arms around her, and cried with relief that someone was there to help us. We stayed in Vallarta a few more days, and then went home with Mama.

***

In San Jose del Cabo, Gaby and I slept in a *palapa* outside the bus and hung out on the beach all day with the girls. Miriam would do her "sasasunts," which was her made-up word for her exercises where she bent her knees and moved her arms around in repetitive motions and then did squats and kicked her legs. Later, we would roll in the sand dunes, laughing. The days were long and hot and the waves we swam in were massive. One day I was standing on the beach watching a big wave come at me when suddenly it crashed down upon me, scraping me on the ocean floor before a strong undercurrent dragged me far out to sea. I fought hard to get back to my stepfather, Alex, who looked tiny and featureless in the distance. I'd get closer to shore, but then the relentless waves would smash me back to the bottom and the current would drag me back out. Eventually, I found my way down-current and swam in. No one seemed concerned and Alex simply remarked, "That was a doozy," or something like that. Those beaches are closed nowadays because of the dangerous rip currents and very high waves, but at the time we didn't know any better. Gaby and I were chatty and easygoing and our sun-bleached hair hung down our tanned backs. We had no trouble making friends and were soon hatching plans to hitch a ride back to the States with two vans of surfer dudes from California. Mama called Grandma to let her know we were coming, and Grandma said if we could get ourselves to L.A., she would fly us the rest of the way home. The absurdity of this hits me now as I think back. Of course, Grandma had a good deal of money; certainly plenty to have us flown home, but instead she permitted us to hitchhike a ride with strangers. After all her years sheltering us from the world in strange and inconsistent ways, this took the cake.

We set off up the Baja 1000 in August, stopping at Punta de Conejo where we amused ourselves watching the guys tripping on mushrooms and surfing the dangerous, choppy waters above sea urchins that clung, black and prickly, to the rocks below. We drove long hours in the heat of the day, stopping on the side of the road at night, or driving out to the coast to sleep on the beach where the warm breezes blew over the pile of our dirty bodies and silent surfboards.

On one occasion, as we drove along through the desert, we saw a black-and-white flag waving way ahead of us in the distance. As we got closer, the flag stopped waving and we realized it was a white van with a black bottom tumbling over and over. By the time we reached it, a black balloon of billowing smoke was boiling into the desert air. It was surreal. We were sure people had died, but we didn't know what to do. The Mexican desert is dangerous. There are *banditos*. One never knows if something is a trap or not, and anyway, the surfer dudes were tripping balls on acid, so we rolled on.

We reached California at nighttime and pushed on into L.A. where we soon found ourselves at a big party with blonde California girls who didn't seem too impressed by our drunken ways. Oddly, despite all my partying, I hadn't gotten drunk in Vallarta, but something about being back in the States made me unguarded and weak. I had lost my superpowers. Too inebriated to stand, I remember lying on my back on the porch while the tanned, Chicklet-toothed girls mumbled over me, "First day back and she's wasted." I didn't like myself very much, but I couldn't think of what to do about it.

***

Grandma sent Gaby back to New Hampshire to live with Debbie and I was brought back to New Milford where Grandma had built a second house for her and the cats. I shit you not.

The Cat House was near the garage and was literally erected so Grandma could be the cat lady she had always dreamed of becoming without messing up Tanty's old house. Though quite large, The Cat House had small rooms, one of which was crammed with cat cages. The washer and dryer were in the kitchen and a large cat run was built off the back of the room.

Much to my embarrassment, Grandma had become known as a cat lady. People dropped off unwanted cats and Grandma would take in every one of them. She would catch sight of a vehicle coming up the driveway and there would be a somewhat dramatic flurry of activity as she pulled on her coat and boots, calling out in a voice wrought with incredible sympathy for "the poor dear." She'd shuffle about, barking orders at Mrs. Collins to get out some wet cat food and then Grandma would spend a good deal of time on her knees coaxing the tiny little orphan in. Soon, the abandoned feline would be deposited into one of the built-in cages that lined the two-story house. Each cat had its own cage where it stayed most of the time. Every day, Grandma would take some cats out of their cages in order to spend time with them. She had a rotating schedule, so sooner or later every cat had received some attention and then she would start over. Locals had been hired to help keep the many cages clean. Meanwhile, Grandma lived like a pauper, although she had millions of dollars.

I took up residence alone in Tanty's old house because there was nothing for me at Grandma's place and it stunk of cat piss. What Grandma focused on and valued made no sense to me and her presence only made me feel lonelier. I was of little interest to her. We rarely spoke and it was clear that was what she wanted. If I started telling her about my day at school, often as not she'd say, "Disappear into the woodwork, dear."

Grandma never came over to the main house, but occasionally she would send Mrs. Collins over to sleep there and make meals for me. Mrs. Collins made her own food at the main house. Sometimes she would make chicken-in-a-pot, which I loved. I couldn't resist sticking my fingers in it before it was ready.

"Girl, I don't know where them hands have been," Mrs. Collins would screech. "They may have been in your coochie!" I'd always laugh and so would she.

If Grandma didn't send Mrs. Collins, I would simply eat what was in the fridge, often taking out a large London broil steak and shoving it under the broiler with a bunch of butter on it.

My only other company was my cat, Ann, a push-faced white and orange kitty with very soft fur and a sweet disposition. She used to kill mice and leave them in little warm, soft piles at my bedroom door, or hide them in the folded quilt at the foot of my bed, which felt like a token of her love.

I got straight A's in school, except for in math because I got sick one day, fell behind, and didn't know how to communicate the problem to the teacher. I was also failing at making friends at the local public school. The other kids knew I had previously gone to the private high school and held it against me. There had always been a strong us-vs-them mentality between the Canterbury prep school kids and the students at New Milford High. I might as well have been the smelly girl.

Bored, directionless, and lonely, I spent long quiet afternoons and nights in my room or watching television: The Merv Griffin Show, All My Children, One Life to Live, and General Hospital. To relieve the tedium, I studied Modern Greek with Berlitz records I played on my cheap plastic record player. I ended up producing a full journal in the Modern Greek alphabet, which later I could not read back to myself.

Arturo sometimes sent bindles of Peruvian Flake or joints of marijuana that I never smoked. I wasn't particularly fond of any of it and it just reminded me of a time when I was happier and not alone. It seemed impossible that I had once danced happily at the discos of Vallarta and I sometimes wondered if I had been better off living with my dad's abuse. Life in Grandma's hermitage was suffocating me and I was starved for human connection. My dissociation was chronic. I felt adrift, separated from myself and the days I was living. Everything was illogical and out of place. There was no substance to ground myself in, no companionship or feeling of belonging anywhere. Bored one day, I went for a run. I had been on the cross country team at Canterbury and loved it. I recalled feeling the wind in my face, and the strength of my body, and the burn of pushing hard and then harder as I crossed the last hockey field to the finish, teammates yelling along the sidelines, and me on a couple of occasions peeing down my legs instead of stopping and possibly losing the race. After that first run, I kept it up. I would run up and down the dirt roads around our house, which gave me a temporary sense of myself. The dirt crunching under my feet, the straining of my body and lungs, my rhythmic breathing, the smell of the earth and the air—all of these things brought me into the moment and helped me to escape the heavy shadows of the New Milford house, and years later they would be the seeds of a lifetime of athletic adventures.

After I learned to drive, Grandma started having me chauffeur her to the store in Sherman, Connecticut, because her Peugeot had rack and pinion steering, which was hard for her to manage with her arthritis. I drove a little too fast for her liking. She preferred I stay under the speed limit, but it embarrassed me to drive like that. Other people did not poke down the road the way she expected me to. She repeatedly told me to slow down, citing newspaper articles she had read about drivers who "failed to negotiate the curve." One day, as we approached a big curve flanked by tall grass, she was going, "Slow down. Slow down. Slow down." Finally, there was no way to go any slower, so I stopped the car in the middle of the road. Aghast, she exclaimed in her best movie star voice, "Sammy, dahr-ling, you mustn't. If you are going to act like this, I won't let you drive!" The rage that comes with powerlessness boiled up inside me, pressing on my chest. I stared back at her angrily as the yellow grass swayed in the summer sun behind her.

Of course, I started driving again, because it was the practical thing to do, but I was enraged. Grandma had done very little to teach me how to manage life, yet she'd thought nothing of sending me to Mexico with Daddy—a man she knew had been violent with my mother—and she hadn't been a bit concerned about me finding my way back from Mexico with surfer dudes I had met in a campground. Grandma paid no attention to whether or not I had meals to eat or got myself to school. I was supposed to disappear into the woodwork and handle things myself. And I did. Yet Grandma never trusted my judgment.

I was actually a pretty conservative driver. In fact, I was innately a pretty conservative person, but no matter what I did, Grandma disapproved and insisted I act some other way. If I obeyed her, other people thought I was weird. If I didn't, she treated me like I was off the rails. I hated every part of my life with Grandma. It was one confinement and frustration after another, and it seemed I could never earn anyone's approval. If I did excel at something—like dancing or horseback riding—she took it away from me. Although she said I was special, I could never meet her standards. The only time I had any peace was when I was alone, running, or learning Greek from recordings–because I never told anybody I did those things.

Grandma likely sensed I was pulling away from her.

In an emergency like that, when she was in danger of losing her influence over someone, Grandma pulled out her wallet. That year, she surprised me by offering to send me to a camp in the West Indies because my grades had been so good. I eagerly agreed and was soon on a plane with a load of rich New York City teenagers on my way to Antigua for six weeks of sailing, tennis, scuba, and delicious food. I felt like I'd been released from prison. I borrowed clothes and swam in the ocean. I fit in there and was liked. My camp friends and I loved telling stories and marveled at the Rastas, disdainful of their women who walked behind them, but willing to let the men force kisses upon us.

There was a *National Geographic* photographer at the camp who took photos of these two beautiful and thin, very rich teenage girls who were with our camp. The photographer told me once that I was beautiful and could have been a model "if it weren't for that scar" on my face from the fall out the window at The Dakota.

"If it weren't for that scar." He had no idea about my scars, but I did. I had long felt set apart by my history, my accident, and my grandmother. The scar on my face was just a visible, disappointing reminder of all the ways I felt different, like I didn't belong anywhere. I went up the beach and sat down where I could watch him take pictures of those beautiful, perfectly scarless girls. I felt tarnished for life.

Upon returning to Connecticut, I was once again isolated, but it felt harsher after the joys of the summer. I found it unbearable. I was like a cat in a metal cage over a fire—desperate and in pain, but with nowhere to go. To make matters worse, Arturo had sent a white envelope of Peruvian flake while I was away and Grandma had discovered it. She was furious with me and "so disappointed, dahr-ling" that I was sure she would never do something nice for me again.

Grandma and I had some terrible arguments after that. On one occasion, she was expressing her disdain for my teenaged ideas and I lost it.

"Fuck off," I spat. I had never spoken to my grandmother like that before, but I no longer cared what she thought. I had stepped off a cliff and felt the free fall start as the words left my mouth. Mrs. Collins, who was standing behind my grandmother in the kitchen, winced and waved her hands at me to stop but the damage was already done. Grandma leapt at me and shoved me into the fridge, which tipped heavily against the wall.

"Sammy, you dasn't!" Grandma exclaimed, sounding like Katherine Hepburn in an old black-and-white movie.

Fury welled up in me. "This isn't a movie!" I screamed. My rage felt terrifying and frightening.

As far back as I could remember, Grandma had told me I was special and promised me that, if I was a good girl, she would always take care of me financially. For years, I had believed her money would ultimately keep me safe, but I didn't care anymore. When I opened my mouth to tell her to fuck herself, I understood I was walking away from a fortune, and I was willing. I had never been able to be a good enough girl for her anyway.

She cut me out of her will, which was just what I expected. Fortunately, I had taken my PSAT's and SAT's at the end of the previous school year and been accepted at Bard College at Simon's Rock—an alternative college in the Berkshires of Massachusetts. I had a way out, at least temporarily.

FALLING UP FROM THE BOTTOM

CHAPTER 10
SIMON'S ROCK

On a beautiful August day in 1983, I started my first day at Simon's Rock. When I met with my guidance counselor, Victor, he told me my grandmother had asked him to keep her apprised of my comings and goings there.

"We don't tattle on our students," Victor told Grandma. "She's in college now."

Grandma had always gone before me, telling people how broken I was and how sad my life had been, making me out to be a pitiful problem. According to Victor, it would not be business as usual for Grandma at Simon's Rock. I liked the sound of that. A sense of freedom washed over me.

"You're in college now," Victor told me that day in his office. "Stick with the winners, choose your friends wisely, do your homework, go to class, and you will do really well."

I nodded, though I honestly had no idea how to do all that. I felt like a fraud.

Life with Grandma had left me woefully unprepared for a college environment. At Grandma's house, a job well done was not necessarily rewarded. Maybe she would send you to camp "because you got good grades" if that happened to serve her purposes, but more often than not, she would put a stop to whatever you were doing successfully. Birthdays and Christmases were canceled over minor childhood infractions, but if someone was really fucking up, Grandma would give them money. It was all just random. So, I hadn't grasped yet that my actions were directly tied to outcomes. I knew on some level I was supposed to show up on time, prepared with pen and paper, having done the homework. I was supposed to listen, assimilate, participate, but that part of Simon's Rock seemed far off to me, as if it somehow didn't belong to me. What I cared about, what I dedicated myself to at Simon's Rock, was connecting with people. I had been so lonely for so long, nothing else mattered very much to me.

I first saw Grey Dey standing in line at the student center on campus. He wore jodhpurs that poofed way out from his thighs to his knees and had a black flattop haircut greased to attention. The sides and back of his head were shaved clean. He was chattering loudly in the registration line waiting to purchase his books and get his class schedule. At first I just stood fixating on him, but then I eased over until I was near him. I listened for a while and then threw in a word or two. "Yes," "No," "I think so. . ."

Grey chattered easily with me. "Hi, where are you from?" "What classes are you taking?" He seemed genuinely interested in my replies and made me feel right at home. He was unusual and I immediately liked him. We were fast friends from that day on, and our friendship would continue for decades to come.

Grey was an artist from Boston whose style back then might be described as cartoonish realism with hints of mysticism. He created with impressive regularity, using colored pencils. Grey's brain never seemed to shut off and we could talk for hours, smoking pot and listening to music: Nina Hagen, X-Ray Specs, Lou Reed, Patti Smith, The Talking Heads, Brian Eno—we loved anything that represented the creative and misunderstood. All of it was played loudly on a low-quality record player hooked up to speakers by wires crisscrossing the walls. His bed was on the floor and his artwork and supplies were neatly placed on a counter beneath a large set of windows. It was a barren, cold room. His bed was always unmade and kind of hard, the lighting was mostly harsh and fluorescent. The punk rock music he played didn't particularly appeal to me, though I really got into Patti Smith and the Talking Heads, but I was fascinated with him and found him relatable.

Maybe best of all, Grey didn't think I was an alien from another planet. He seemed equally entertained with me and spent long hours painting my face: eyelids a shocking sky blue, bright red lipstick. He teased my hair into a blonde afro and then put cigarette butts in it. I preferred a lower-key psychedelic punk look, which I slowly pieced together out of thrift store finds. I was often seen walking around campus in a pair of knee-high rubber boots, tights, a red paisley knee-length skirt, and a tan suede vest with long fringe. At some point, Grey cut my hair shorter on one side than the other with a long wisp remaining to hang in front of my face on the left side. We wore our oddness like a badge of honor.

Grey eventually introduced me to John Estabrook, whom I immediately fell in love with. John had long curly light-ginger hair, chain-smoked cigarettes, was quiet and mysterious, and wore a long black wool coat and big black engineer boots in all seasons. He was brilliant at mathematics. Much to Grey's chagrin, John and I became immersed in each other, often excluding him without realizing it. We would spend long hours in John's "closet single" room on the floor beneath mine, listening to Patti Smith and letting cigarettes stand on the record player until they turned into ghostly ash towers and toppled over. We rarely showered and I took to buying new clothes at the local secondhand store, which were eventually added to the pile of dirty clothes in my room. I'd have to push hard on the door to move enough clothes to enter the cramped space largely occupied by a mattress on the floor. John, Grey, and I had lots of adventures, many of which involved taking acid. Or we'd hitchhike to the Roseland in New York City to see Public Image Limited, sniffing Amyl Nitrate as the 18-wheelers sped by, and hitchhiking back just in time for a class on the subject of Madness in Literature taught by a very cool intellectual named Hal. My acid-addled brain would follow the rabbit hole of his ramblings on Clarissa Dalloway's life or the lack of punctuation in *Autumn of the Patriarch*. I found his class fascinating, but not enough to actually read the books all the way through in time for class.

Victor, the guidance counselor, noticed the changes in me and warned me that "I needed to be a nice young lady" who didn't swear and wear chains and hang out with John and Grey. But I didn't want to be a nice young lady, and now he annoyed me. Trying to be a good girl had gotten me buried alive at Grandma's house. In the company of John and Grey, I felt resurrected. I certainly didn't feel like a bad girl, per se; I just had no interest in being contained by societal norms that I completely couldn't fathom. And besides, I didn't really know the rules and I was tired of beating myself up over it.

At some point, I had read Edie Sedgwick's biography and thought her life was everything I wanted mine to be. Known as an It Girl in 1965, she had an intense relationship with Andy Warhol and hung out with the artists and intellectuals at the Factory. She was sexy and sophisticated in a very New York kind of way I could relate to and wanted to emulate. Most importantly, I felt she had been genuinely loved by the artists she inspired. I got the sense she was dear to them and I wanted that most of all. I neglected to take into account her death from a drug overdose. After years of having every dream squashed until I gave up having dreams at all, I dreamed of Grey, John, and I becoming great artists together and of being genuinely loved by them. And so it came to pass. . . sort of. We all really were creative and artistic, but at the time, not always as productive as we might have been. And what's funny is that years later, my sister Gabriela would marry Edie's cousin, Nikko Sedgwick, an affable artist who studied at Bard College, to which Simon's Rock was associated. They're still happily married to this day. Whenever I tell him good news about my life, he says, "Sammy, it couldn't have happened to the sister-in-law of a greater guy!"

***

I was back at Grandma's between terms at Simon's Rock

when she took me out for a fancy lunch at The Iron Kettle in New Milford. There, where she calculated I wouldn't have the nerve to make a scene, Grandma broke the news to me that Mrs. Collins had died of cancer. Grandma had just returned from the funeral in Mississippi. I was heartbroken to lose Mrs. Collins and upset to learn Grandma hadn't told me Mrs. Collins was dying and hadn't taken me to the funeral.

"Why didn't you tell me?" I asked.

"Well, I just couldn't deal with it," Grandma said. "I couldn't deal with telling you and the emotion and taking you down there. It was just too much." Then she warned me not to make a scene.

I felt sick and incredibly alone. Mrs. Collins was gone and I hadn't even known she was sick. My heart ached and I felt entirely misjudged by Grandma. She really had no idea who I was or what I needed. I felt like I had a pile of coal in my stomach.

Grandma had other things on her mind. Apparently, the Reverend and Mrs. Collins had built a nice middle-class life for themselves and Grandma felt "betrayed, horribly betrayed." Grandma had sometimes given Mrs. Collins money and gifts. It turns out those weren't out of gratitude for all Mrs. Collins' work, they were charity because Grandma thought Mrs. Collins didn't have anything. Grandma was appalled when she arrived in Mississippi and found a nice family home where she had probably expected a tin shack.

"They even had some nice paintings on the wall," she said, astonished.

There, Grandma had been trying to rescue Mrs. Collins like some stray cat and Mrs. Collins hadn't needed the rescue, which royally pissed off Grandma. So, that's what we talked about while I picked at my meal and digested the news that Mrs. Collins was gone forever. It burdened me that I would never be able to say goodbye.

***

John and I spent the summer after my freshman year at Simon's Rock in Boston. We occasionally took acid and talked through the night. One night, I had a bad trip that caused me to disassociate randomly for months. I'd find myself sweating as the rays of the hot sun shone onto me through the window of the train from Dorchester to Harvard Square. I'd feel the sweat bead on my upper lip as I stood there stiffly in my black rubber boots. Riders on their way to work would glance askance at me, sensing my awkward suffering, but unable to determine exactly what was wrong with me. I would have a flashback and suddenly be terrified and forget where I was going. A few stops would go by as I searched frantically for reminders of where I was, and then I'd suddenly remember, my muscles would relax and a relief would wash over me. A moment later, I felt like just another person riding the train.

On dull afternoons, I would pick up one of the books I should have read months before for my college classes, lie down in the warmth of the sunlight coming through my window, and read until I finally got what my teachers had said about the assigned literature. I related to the odd, lonely characters, like Meursault, from *L'Etranger* by Camus, who was judged harshly because he did not weep at his mother's funeral. And Artaud, who wrote about his madness and opiate addiction in *Artaud Anthology*. I felt like I was starting to get my bearings as a college student and thought it would be cool to go back to Simon's Rock and do my second year in a different way.

Sometimes, I'd hitchhike to New York. Grandma was always appalled when she opened the door of her apartment in the Dakota to find me standing there in ripped jeans and chains. Eventually, she broke the news to me that I needed to enroll in business school. Disgusted by my freshman performance at Simon's Rock, Grandma refused to pay for any more expensive private school education.

So, I spent the next year in Boston, attending business college and hanging out with John. He was taking art classes and doing a lot of reading, but overall, our lifestyle could best be described as lackadaisical. We'd lie around on his mattress on the floor in his attic bedroom, listening to Patti Smith and smoking cigarettes. Then we'd go to Harvard Yard or meet up with friends. On weekends, Grey, John, and I would go to 1270 Club or Spit, or wherever there was a good punk show.

Grandma was not paying for my room and board and I had no money, so I was basically homesteading at John's parents' house. John's mother and father were academics and all John's siblings were attending Harvard. The family must have wished John and I would hurry up and find some direction in life, but they put up with us kindly.

CHAPTER 11
HEROIN

By the summer of 1984, Grandma was ready to ship me off again. This time, she sent me to Mama, who was living in San Francisco with the girls; Mischa; and Michael Pincus, Mischa's father.

John and I refused to be separated; he wanted to spend all his time with me and I feared being alone. Unfortunately, we were broke. John's parents were not enthusiastic about him going to San Francisco with me and didn't seem likely to fund his trip, so I begged for a second Greyhound ticket from my grandmother.

John and I spent that night at the Dakota with Grandma, relieved to know we would be leaving together. The next morning, we hurried to Grand Central Station, weighed down by bags stuffed with clothing and books. The city was bustling and we felt alive with possibility. Once on the bus, we wrapped ourselves around each other.

Five days later, John and I arrived in San Francisco, dirty and exhausted. The bus ride had been long and boring and we'd had to get off every morning at 5 a.m. to let them clean the bus while we sat in shitty spartan bus stations along the way. We'd passed hundreds of miles of corn fields, salt flats, and mountains and we smelled like it. My mother picked us up at the station and took us home to her house on 24th and Harrison in the Mission where the girls buzzed around, excited at our arrival. They had always admired my older sister Gaby and me. I thought they were foolish. Instead of being interested in them, I judged their innocence as stupidity. Honestly, I don't think I knew how to see them.

We were given a small room off the hallway near the girls' room. I spread an alpaca blanket John's parents had given me for Christmas across the mattress on the floor and our move-in was complete. We stayed for a couple of months.

My family seemed happy. Mischa's father, Michael, owned a socialist bookstore and loved corny jokes. He was missing a quarter of one of his fingers, so he'd give you a high five and say, "Slap me 4 and 3/4!" He brought a degree of levity to my family that I had never seen before, and I liked him.

John happily hung out with me and my sisters, telling jokes and talking about life. He even took Ayin to see *Purple Rain* repeatedly, since she was completely enamored with Prince. My sisters and brothers were all attending Urban School up in the Haight, which was paid for by Grandma's dear friend, Tanty, and they took circus classes at the Pickle Family Circus. Ayin studied dance with an intense man named Ed Mock in the Mission, who would later die tragically of AIDS during the terrible epidemic. His community would mourn him greatly. Lhasa had

All of my mother's children on the Harrison Street stoop in San Francisco

(Top row, left to right: Mama, Sky, Lhasa, Ayin, Miriam, Gabriela; Bottom Row: me and Mischa)

started singing while at Urban and was performing in a Greek cafe on 24th near Harrison. Back then, she sang in a high voice and I wasn't super impressed, but I had fun seeing her sing.

At the end of summer, John left. His mother, who had tenure at Syracuse University, got him into school on the east coast. I was devastated by his departure and the realization we were not going to become great artists together. I cried in my room for a week, feeling like I just couldn't have nice things or love and was perfectly alone. I found little sympathy, though, so I finally emerged from my room, puffy faced, and called an old Simon's Rock acquaintance named Emily to see if she was doing anything interesting that didn't involve despondency. She invited me to accompany her to a show at the Mabuhay Gardens nightclub, affectionately known as The Mab. After the show, we went back to Emily's spartan apartment in The Haight to sit on her hardwood floors and talk about life in San Francisco. Soon the conversation turned to drugs and Emily mentioned she had tried heroin.

I had spent the previous couple of years immersed in the lyrics of punk legends like Patti Smith and The Velvet Underground, romanticizing heroin addiction. I had built an extensive thrift store wardrobe emulating Edie Sedgewick's fashion sense and idolized her drug-and art-fueled lifestyle. I had read Atonin Artaud's description of heroin withdrawal as a "corrosive sensation in the limbs" and did not recoil. I was not introduced to emotional pain by the depressing imagery conjured from the depths of the music, literature, and lives I admired; the desolation was already within me and I had seduced myself into believing heroin would save me from it. I thought it would make me stronger, that it would give me the superpower of not giving a shit. The possibility of finally living what I had merely imagined animated me.

"What's it like?" I asked. And then, "Where do you get it?

"It's warm when it goes in," she said, nonchalantly. "I got it from Jonithin Christ of Code of Honor. He doesn't live very far away,"

Code of Honor was a hardcore punk band, well past its time, and Jonithin was a faded, depressed junkie.

"Let's go!" I said.

We walked briskly up Divisadero, the anticipation

crackling between us thick in the warmth of the summer night. We chatted cheerfully, young and carefree, as if we were headed to the candy store and not to shoot heroin for the first time. At Jonithin's building we were buzzed in. We trooped up to his apartment, our Doc Martins causing the sagging wooden stairs to creak tiredly. We ascended to a dark hallway where the scent of many years hung between cool, lumpy walls. We turned right, Emily knocked on a dirty apartment door, and we waited with hushed expectancy.

After a bit, a guy named Deogee cracked open the door and leaned into the hallway. "What's up?" he asked.

"We're here to see Jonithin," we said.

Jonithin's head popped out and he cheerfully invited us in, recognizing that we were about to give him money to get heroin. He was probably dopesick that night and overjoyed to have someone to rip off.

Emily and I hung around for about an hour while Jonithin was out copping the dope. He finally came back and pulled a bindle out of his pocket and pushed us all aside to get to his bedside table. He grabbed rigs and a spoon, a lighter and lemon juice. He dumped a matchhead-sized amount of dope into the spoon, squeezed lemon over it, and lit up. When it started to boil, he flicked the lighter off, pulled the plunger out of a syringe, and stirred the dope until the last bit of powder dissolved into the lemon juice. Then he tore off a piece of cotton from an old cotton ball on the table, rolled it between his fingers, and dropped it into the warm brown liquid. Within seconds, he had pushed the plunger back into his rig, drawn up most of the fluid, and popped it into his arm, leaving a little for the rest of us to split. Since neither of us knew how to shoot up, Jonithin did the prep and injecting for everybody.

The Persian heroin was strong. At the time, I didn't know it, but it had come directly from Afghanistan. Although Emily and I split the remaining dose, we both felt the warmth of it spread through our chests and into our stomachs as we lay back on the bed. A blanket of peace descended upon me and I closed my eyes.

Emily walked herself home later that night, but I stayed at Jonithin's, passed out, in and out of dreams, enveloped in comfortable sensuality. It was like dying and not caring you were dying, but in a good way.

Walking to the store the next day, still feeling the effects of the heroin, I thought, "No one knows I'm high. No one can touch me anymore." I could easily shrink inside of myself and the harshness of the world could no longer touch me. The years of isolation and despair no longer reached through the ethers to suffocate me. I was free.

***

For the first couple of years of my addiction, I was still able to hold down my job as a troubleshooter at a courier service. I liked it there. The office was full of witty banter and folks having a good time with life, earning a paycheck, and paying their bills. I longed to be one of them, but I was strung out and jonesing hard every single day. I'm sure they didn't know exactly what I was up to, but they had to wonder about my behavior at times. Every now and again, I'd go into work dopesick in the morning, then Jonithin would manage to cop during the day and he'd call me at the office and tell me to meet him at his work, which wasn't too far away. I'd race over there on my bicycle and we'd get loaded in his work van in the alley outside. Then I'd ride back to my office, happy, feeling good and energetic. I expected people to notice, but they never picked up on it.

I'd moved in with Jonithin and his housemates Tina and Doegee (a play on the word DOG) in order to pursue my addiction full time. We lived in a run-down punk rock apartment with seedy yellow lighting and filthy carpets, but it was safe and warm and off the streets. Tina and Doegee would chip in on heroin now and again, but they weren't strung out anymore. They held down jobs and did things like cooking meals and taking baths. I envied their quotidian lives. They'd get home from work—Deogee was a bike messenger and Tina worked at Glide Memorial Church with Cecil Williams—and they'd prepare some dinner, eat it in front of the TV, and then Tina would take a leisurely bubble bath. I wanted so badly to live a simple life like that, but my addiction was so intense that the withdrawal was unbearable. First my skin would crawl. As time went on, my bones would start to ache so intensely I thought they would shatter. Each minute would drag on, interminably. I would be sleepless and throw up for days, an extreme anxiety in my legs, as if they were going to run away like skeletons, all on their own. My body felt drained and thin, and I could barely lift my head half the time. Each moment crawled on like tarantulas. After a week or so, I'd give in and find a way to get more heroin. I was terrified and stuck.

All I had wanted as far back as I could remember was to feel alive and connected to the living. When I first started using, I thought heroin addiction was a choice. At 18 years old, I thought dope was a romantic act of self-defeat, a way to shout to the world, or at least my family, that I was in pain and had given up somehow and I needed someone to help me find my way into the living, connected world. But using heroin wasn't my choice for long and it set me apart from the world far more completely than Grandma ever had.

As a girl, I had a recurring nightmare where I'd find myself in a horrible, enclosed tube with eerie yellow lighting. The tube wound around relentlessly, and I'd be sliding down it at a high rate of speed, banging into the walls and ceiling. Suffocating in the tight air, bathed in the depressing yellow light, I plunged to some unknown destination I sensed could not be good. That's how it felt to be strung out. I was suffocating and miserable, plunging to nowhere good, and I couldn't figure out how to escape.

***

With money borrowed from his parents, Jonithin managed to score an apartment on Ringold Alley. I thought it was sweet of them to help him. I could tell from listening to him on the phone with him that they really cared for him. After living so long in the one bedroom with Tina and Deogee—its gray walls and dingy carpets constant reflections of what his life had been reduced to—Jonithin was giddy when he unlocked our new door the first time. It was a railroad flat with a bedroom, a bathroom with a claw foot tub, a living room, and then a kitchen, all in a row. We had no furniture, so there was nothing to move. We had jumped on the bus with a single duffle that held our possessions. Jonithin simply set the bag down and we were moved in. It seemed a little anticlimactic, but we covered that with some magical thinking. Jonithin chatted happily about how life would be now while I pictured the apartment filled with furniture, a refrigerator stocked with food, clothes in the closets, shelves of books, Persian rugs on the floor, and bubble baths surrounded by candles.

In a minute, all that vanished as Jonithin knelt on the floor in the bedroom and pulled out his spoon and a small bindle of Persian heroin. On the way over we had stopped at Janie's and Tommy's to grab some dope. Whatever else we were doing, our primary goal was always to get fixed. Jonithin was happy and chatty because he was always happy and chatty when we were getting ready to fix. We referred to fixing as "getting well," because most of the time we felt so sick. The dope would just barely get us well enough to find a way to get another fix.

A few months later, I overdosed for the first time in that bedroom. We had been dopesick that day, of course, and Jonithin had gone to cop. As always, upon his return, he scurried through the door, intense focus on his face, and rushed through cooking the heroin. When the dope was ready, he fixed himself while I prepared my arm by wrapping a tie tightly around it. He quickly sucked the remaining brown fluid through the cotton, grabbed my arm, and shot me up. I felt a strange coolness pass through me—like a ghostly mist—and then the warmth as I lay back on the bed and the room disappeared into thin lines around me.

I heard Jonithin say he was going to the kitchen for crackers and cheese, but my head was standing in the cool darkness of an imaginary room. The room was empty and entirely dark, but I could see through my mind's eye, even what was behind me. It was so real I shook my head and started up off the bed. Comforted that I could bring myself back to the real world, I let myself sink into the dream. A door behind me was slightly ajar and, beyond it, pure blackness, the cosmos. Ahead and to the right was another doorway. A bright white light filled the room behind it. I felt one with all of it, completely at peace, no sensation of pervasive fear, but with a certain curiosity and purpose. I reached back and felt the cool hard surface of the wall behind me. I slid my hand over to close the door and then started walking toward the light. Three steps later, I felt a sudden, violent tug at the back of my neck. The door and the wall disappeared, and I was falling backwards into space at a high rate of speed. I slammed onto the bed, sat bolt upright, and a voice that came from my lips but wasn't my own said, "Who are you? Where am I?" to Jonithin, whose astonished face was just a couple of inches from my own.

He had gone into the kitchen to prepare the crackers. When he returned, he found me unconscious on the bed, not breathing, my veins bulging under my blackening skin. He slapped me repeatedly, shook me, and yelled. Finally, thinking I was gone, he let me drop onto the bed. A few seconds later, I started gurgling and choking before sitting up and asking where I was. Jonithin wept. He grabbed me and held me, saying, "Thank God, thank God. I was so scared." We talked for a long time that night about what happened, what I had seen—the room, the doorway with the light, everything behind me and around me as if I knew everything at once—and how close I had come to dying. I was astonished, and yet for the first time, unafraid of my own death. It seemed so peaceful and inviting, so completely comforting. Like daily living, but without the fear and the pain. I felt childlike.

The apartment on Ringold never became the good home we had hoped for. We didn't eat a lot because we spent all our money on heroin, but what food we did cook sat dried out in pans on the stove and abandoned dishes. In time, the pans became alive with tiny roaches spilling over the rims onto the stove and then the floor. Some of them scurried around with giant egg cases attached to them, which looked like bulbous tails and eventually burst, jettisoning more roaches onto the scene. We had moved the mattress to the back of the apartment near the kitchen because of the noise and light from the street, and we could hear them crawling around as we lay on our mattress on the living room floor at night.

Ringold was known for being a "leather alley." After the gay bars closed for the night, leather fetishists would line Ringold for quick trysts. We used to peer through the slats of the blinds, watching their muscular bodies and shiny leather move rhythmically in the glow of the streetlamps.

Our landlord lived upstairs from us. He was a friendly gay witch activist who had created a stencil template that said "CIAids" over stars and stripes. He used to spray paint it around the city in red, white, and blue. The implication was the CIA had started the AIDS epidemic. Whenever I saw his stencils on walls around the city, I felt subversive by association. He was kind to me and never seemed to judge me, even though I was clearly not in my most cheerful headspace whenever he saw me. He gave me hope that there were good people in the world, and in some way, he made me feel okay, even when I wasn't.

Below us, a photographer named Victor Arimondi

had his studio. Victor had once been a high-fashion model in Italy and later photographed for fancy mags such as *Vogue* and *Harper's Bazaar*. The walls were lined with black-and-white photographs of famous people he had photographed over the years. Victor knew what was going on with me and I could sense his compassion. Once, when we talked in his studio and I cried about my deplorable situation, he asked me to stand in the alley so he could photograph me. He hung the photo on the wall of his gallery between Norman Mailer and Grace Jones and said to me, "Now, that ought to make you feel better."

But how the hell can an addict feel better? All day every day and all night every night was hard at the Ringold house. Jonithin and I were always short on money and, consequently, dopesick. At his wit's end one night, Jonithin jumped up, threw on a black turtleneck, black pants, and a black hat. He tied a black handkerchief around his face and raced out the door. He had a fake pistol in his right hand. Soon after, he was home, pumped on adrenalin. He dropped a handful of bills on the floor and ripped off his clothes, stashing each piece of clothing in a different part of the house. He had robbed a man who stopped to take a piss in the street, holding the plastic gun to the man's back and shouting at him not to move. The man panicked, threw his wallet on the ground, and took off running while he was still pulling up his pants. As it turned out, Jonithin had just robbed an off-duty cop of a wallet containing 18 dollars, which wasn't even enough to buy a bindle. We spent the rest of the night in torment, kicking hard and ruing the day we were born.

***

The sun was bright as I stepped out into Ringold Alley. The muscled leather men from the night before were gone and the street looked bleak and hard. The cement itself seemed to emanate hopelessness, its filthy coarseness rejecting me at every step. I walked up the alley to 9th Street and turned left, heading to the pay phone near Club 9. I picked up the receiver, dropped my coins, and heard them clank against the metal within. I dialed the number. As I stood listening to the phone ring, I kicked nervously at something on the ground, pushing it back and forth with my foot. After a while, Janie answered and I humbly asked her for a front. This wasn't the first time, and I hated to ask, but we were in pain and there was no other option. I had $10 now and would hustle to get the money to pay her the other $15 later in the day, but I needed a fix now.

Janie was a slight blonde woman with the gray skin of a heroin addict. She lived with a guy named Tommy, who traveled to Afghanistan periodically for Persian heroin. Tommy would mail it back to Janie in an envelope, which she kept hidden behind a mirror in their cluttered South of Market apartment that smelled of things that hadn't been used in a long time. They kept a pistol-grip pump shotgun by the door so it was one of the first things visitors saw. Every time I copped from Janie, I pictured her grabbing the shotgun, the weight nearly too heavy for her skinny arms, the blast shoving her back through the wall, smashing the plaster, and leaving her in a white cloud of dust. I wondered which would come first for her: death by gun blast or death by dope. She was weak and sickly. The only power she had was possession of the dope. Someone coming in the door could take an easy shot at her and, *BAM*, she'd be done for.

Janie said she'd front me, and I turned to head home to tell Jonithin, glancing quickly at the object I had been kicking on the ground. It was the remains of a goat's head, horns and all, the leathery skin jagged where it had been severed. I had heard of Satanists in the city, but only knew of one who lived in the Haight, the son of a wealthy oil baron in Texas who received $1,000 a week from a trust fund. He talked of being involved in some cult where people would shit on altars, but he had struck me as simple-minded and pathetic. He was completely obsessed with drugs and his boy toy du jour, so I really couldn't imagine him being heavy enough to engage in anything as intense as animal sacrifice.

I flicked my finger in the coin return to see if there was anything there, then turned away from the goat's head and started toward Ringold Alley. I noticed a thin Nordic-looking man with close-cropped blonde hair standing by the bus stop and then suddenly he leaned toward me and held out a lollipop. No way did I trust him.

He explained that he was a photographer and would love to shoot photos of me. Then he reached into his pocket, pulled out a pen, wrote down his number, and handed it to me. I took it with the same caution one reserves for touching any potentially hazardous substance.

"I might call you," I said warily, before scooting off down the street.

His name was Stefan, and he was a freelance photographer who was working on a shoot for *Fad Magazine*. I agreed to let him take my picture because it gave me a break from the boredom and hell of my existence, and also I hoped he'd give me money so I could buy more dope. He never paid me, maybe because he knew what I would do with the money, but it was probably because he was just another starving artist like the rest of the creatives in San Francisco. He sometimes talked to me about hope and options. I enjoyed working with him, but thought Stefan was a bit daft to imagine I would ever quit heroin. His kindness warmed my heart, though, and it felt good to have an inkling of compassion anywhere near me.

Sometime after the photoshoot with Stefan, Jonithin moved away from San Francisco, leaving me alone in that cockroach-infested Ringold apartment with a horrific heroin habit.

***

After Jonithin left, I was totally strung out. I didn't know how to shoot myself up and had no idea how to get money for dope because I wasn't a thief and I was too sick to figure out other options. One day, I was sitting in my apartment, dopesick, when someone knocked on the door. Paul was on my steps, smiling and saying he'd share a fix with me if I let him shoot up in my place. I let him in.

I lost the apartment on Ringold pretty quickly, but talked my way into a loft bedroom in an apartment next door to Tina and Deogee's place. Soon after, Paul moved in with me. We didn't understand boundaries or respect for roommates so we never asked if it was ok, Paul just started sleeping there one day and never stopped.

When things got particularly desperate for us, we would go to Paul's mother, Pat, who lived in the Lower Haight. She had a one-bedroom apartment with her Rasta boyfriend, Roland, from Chicago, and his baby son, Isolat. Pat was a Nichiren Shoshu Buddhist who did the *nam-*

myoho-renge-kyo chanting thing and made offerings on an altar in her bedroom, but her spirituality never saved her from the ravages of addiction. She was pale and gaunt and her face was blotchy. Roland was mean and unhappy and his son was always dirty. Still, I often envied Isolat because at least he had Cheerios to eat in the morning while Paul and I were so hungry all the time. Their apartment was filthy and depressing and we slept on a closet floor, sometimes sharing it with an annoying guy named David-something. We were always dopesick.

It was around this time that I met Mignon Haggard, who was an acquaintance of Paul's. She had come up from LA, where she lived with her Mexican boyfriend Luis who was a big heroin dealer in Santa Ana. We met Mignon at the airport, and she immediately pulled me into a bathroom stall to shoot up a speedball—a mix of coke and heroin. Mignon dressed in the typical LA rocker fashion with tight mini skirts, lacy bras, and sexy little ankle socks with pink, super-high heels. Her bleached-blonde hair hung in a huge mane around her face, and if she wasn't burning her hair with her cigarettes, she was burning a hole in the carpet as she nodded out. She always had tons of heroin, and we became thick as thieves right away. I spoke Spanish so she had me call Luis every day and tell him all sorts of stories to convince him to send hundreds of dollars to us through Western Union. Then she and I would hop into a Yellow Cab and run downtown to Howard Street to pick up the money. The Western Union guys knew us by name. We were in there every freaking day for weeks on end.

Mignon was Merle Haggard's granddaughter. She and her brothers were both addicts, and unfortunately both died of overdoses around that time, but not before selling all the furniture in their parents' house while the parents were away on vacation.

***

One day when Paul and I were particularly sick and bored, we hooked up with David and headed out walking toward the Mab on Broadway. The Mab was a shit heap of a club that housed a variety of punk rock shows. That day, The Mentors were playing, and since Paul and I were dopesick, Paul had hustled up some Benadryl and a 40-ounce St. Ides for us to take the edge off. I popped two pills and guzzled the beer. Not a brilliant idea. By the time we arrived at the Mab, the effects were just hitting me. The Mentors were abominable—big fat guys with ugly, messy beards and filthy t-shirts hanging loosely on their puffy bodies. They sang misogynist and racist lyrics with videos of murder playing in black and white behind them. I was so wasted from the Benadryl that I was unable to get up from my chair, and was instead stuck like the protagonist of *A Clockwork Orange* in the torture scene where they prop his eyes open with toothpicks and force him to watch appalling movies. I was horrified at my condition, and disgusted that Paul had left me and never came back to make sure I was okay. But of course he didn't. It would never have occurred to him. Boy, I sure knew how to pick 'em. The show seemed to go on forever, and I watched, awaiting the moment when my paralysis would run its course. Paul found me as the club staff cleared out the crowd after the show, and he laughed hysterically when I told him what I had experienced. I wanted to punch him in his stupid laughing face. I hated him, but he was all I had.

Eventually, Paul's mom kicked us out, sick of our dope-sickness and our lying around in the closet plotting ways to get high. We would roam the streets finding ways to hustle people, hoping to run into some junkie looking for dope or to meet someone new that Paul could scam. Once, he and I spent the day roaming Polk Street like hungry ghosts, our veins aching and unfulfilled, and came up empty-handed. Finally, in the afternoon, we stumbled across our friend Peter, who was now staying in an apartment near the Tenderloin on lower Polk, and he offered us a place to stay for the night. We tagged along with him as he led us down the street, opening a heavy wooden door that led us into a musty foyer. Paul chattered on as he and Peter moved toward a creaky black elevator. Peter's black curls flopped into his face as he pulled a metal accordion door open and then slammed it shut behind me. Reaching past me, he pushed a protruding brass button for the third floor and the elevator heaved into action, gears turning reluctantly as it ascended. Soon we were standing in the apartment, light from the living room exposing dust particles in the gloomy thickness of the afternoon. Tired and cold, I lurched forward, placing my hands on the floor and easing myself down onto the carpet. The apartment was small, just one room with a kitchen and a tiny bathroom. There was a small bed in the corner, which Peter sat down on as he waved to us to make ourselves comfortable wherever we could find space. I pushed aside a pair of sneakers and a few items of clothing, grabbed a small hard couch pillow that was lying on the floor, and shoved it under my head, closing my eyes and wishing for sleep to take me away from the bland misery of the day. It was still daylight, but we didn't have any dope and we wanted the day to go away. Our silence blasted in my ears, and the muffled sounds of the street outside made me feel unbearably lonely. I sank beneath my thoughts to the bottom of a well, lying on the ground, looking up into the void of the bright day above. I couldn't tell how long I lay there, but after a while I felt a strange pressure on my chest as if someone were sitting on me. I tried to open my eyes, but they wouldn't budge, and when I attempted to turn over to relieve the pressure on my chest, I found myself immobile and powerless. I wondered if I was asleep but I felt awake, just unable to open my eyes. When I tried to murmur a request for help, I found it impossible to speak. After a few long moments of pushing hard, I was able to squeeze out a barely audible "mmmph" sound and break the spell. Suddenly, the pressure disappeared and I was able to talk again. I exclaimed loudly, nudging Paul, who was lying beside me with his arm over his face. We talked about what might have happened. Peter suggested it might have been a psychic attack from someone or something close by. I never knew what happened or if I dreamed it or if some strange being was sitting on my chest sucking the life out of me. It was just another random, terrifying thing that happened like the random terrifying things that had been happening all my life.

From as far back as I could remember, I had lived with the idea that something dreadful could happen at any time and there would be nothing I could do about it. And truthfully, there had been terrible moments: being molested by Bill, Glenn's family burning to death in the fire, Bobby Johnson falling off the truck and dying in front of my eyes, and long periods of extreme dissociation. There had been nothing I could do about any of it, and I had no one to help me make sense of things, so I had come to believe the world could assault me at any time and I was simply at its mercy.

Paul and I eventually got a room at the Leland Hotel and paid for a couple of weeks with our General Assistance checks. I was still working as a troubleshooter at US Courier and was trying hard as hell to keep that job, in spite of my heroin addiction. I would wake up dopesick, ride my heavy messenger bike to work, and sit at the U-shaped dispatch table with the dispatcher and other troubleshooters whose job it was to track down lost packages. I actually enjoyed the job because I was good on the phones and had a knack for stubbornly figuring out even the most complex issues, and I was great with customers, but it was brutal when I was dopesick. First, I would feel icy, then weak. My legs would get restless and start kicking involuntarily. I would pour sweat and eventually vomit. But I had a lot of practice acting normal when life was hard.

At one point, soon after seeing "beware of lice" signs in the office, I felt something crawling on my neck and went into the bathroom to pick it off. Horrified to see a fat bug squirming in my fingers, I ran out and told the manager, Mickey, that I had lice. I asked him if I should go home, and much to my chagrin, he said, "No." Sad, lonely, and hurting, I couldn't keep my deep, dark secret anymore and confessed my heroin addiction. Mickey fired me on the spot.

I had felt like an outsider for the majority of my life, set apart, expected to "disappear into the woodwork," and largely left to shift for myself in my grandmother's world. The pain and shame of my addiction added a new layer to my separation from everyone around me, but my job had supplied normalcy and some hope that life could be different for me someday. I lost more than the job when I got fired. It was as if I had been struggling in the ocean, trying to stay afloat and keep my head about the waves, swallowing sea water, burning in the hot sun, fearing sharks and the darkness of the depths, but keeping a far-off ship in sight and suddenly the ship had disappeared beyond the horizon. I released myself to the watery depths of my addiction and only on rare occasions after that did I try to make my way to shore.

From there on out, I focused on staving off the agony of withdrawal, without regard to where that took me and who I spent my time with. There were seedy hotel rooms with zombie-like junkies tearing at their flesh and poking needles into the remains, ignoring the disaster of their dying bodies to relax into the warmth of relief as the heroin hit. There were gangly meth addicts and broken TVs, neither with any hope for reassembly. And there were coked-out prostitutes with blood under their nails and dark track marks crisscrossing their arms, strategically following the outline of their vascular mapping.

Once when I was staying at the Phillips Hotel in the South of Market district, my sister Gabriela sent me a birthday package. I recall opening it on the bed, atop my old alpaca blanket that John Estabrook's parents had given me in another life, and feeling a sense of pride and belonging when I saw the fancy black-and-white checkered toothbrush with natural bristles she had sent, along with a few other small gifts. I used it with pride at odd hours of the day and it reminded me that someone somewhere loved me and knew me as Sammy and thought I was worthy of a birthday gift.

FALLING UP FROM THE BOTTOM

***

Sometime in 1988, I became the joyful recipient of thirty thousand dollars from Grandma's dear friend, Tanty, who had passed on to a more peaceful existence. I quickly moved out of the shitty hotel circuit and rented a one-bedroom shotgun apartment on Fell and Divisadero. It was a huge relief to not feel terrified of becoming homeless and to be away from all the sad and fucked-up denizens of the San Francisco hotel life. Soon after, I decided to use part of the money to go to inpatient drug treatment at Garden Sullivan on Geary Boulevard. I was nervous about what was in store for me there, but also ecstatic to be safe and well cared for. I had my own bedroom there and we had groups where we would learn about addiction behaviors and discuss solutions for dealing with our feelings, unpacking the past, and looking toward the future. In the evenings, we'd venture out in white vans to go to Twelve Step meetings around the city. The girls would get dressed up as best we could so we could flirt with the guys. I don't think I absorbed much of what was said at those meetings, but I relished the feelings of hope, safety, and joy I found there. Unfortunately, it didn't last. At the end of the 30-day treatment program, I returned to my house on Fell Street and found a young woman named Rachel lodged in the bedroom next to mine. Paul had moved her in and was using her rent money to buy heroin. Within a day of telling Rachel I had just gotten back from treatment, we were shooting up together. Not long after that, I got in a huge fight with Paul. Finally sick of his drama, I threw him out.

I never saw Paul again, but Rachel and I stuck for a while. She was 19 and came from a good family in San

Francisco. Her father was a luthier and they had a nice home nearby. Her parents obviously cared for her and couldn't understand why she'd prefer a life of madness when she had a loving family waiting for her at home. It appeared that Rachel was a pretty happy person in general when she came to live at my apartment. Paul must've bumped into her at a party or something while I was in treatment, then he swooped on the opportunity to draw her into copping dope from him. That way, he could take most of it and give her and her cheery friends a little bit to shoot up, and they'd be satisfied. They were too naive to assume he was ripping them off. Let me tell you something: every junkie who cops for you is ripping you off. Anyway, he had a way about him that made him attractive to people and he consistently had a connection when everyone else was dry. He always had a shit-eating grin on his face, and he was energetic and looked like a cool, bleached-blond punk rocker, which was super "in" in the early 80's. Rachel was probably a lot like me in that she was young and looking for fun. Heroin seemed cool and tough and I imagine she thought it would give her an air of mystery. She probably wanted to look more adult too. That's a common theme among young naive girls. Being punk rock was also considered cool, and lots of rockers did dope. A childish oversimplification of heroin abuse and a lack of real knowledge of the imminent tortures of addiction probably led Rachel to shoot up with Paul for the very first time. And the thing is, you can toy with heroin, but it doesn't take long for it to grab you. Especially if you have any deep-seated woes hiding in the crevasses of your brain. To my knowledge, Rachel hadn't been abused or sexually assaulted as a girl, and she hadn't been neglected, like I had been. I figured she was just a happy-go-lucky party girl who got caught in the clutches of a monster before she realized it was happening.

She had a younger brother who seemed well-adjusted. Always baffled by well-adjusted people, I'd sneak glances at him during brief visits to her house to pick up clothes. Her parents never really talked to me, but I am sure I was weird and stilted. I felt guilty, like I didn't belong in their home, and although I imagined they didn't know what Rachel was up to, I was aware I wasn't doing her any favors. I wondered why they even let me in the door.

Rachel was generally cheerful and had some fun friends from high school she brought over now and again. They started dabbling in dope too, and before long we were all getting high together way too often. One of them who was particularly dear to me was Sandy. A tow-headed surfer type kid with a great sense of humor, Sandy always made me laugh. He would look at the tracks on my arms and run his finger along them saying, "Ticka-ticka-ticka" as if he were drawing a line with dots of my blood. A few years after he started using heroin with Rachel, Sandy killed himself by jumping out the sixth-floor window of an apartment building during a party. I recall a friend telling me his spine had been crushed like an accordion in the fall. I envisioned all the party goers leaning out the window, their rocker hair tumbling over their stunned faces. Sandy had tried to commit suicide multiple times before, once slamming himself into a large picture window, which refused to break. He had a big bruise on his forehead for a while after that. I think Sandy just couldn't take the pain and isolation of heroin addiction and failure. I'll never know what initially brought Sandy to this heinous world addiction, but I imagine that, much like Rachel, he just wanted to have a little fun.

The apartment deteriorated. We never used the kitchen, but the toilet became so stopped up we had to call the landlord, and he was thoroughly disgusted we had let the place get so bad. I was embarrassed. He was a good guy and we had screwed up his apartment. We just didn't know how to live, and even the simplest things were ignored because we were so strung out. It was utterly humiliating to be repeatedly caught in the act of being a total idiot, and that part never got easier for me. Regardless of how far down I sank, I always yearned to be a part of the society around me, and wished I could figure it out so I could fit in. The more dysfunctional I became, the more my shame grew, but I was in so deep by then that getting better seemed about as possible as digging the Grand Canyon with a teaspoon.

When I was still living with Jonithin on Ringold, I got a series of kidney infections and eventually ended up in the hospital with 106-degree fever. One of the ER nurses said she could feel the heat coming off me from across the small examining room. Tests revealed I had been born with a deformity in my urological system that had created a serious blockage, hence the infections. Surgical repair was required, followed by a stay in the hospital to recover. I didn't mind. The hospital was comforting, clean, and hopeful. While living at the Fell Street apartment, I began to get sick again. The pain would start in my side and over a period of a few weeks it would become unbearable. A horrific fever would develop and I would drag myself to the ER where I would be hospitalized and dosed with antibiotics. This happened over and over. Every time the hospital announced I was to be discharged, dread would settle over me at the thought of going home to my life as a junkie. I started to wish I would get sick to get a break from my addiction. Every admission to the hospital was a temporary reprieve, a retreat to safety.

***

One night, I went to cop from a guy named Piak who used to sell me weed. Although he had hair down to his shoulders, a nice bohemian-style apartment, and sold drugs, Piak simply could not get laid because he was too small and the ladies weren't attracted to him. He mentioned his frustration now and again, but I never offered to help.

When I arrived at Piak's, a guy named Rob was there, chatting energetically. His teeth sparkled as he spoke, and his stunning blue eyes twinkled in my direction. I immediately liked him, assuming he was just a pothead. He didn't have that junkie stare and look of misery. He spoke loudly, laughed a lot, and called himself Rat Fink after some cartoon rodent. He liked guns and Harleys and listening to Scraping Foetus. I figured he wouldn't pay attention to me since everyone knew I was strung out, but to my surprise, he hung with me from day one. I was dopesick when I arrived at Piak's that night and Rob was there buying a large bag of weed. He was vibrant and funny and happy. Rob and Piak were heading over to the East Bay for some white and I assumed they meant coke. Piak didn't do heroin to my knowledge and Rob didn't seem like the type either. I didn't want coke, but was happy to go along for the ride because anything was better than nothing.

We exited Piak's bohemian abode, Doc Martens hitting the worn red velvety carpet in the old San Francisco building, and descended in the elevator, staring through the accordion doors as we passed from floor to floor. My stomach turned and I hoped I wouldn't shit myself. Sweat was rolling down me by the time the elevator opened in the cool hollow lobby and we headed for the exit. I was to ride on the back of Piak's motorcycle with him and Rob was going to drive a little red crotch rocket. He had built this bike himself and it stood 18-inches off the ground with the shifters in the rear instead of the front. When he laid down on it, he looked badass and his mohawk made him look fast. He was Rat Fink! He revved the engine with one hand on the bike, right foot on the ground and left foot on the rear shifter. His left hand was propped on his hip, waiting for us to mount Piak's bike. Then we were off, heading toward the Bay Bridge through the city streets. The air was summer cool and I pulled my jacket more tightly around me as the air cooled even more on the bridge. Piak opened up as we hit the bridge. Rob and Piak dodged in and out of cars as we sped along. I felt alive and content, the dope-sickness temporarily replaced by adrenaline. Velocity and wind whipping my hair around me were my drugs and I was momentarily transported away from the mundaneness of my life as the city fell behind us. Rob, who had been ahead of Piak, was now riding close to the trailer of an 18-wheeler and was weaving closer to it, then moving back away. Suddenly, and without fanfare, he ducked his head down and went under the back of the trailer, coming out the other side. I was astonished. Piak saw it too and we both howled into the night air. I had to have this guy. Rob symbolized freedom and throwing caution to the wind, but what I didn't know that night was that he had no limits. None.

Rob copped quickly and we were back in San Francisco in no time, Rob doling out small white lines for each of us. The lines were so tiny I thought he was a lightweight yuppie, but it was free and who was I to complain? So, I snorted the line and lay back in my chair. My stomach had been turning and I had been cold and sweaty, but suddenly a familiar warmth spread through my body, hitting my stomach and soothing the ick. Within a couple of minutes, I was starting to nod out and realized that we had just snorted China White—heroin, not cocaine. I was in heaven and knew Rob was going to be my person forever. We went back to my apartment that night and he never left.

I thought I had won the boyfriend lottery. Rob was sexy in an old-school Rockabilly way, had money, motorcycles, guns, a sense of humor, and he liked heroin. I found out much later that Rob had earned his money in a car accident. He ate cement and lost all of his teeth. After weeks in the hospital and multiple surgeries, he was well enough to get around and had a brand-new pair of pearly whites. He got a chunk of change out of the deal. The minute he was well enough, he bought a Harley Davidson 1340 Sturgis lowrider with a wide-glide front end and an AMF backend. It was heavy and rattled like crazy when the engine was going. In fact, it rattled so much the bolts would rattle right off it and Rob would have to tighten them down after each ride. He loved tightening the bolts on his hog. Once, when we were riding the Pacific Coast Highway, enjoying the beautiful ocean view, the bike died and he had to push it for about a quarter of a mile. He was furious that it was so heavy and he propped it against his skinny hips and cussed the whole way back.

"Stupid fucking hog. Fuck this shit, fucking piece of shit."

He loved that bike and I loved to ride bitch on it. I was super turned on by the sound of the engine and the feel of it vibrating between my legs. I would lean into his back and hold on tight.

We spent our days doing drugs and blasting Scraping Foetus on my record player while Rob shot bullets through the closet walls of my house with his Enfield 303 "anti-people weapon", as he called it, which sent wood chips flying. We went to a pawn shop and he bought me an olive-green shooting jacket with a shoulder pad to lean the stock against. He also bought a pistol-grip pump shotgun and a 22-gauge sniper rifle that broke down and fit into any stock. He would clean his guns, taking them apart on the floor of my bedroom and say, "This is the giver and taker of life." I was dumb enough to be impressed by that at the time. The fact that guns couldn't give birth or impregnate anyone didn't even cross my mind.

But Rob was dishonest. I came to understand the full extent of his chicanery soon after we started dating. My image of him as a good-looking, gregarious guy who had his shit together was completely shot down after he plotted to steal Piak's stash and all his money, then carried out the horrible deed. I had always liked Piak and didn't steal from my friends, but Rob was going to get us some dope, so I let him go about his business. I told myself it wasn't me doing the theft and buried my head in the sand, but I still felt complicit and didn't like it. Piak eventually guessed it had been Rob and hated him from then on out. I was guilty by association and Piak never talked to me again. Months later, I heard he was arrested with a sheet of acid and had been sent to prison, then deported back to Thailand. I never verified the story, but always wondered about him and kind of missed him.

Rob's negative traits surprised me, though my naive understanding of his character was quite superficial. I had never been taught to be discerning with men, so I found Rob intriguing based on his appearance, what boots he wore, the Harley he rode, his ready sense of humor, and the heroin he had in his pocket. Rob was my junkie princess dream. When Rob would tell me stories about his family and how they judged him, I thought he was just too cool for them. He'd tell me about his older brother who was super controlling, and how the whole family looked at him like a pariah when he'd go home for holidays on occasion. I assumed they were foolish for misunderstanding him. Never occurred to me to wonder. . .

Many years later in my 40s, I'd learn with the help of a therapist who taught me things a mother might teach me that there were questions one should ask oneself before hooking up with a guy. Like, for example: What was he like under duress? Was he kind to his mother? How did he treat his female friends? Did he have female friends? Was he consistent? Did he have a healthy relationship with his parents? Could he manage through stress without going nuts? Was family important to him? But at this early stage in my life, a superficial image and one night of coolness was all I needed to move in with someone.

***

The day came when Rob decided to sell his Harley, buy a used truck, and drive down to Culiacán to see my dad and kick dope. The truck he bought was so high off the ground it didn't have a good center of gravity. Not long after he bought it, I rolled the truck while barely turning a corner on my block. Nevertheless, we drove the truck to Mexico along with the Enfield 303, the shotgun, and the sniper rifle. Naturally, we had no permit to cross into Mexico with those guns and I was completely clueless about how much trouble we'd be in if we were caught with them. The guns were just loaded into the truck with the rest of our baggage and off we went, driving down the Baja 1000 toward La Paz, where we planned to catch the ferry to the mainland. We thought we'd probably go to Puerto Vallarta and then drive over to Culiacán from there.

There was snow on the ground when we reached Tijuana after a long day of driving. We rented a room in a tarnished hotel. Even the walls of the place looked jaded, as if they had seen too many years of tired prostitutes and horny truck drivers with bumps of coke and bottles of tequila. We paid the clerk and dragged our bags from the truck into the room. It was unheated. Rob pulled the stiff curtains closed as I climbed into bed fully dressed, shivering and pulling the blankets over my head. We spent a restless night and were up at the crack of dawn, anxious to get into the warmth of our truck.

Sometime around six a.m., Rob pulled into a gas station about an hour south of Ensenada, his mohawk and leather pants instantly drawing attention. Two Mexican men eyed him with curiosity and barely disguised disgust. Fearful, Rob pulled the pistol grip pump shotgun out from under the driver's seat, loaded it, and stuffed it back under the seat. The Mexicans looked away in a second-nature act of self-preservation. What gun?

When the gas tank was full, Rob pulled himself up onto the seat where I lay beside him still wearing my leather jacket, leather pants, and 20-eye Doc Martens, my bleach-blonde mohawk leaning on my bent arm. The truck started and we were off again, careening south at 90 mph as Rob slipped in a cassette of Scraping Foetus. "Fee Fi Fo Fum, it takes two to tangle, it takes one to cum. Some things are better left unsaid, like a pound of protection beats an ounce of lead. . ."

We drove for about an hour, when suddenly Rob shouted, "Oh shit, Sammy!" and I felt the truck lurch to the left, then spin. Hazy, sleepy, and drug depleted, I didn't move. The truck listed, then spun around and went backwards down the highway for a second. Then it hit dirt on the side of the road and caught air. It flipped once, twice, then hit the ground rolling, the aching metal creaking while I calmly waited for something metal to impale me. The truck finally came to a stop, upright on the tires. Still, I lay there, quite still, in the same place I had been when the accident started. I could hear Rob yelling as fire broke out under the hood. The gas from the tank had spilled onto the manifold when the truck flipped and was now burning. Rob pushed open the door on his side. It made a loud popping noise where the roof had caved in. I was still immobile, stunned. Rob started pulling things out of the truck and dragging them up to the side of the road, dropping them in the desert dust. Finally, he tugged on my leg, yelling at me. "Get out! Get out of the truck!" and dragged me out of the burning truck. He had a big gash in his forehead above his left eye and he was bleeding profusely. His mohawk stood up above the gash and his green eyes flashed with fear. He grabbed the shotgun from under the seat, thrust it into a pillowcase and handed it to me, telling me to get up on the highway and stop the next car that came. I wondered for a second what the pillowcase was for, since the gun was obviously supposed to help me stop someone. What was Rob thinking? Was I supposed to kinda try to hide it, then whip it out if there were trouble? But I was tired and the desert seemed bigger now, and I didn't want to spend a lot of time there, so I hoofed it up to the side of the road and sat down for a minute in the dust and rocks, the heavy metal feeling hard in my hands through the pillowcase.

Rob proceeded to run back and forth to the truck, grabbing as many of our belongings as he could, while I sat on the side of the road screaming at him to get away from the burning truck. I imagined the whole thing was going to blow, killing him and leaving me standing there holding that damned shotgun. I looked up the highway now and again, sure no car would come, given that we were who knows how many miles off into the desert, but to my surprise a little red 1960s panel van came trundling down the road. I stood up on the road, my blonde mohawk pouring down my back, my black leather pants and boots covered in dust, and the shotgun hanging partially out of the pillowcase, and waved down the driver. The van stopped and two wrinkled old men got out of it—the driver smiling and telling me to put the gun away. They had seen the truck burning and that's why they had stopped. Nothing to fear, no guns necessary. What the fuck were these guys thinking? I had a freaking pump shotgun in a pillowcase. Nothing made sense.

They agreed to give us a ride to Constitución, near La Paz, because that was the closest town with a phone and a hospital. Mind you, it was 15 hours away. We loaded as much as we could fit into the van and climbed into the back amidst what was left of our worldly goods. The journey was long and Rob's head continued to bleed. Occasionally, I would start crying and say, "He's bleeding so much!" Rob would tell me to shut the fuck up because he didn't want the old men to get nervous and dump us in the desert. Each time we would arrive in another no-phone-having tiny town, the old men would suggest we get out and we would protest, begging them to take us on to Constitución.

When we arrived there, we thanked the men, gave them everything we couldn't carry, and limped to the hospital. The hospital was a plain building with very little furniture and only one nurse. Rob was in pain and requested drugs, and the nurse prepared a shot, first dropping it on the floor, picking it up and wiping it off with a rag, then injecting him in his upper arm. We were disappointed after such a long journey that there wasn't more fanfare upon our arrival at the hospital and soon found ourselves walking around town looking for a hotel.

Coming to a crosswalk, I stopped to let a car pass, and realized it was the local police. They smiled at me and said hello through the open window of their car, and I asked them if they knew where we could stay. Rob was terrified when he saw me speaking to the cops and pulled back with his hand on the blanket that covered the guns, but the cops were young men who were more intrigued by us than anything, and pointed down the street in the direction of a two-story white building.

We ambled down the dusty street and arrived at the hotel, a couple of blocks away on the corner of the main avenue. We paid for our room and hobbled up the tile stairs with our bags in tow. We had brought the guns with us from the truck and did our best to conceal them under blankets as we bumped up the steps with our things. The door was half metal and half frosted glass with bars on it, and it creaked as it opened into a sparsely furnished room with a blue-tiled floor. Sun streamed in the slatted windows and the heat made us feel lazy.

We set our things down on the floor and Rob dropped onto the bed, exhausted. Suddenly the day's events came to a screeching halt in that little room and we stared at each other, speechless. Since the moment of the accident, there had been a flurry of events, culminating in the silence echoing in this space. The bed squeaked as Rob shuffled the two pillows into position behind his head and stretched out further, crossing his legs, his combat boots casting small piles of desert dust onto the bed.

I felt bored, yet relieved to have a place of our own to escape from the world, while also dreading the complexities of our situation. Our predicament was obvious: no money, no car, Mohawks and Doc Martens, and three guns in a foreign country while injured.

Our thoughts went immediately to how to make money and get some food. Rob wanted a bag of weed, which I cared nothing about, but he was insistent that we track one down to deal with his dope sickness and pain. We decided that, since I could speak Spanish, I would go to recon, leaving Rob to lie down in the hotel and rest.

It took me just a few minutes before a boy around 12 years old approached me and asked if he could help us with anything. His name was Abel, he said, and he could get us whatever we wanted. Within no time, Abel and I were standing next to the bed, and Rob was doling out a five dollar bill for a large bag of shitty weed—about two ounces—which Rob proceeded to puff on all day long. I felt lonely.

Our next concern was how we would get back home. There was nothing to do but call my family and see if they would help. I sat in the phone room in the hotel, kicking my foot nervously back and forth as I dialed Tanty. She had been there through thick and thin during all the years of craziness with my mother, my Uncle Wiley, us girls, the fall out the window, everything. I had never asked Tanty for anything before, but I trusted she would help me. After hearing me out, Tanty said she would send me $2,000 to buy a car and I breathed a sigh of relief, some of the tension finally receding from my body.

A few days later we headed home in a dusty blue Datsun B210, our tails between our legs. So much for the glamorous Harley, the 4-wheel drive truck, and our delusions of kicking dope in Mexico. When we got back to the States, we headed straight for a dealer.

Honestly, my dad would have kicked Rob's ass had we made it to Culiacán. My father, in spite of his unorthodox ways, was a man of principle and he was powerful. Rob would have had to shape up fast or he would've been out on his ass in a Mexican city that doesn't suffer fools. I once read that Culiacán was one of the top 20 most deadly cities in the world. Don't mess around and find out. Of course, I've always cared deeply for Culiacán because my big beautiful family is from there and they are people of great loyalty and heart. It's a home to me.

***

After the Mexico debacle, Rob and I returned to San Francisco. We found a small studio on the first floor of the same building Piak lived in on Divisadero and furnished it with great finds from the streets, including a big wooden desk that made the place look quite homey. I soon became pregnant with my first child. I got on a very low dose of methadone so I could stop using heroin and be relatively healthy for the pregnancy. Glad to be off the dope, and excited to have this new life to focus on, I went to prenatal appointments, wore clean clothes, and felt some semblance of normalcy for the first time in a long time. Rob still had a habit, though.

Broke, we had gotten into the scrap metal business, even being so bold as to drive our truck down Divisadero Street, stopping at each light post in the median and popping off the base caps with a crowbar. They were pure aluminum and we found a fence to buy them, an old black man who purchased items out of his garage in Daly City. We sold to him for many months before we saw him on the news one day. He had been indicted for purchasing city property and went away to jail. That was the end of that. We took to jumping into the scrap metal yards in Hunters Point and hit one particularly lucrative spot more than once. That ended after the owner got a Doberman. The dog met us about 100 feet inside the chain link fence we had just hopped. I ran for my life, grabbing the fencing and pulling myself up, heaving my pregnant belly over it and dropping to the ground six feet below. By then we had pretty much emptied the lot and it wasn't too hard to say goodbye to it, what with lean pickings and the killer dog and all.

When I was in labor, on my way to the hospital, I

called my mother. She and my sisters, Sky and Miriam, came to be with me. I labored for 18 hours, holding my mother's hand and looking up at her in misery. The young male doctor had curly blonde hair and treated me with disdain. His lack of respect was predictable, since everyone knew I was addicted to heroin and Child Protective Services was involved in my prenatal care. They tested me periodically for drug use. I stayed relatively clean during my pregnancy, but had taken Vicodin once before they tested me, so I was definitely on everyone's radar. Thankfully, for her sake, my daughter was born healthy.

I was instantly in love with Simika. She slept near my bed in a little basket and the nurses gave her to me every so often to breastfeed. She had tiny white dots on her nose, as all babies do, and I marveled at them. Snuggled into blankets, her miniature face was perfect. I breastfed her and held her so much I sometimes fell asleep with her in my arms. But I was still an addict and completely incapable of being a good parent.

After Simika was born, I went back to using, and my daughter was at risk. Rob and I lost our apartment and were eventually forced to give up our precious baby. Simika went to live with Rob's relatives in Chicago who could take good care of her and keep her safe. Heartbroken and mortified, I went off the deep end.

***

Bibiano stood solidly in the doorway, his feet shoulder width apart, eyeing me in a predatory fashion. I could see the calculations reflected in his features, small shifts in his demeanor, and subtle changes in his facial expression as he assessed what advantages he had over us. He would tell me later he had been a librarian back in Cuba—a nice guy—until he came to the States, where he became a heroin dealer. The trajectory didn't faze me. Given the situation I was in, it made all the sense in the world. He had holed up in the Star Hotel, a sleazy downtrodden building that listed to one side and housed a rotation of the most tortured junkies and hookers in the city. Looking past him, I could see a cracked window that opened onto a small roof in the center of the building. It was littered with broken syringes and a pair of discarded pink underwear that had long ago lost their allure. A heavy black curtain hung over the right side of the greasy window. It was covered with dust, bare only where Bibiano's hands might touch it if he were peeking outside in a moment of coke-induced paranoia.

My friend Rachel and I stood in the hall ignoring the gloom of our surroundings and the pain that had soaked into the walls over time, focusing simply on the small bags of heroin in Bibiano's possession. We handed over the cash and Bibiano handed over the drugs, and then invited us in to get high with him. He would use his drugs and we would use ours, but he was willing to share a bit since we had purchased so much. We quickly shoved aside the clothes on the greasy green carpet and pulled a chair up beside the dresser. Out came a dirty spoon caked with old burnt heroin and a piece of used cotton. With one quick sweep, Rachel scooped out the cotton, tossing it into the garbage, grabbed a Q-tip from her little metal mints can, and pulled a piece of it with her teeth. Simultaneously, she opened the bag of heroin and mashed its stickiness onto the cold spoon. It stuck there as she drew up water into the syringe and shot it into the spoon. Bibiano was ready with a lighter and leaned toward the dresser and the spoon in Rachel's hand to heat the brown liquid. In a minute or so, the heroin started to boil and Bibiano flipped his finger off the lighter, pulled out a bindle, and dropped in a heap of coke. Rachel pulled the plunger from a syringe and stirred the mixture vigorously—one, two, three, four, five times. For a split second I thought, "That's a lot of coke," but Rachel was already drawing up the elixir into the rig.

I had a hard time with my veins and didn't have a needle of my own with me, so Bibiano generously offered to let me use one of his old ones. Pulling out a small bottle of bleach provided by the needle exchange folks on the corner of Mission and 14th, Bibiano drew the bleach into the needle, shook it a few times, and squirted it out, following this with a few rinses of water through the rig. Then he drew up some of the speedball for me. I was nervous because I was dopesick and something about the relief of knowing my next hit was coming made my stomach turn every time. I had no veins left in my arms so Bibiano offered to shoot me in my neck. He sat on the creaky bed, which doubled exaggeratedly under his weight. I sat next to him, leaning back into his lap and held my breath tightly, pushing hard so the veins in my neck would bulge. He found the one I normally used in the front of my neck near my Adam's apple, and stuck in the dull needle. The fluid shot directly into my brain and I reeled, sitting up briefly, and then dropping to the floor.

"I think it's too much," I said.

***

It was dark when I woke up. I felt numb, but soon the awareness of the cold air around me crept in. Cramped and unable to move, I looked up at the night sky where stars were twinkling way off in the darkness. I was in an eerie dream, and though I felt no fear, a sense of evil enveloped me. Almost as if I was being born, and with confusion and wonder, I crept out, my body moving on its own, awkwardly seeking space to leverage another small movement. What the hell?

It was a garbage can. I was in a garbage can. I don't know how long it took me to get out, but it seemed like hours. When my feet finally touched the floor, I realized I was on the cold metal stairs of the fire escape behind the Star. The heavy back door, rusted corners rounded from years of neglect, stood ajar, so I pulled it open and stepped up into the dark hallway. Yellowed bare bulbs sizzled overhead as I crept silently down the hallway, still unsure of my surroundings. The muffled voices of paranoid drug addicts, well into their fixes by now, reached me from behind the thin wooden doors that lined the hallway and then subsided. I finally came to a closet-like shower and was suddenly relieved to recognize exactly where I was. I pushed open the thin metal door and stepped up about a foot into the darkness onto the wet tiled floor. I sat on my haunches in the tiny tiled chamber, leaving the door slightly open to allow some light to come in. As I sat in that clammy room, memory seeped back in, then suddenly flooded me. I saw the bright light, the dresser, Rachel and Bibiano, and the syringe. Realizing what happened, I bolted up and headed down the gooey red carpet to Bibiano's door, across from the back door of the building.

I stood outside listening and there suddenly was Rachel's voice. I reached my hand up, balled it into a fist, and knocked lightly on the door—one, two, three times. Bibiano opened the door. Rachel was peeking out from behind his shoulder.

Sheepishly, they asked, "What do you want?"

Seriously? After they threw me in a trash can when I was overdosed?! That's it? What do you want?

I looked at them quietly and asked, "Is there any coke left?"

SAMANTHA DE LA VEGA

FALLING UP FROM THE BOTTOM

Sweet little roly poly Simika

*Me during the painful drug years
The amazing thing is, people can recover*

CHAPTER 12
WHITEY AND THE FRÄULEIN

A few weeks later, I was back on Mission Street in the heat of the day. The hot sun beat down until my black sleeveless t-shirt was soaked with perspiration. I was thin now, and ashamed, walking with determination and trepidation toward the Star Hotel. I rang the buzzer. Patel buzzed me in the door from the upstairs office. He had been there forever. His dead eyes looked down at me through the thick, pitted glass of the office window, his face registering disgust.

"I need to see Bibiano," I called.

Mumbling something about "all hours of the day," he buzzed me in and then turned back to his television, which blared a chaotic music medley from another era.

I climbed the creaky black staircase. The carpet had long since worn through. Strips of material hung down like limp dead souls as I moved heavily up the stairs. By the time I reached the top, I could feel sweat coating my upper lip and dripping down my back beneath my shirt.

It was quiet. Most people stayed up all night and slept well into the next day, only getting up when the sick was upon them. Until then, they hid like cockroaches, ashtrays brimming over, bodies jumbled in quiet disarray, abandoned paraphernalia strewn about, dry and smelly in the stifling air.

I turned the corner, took a breath, and knocked lightly at Bibiano's door. It looked the same, and the sameness made me tired. I heard the bed squeak as he set up and listened as he stepped across the floor and opened the door. He didn't say a word. Until now, he had masked his diabolical insides by smiling. On this day, he looked at me plainly as I struggled to say, "I'm sick. Can you front me a twenty?"

I felt like an idiot, but I was driven by the pain beneath my skin—a cracked glass feeling. I shifted in my monkey boots and the glass dug in, small fragments shifting and crackling. The unbearable waiting became a raging fire. I breathed slowly, my heart racing, my body weak and my arms heavy. My legs were sweating in my pants and even my forearms were covered with a thin layer of perspiration.

Bibiano motioned at me to come in and closed the door as I stepped quietly into the room. I figured best-case scenario he was going to give me the twenty and chew me out about bringing the money back soon. Instead, he toyed with me. Since standing even one more second of the pain felt impossible, the worst case scenario was standing there listening to him talk about the morning and what he planned to do with his day. He took off his shorts and lay down in bed again, motioning for me to lie down next to him. Whatever. I started to move toward him, and then he told me to take off my clothes. My skin crawled. I struggled out of my pants, which were stuck to my damp body, and sat down on the bed. Bibiano reached over and pulled me down next to him, spooning me. He was grotesque. The warmth of his body against my sweaty misery repulsed me and I tried to hide inside myself, but the rawness of jonesing kept me ever present. His hands reached down and cupped my breasts. I gritted my teeth thinking, "Just get through it." I could feel his erection behind me, and then I felt him penetrate me. He moved slowly, taking pleasure in my misery. I wanted to die. When he was done, I moved quickly away from him, wiping myself on the sheets and pulling on my pants hastily. At least I had a fix coming. Or so I thought, until Bibiano told me to leave dismissively. I screamed inside my head, and protested slightly, but there was nothing to do. He wasn't playing by the rules, because there were no rules. There was just me in my dopesick misery walking toward the door, hating him and wishing I was dead.

When I opened the door, Whitey was standing there. Whitey was a tall, light-skinned black man with beautiful blue eyes and a dastardly heart. His moniker was the result of his bleached blonde hair. Rumor had it that Whitey had just gotten out of prison for stabbing a pregnant woman in the stomach. He didn't yet have a habit; he was just slinging dope for Bibiano and serving as his muscle. As I stepped past Whitey, headed toward the exit and thinking about what to do next, Bibiano motioned to Whitey and said the unthinkable, "She's yours."

At first I couldn't grasp what he said. By the time I realized what was happening, it was too late. There was no fighting, no yelling, no pleading, no asking for help. No one would have helped anyway. Everyone was afraid of the horrors of violence in the Star. It was a lonely walk down the hall to Whitey's room.

Days passed in Whitey's room. He smoked crack and used me. Occasionally, he'd get angry and burn me with a cigarette. The unspoken truth was I was there; he had me against my will. If I tried to leave, he'd beat the shit out of me. I'd seen him do it before, and I knew the pregnant woman story. More days went by and the dope sickness started to pass. I was feeling stronger in spite of the constant lack of nourishment. My thoughts turned to escape. He had to sleep at some point. Whitey smoked and smoked, only leaving the room for a few minutes to purchase crack after selling some dope. The rotation seemed endless. Finally, there was an interruption in the cycle when a dark-haired German woman with a scar across her face came in. She was loud and confident—strong too, since she had just gotten out of prison—and was looking for action. She would have been beautiful had she not been so cruel.

The Fräulein and Whitey plotted. Soon after, she found a target: a small Asian man she had picked up on the street. After dark, she brought him to the room at the end of the hall past Bibiano's door. A few minutes passed, and then Whitey grabbed me.

"Let's go," he said.

We walked quickly and quietly down the hallway, the thick silence intermittently broken by the murmur of voices behind closed doors. Whitey knocked on the door we wanted. I shrunk quietly into myself, feeling small behind Whitey. The German woman opened it and Whitey pushed passed her, dragging me into the room behind him. I moved to the side as Whitey turned to the small thin man, demanding his money. Then, the Fräulein woman punched the little Asian guy in the back of the head as Whitey pulled out a large cleaver. The little Asian guy jumped jaggedly in disjointed movements, reminding me of a rat trying to run on water. The Fräulein and Whitey made quick business of getting Water Rat's money, but things didn't end there. Whitey slashed at the man standing naked before him and his skin split impossibly to reveal lumps of fatty tissue, but to my dismay, the man didn't fight back. He was a pervert and he didn't want to be seen, so he only protested quietly as the blood dripped down his body where Whitey had cut him. I reeled from the intensity of the moment, terrified for the loathsome little man, yet unable to help him. I was sure I was next. The brutality was unwarranted. The poor guy would've given them the money without any violence, but they were on fire. They danced like pagans, slicing the man here and there, the eerie green walls and the yellow light floating around them as they moved. The room spun and the yellow light dimmed as I lost consciousness.

When I came to, I found myself back in Whitey's room. He and the Fräulein were laughing loudly and talking feverishly about the incident. It had gone well from their perspective.

They sat on the floor, crouched over a spoon, and shot tangy hot heroin into their veins. Before long they nodded out and I became aware of my chance to escape. Quietly, I stepped over their bodies as they drooled into the carpet, their cigarettes capped by long ash caterpillars burning holes in the rug. I opened the door, and made my way down the hallway, my torn jeans and the white cotton shirt my dad had designed years ago in sunny Mexico covered in the blood of the man they had just hacked up.

Outside, the sun was shining and the day was bustling around me. I heard a cheery Mexican Norteño song blasting from a restaurant nearby, and was transported briefly to a few years earlier in Puerto Vallarta—a lifetime ago—when I had been so happy and felt so free. The sun warmed my shoulders as I stepped into the heat and started walking, increasingly aware of how broken I was. I walked up Mission Street, limping slightly and hungry for food, hunched over and squinting in the bright noon light. I had been in captivity a week or more and all I'd had to eat were nibbles of junk food Whitey had thrown at me. Shiny people with clean clothes and well-fed bodies passed by me as I walked. They laughed and talked. Their sneakers were clean, their purses new. They reached into wallets for coffee cash and waved down buses. I walked, directionless, into the new day.

***

I had nowhere to go so I ambled over to Dolores Park and sat in the sun, eyeing the people as they played with dogs, talked, walked, and laid on blankets reading books. My knees protruded from my torn pants. Blood from Whitey's victim mixed with my own, staining the top half of my pants. In a fog of hunger and fear, my chest heavy, I leaned my elbows on my knees and thought of my childhood cat, Ann, with her soft white and orange fur. I pictured her sweet face, her eyes squinting at the sun as she looked up at me in the Towners silence. The distance seemed so far from there to here. How did I get here? But something about that childhood thought stirred a sense of hope. Although I had no idea where to go or what to do, I was free from Whitey and realized I at least had some choice about my next move. I looked up again at the happy, well-fed people in the park and my hope faded into longing. I so wanted what the park people had. There it was. I could reach out my hand and touch it, but the layers upon layers of magic it would require seemed so far out of reach. I knew I had to get food and get off the streets so I could rest. I had fallen asleep in Dolores Park before and had awoken to the sound of *cholos* having an argument with a really loud girl nearby. I was terrified to sleep outside, even in the day, and I had to get out of my godawful clothes with the memories of my time at Whitey's soaked into them. Remembering the Salvation Army on Valencia Street had a policy of giving a free set of clothes to the homeless, I headed over there.

I opened the glass door of the Salvation Army and stepped into the cool shadowy room. It smelled of dampness and summer. The sole of my right shoe flapped against the floor and there was a big hole where my toes stuck out. Shame washed over me, but I was desperate for a change of clothes. I asked a man standing amid the aisles and he waved his hand saying, "The store is your oyster!" His kindness made me remember love. For a second, I felt human.

Moving around the store apologetically, I picked out a pair of jeans, a tee-shirt, and a long-sleeved shirt. Then I looked around for a changing room. The salesclerk, who had been peeking over at me now and again, pointed me toward the dressing rooms at the back of the store. Changing my clothes was almost as good as pouring a can of white paint over the memories of the previous days. I stepped out of the dressing room and the nice man gave me a plastic bag to put my old clothes in. I walked out of the store and dumped the bag of blood-soaked clothes into the first garbage can I saw. It felt like performing an exorcism.

I spent the next two years living in the Sierra Hotel on 20th and Mission, smoking crack and trying to figure out how to unwind my bad choices before those choices killed me. Everyone in the Sierra was dying of their bad choices. Being an addict is a pitiless task. You do it to yourself with zero idea of what you're setting yourself up for until the steely addiction scrapes your insides and crushes your bones. Then it's too late and it feels like it just happened to you by some accident of fate. Most of the people I knew got strung out on drugs when they were young, dysfunctional, confused, and directionless. They were the perfect prey, bumbling through life randomly, just looking for a way to feel better, only to find themselves in anguish, alone, and dying a few years later.

I was sitting in the Sierra one morning, in yet another dark and stale room, listening to the murmur of junkies around me when someone came in and commented there was a guy dying of an overdose down the hall. I was high as fuck on crack and had been up for days, yet I still remembered the CPR I had learned in the West Indies the summer Grandma sent me to camp. I didn't miss a beat. Standing immediately, I crossed the room and headed down the hall to find the guy.

I found the guy lying on his back with his mouth open. I could tell he wasn't breathing. The veins bulged black in his neck and his face was an odd gray color. I leaned over and shook him. Nothing. I could see his tongue was not down his throat and it didn't look like he had aspirated vomit, so I decided to try to breathe for him. I leaned over and put my mouth over his, holding his nose with my left hand, and breathed into him. His chest rose. I breathed for him for a minute or so before he started to stir. When I could tell he was breathing on his own, I stepped away from him. A few seconds later, I heard the cops coming down the hall, their radios blaring static and intermittent communiques from the dispatcher. I could hear them talking as they approached the room, so I dipped out and scurried quietly down the hall, slipping into my friend Larry's room. I peered guiltily through the eyehole in the door as they took the man away in cuffs. The cops looked like Cagney and Lacey from the TV series of the same name. They were undercover cops but known around the Sierra. Once before I had given life-saving breath to a good-looking Hispanic guy in another hotel at 16th and Mission. He sat up right when the paramedics arrived and said, "Daaaaamn, man! You didn't have to call the cops on me." No gratitude. I imagined this guy felt the same, but I knew I had saved his life and that did something for my soul, even in that dark and terrible time when I felt so trapped by my addiction. I still valued life and it reminded me there was good in the world, even if it emanated from me.

Before I was addicted, I thought heroin would make me a better writer. I had been writing journals and poetry for years, reading Artaud, listening to Patti Smith, and I had managed to romanticize heroin, associating it with profundity, intensity, and being truly alive. I believed heroin would connect me to the living self I had buried in order to better "disappear into the woodwork, darling" as Grandma had instructed over and over. Thus, delivered from the aimless nothingness of my childhood, I thought I would finally become compelling enough to interest someone else—anyone else—to care about me, stay with me, keep me safe, and handle daily life for me. But heroin is a psychopathic, possessive lover. It promises peace, stops terror in its tracks, softens the broken glass feeling it creates itself, and whispers, "Rest, rest, you can deal with everything else tomorrow." And while you are asleep in its arms, it steals any semblance of self-esteem you have left, kidnaps your babies, rapes you, and disguises you as a worthless piece of shit. Heroin finally accomplished what Grandma never entirely did: it made me, Sammy, disappear into the woodwork while the shell of me served it at its whim.

CHAPTER 13
MEXICAN REHAB IN TWO PARTS

Mama's voice on the other end of the phone sounded worried. I had called her from the payphone in front of the Mission Hotel, where I had been staying for a while. "I'm not okay," I said.

I heard her take a deep breath. Mama was always kind to me, even when I was at my worst, and she had a way of listening that made me feel heard. She would furrow her brow, tilt her head down, and watch me as I spoke. We'd sometimes talk about philosophy and the meaning of life, or sometimes discuss old times and our unusually similar childhoods growing up with Grandma. By this time, my siblings had grown up and started lives of their own. Lhasa was singing professionally in Montreal. The girls were there too, training as acrobats in the circus school, and Ayin even did a stint on the tight-wire in the Cirque du Soleil in Japan. Years later, the girls would move to France where they would do circus and perform throughout Europe, and end up living there indefinitely and making families. Gaby had married Nikko Sedgwick and moved back to New York City where she was designing jewelry. Her beautiful necklaces and earrings appeared in *Italian Vogue* and *Marie Claire*, as well as on the TV series *Gossip Girl*. Mischa was living with Mama and was in school. He would state later that he felt abandoned with all of us out of the house doing our own thing. He had grown up with a big family of sisters, and now he was living alone with Mama. But Mama was great with him. She kind of doted on him compared to the rest of us, and he always had a nice meal at the table with her. In general, it was the season in Mama's life to rest and enjoy some peace and quiet, yet there I was on a payphone telling her I was once again in a mess and needed help.

I didn't think I was going to make it. I had been in and out of San Francisco General Hospital with septicemia and a PICC line IV directly into my heart to kill the infection, and I was dying. I weighed about 85 pounds and even size one pants floated around my bones.

"Maybe I can talk to your father and see if he can help," she said.

A couple of days later, my mother called the front desk at the hotel and asked to talk to me. I walked down the hall to the phone. The TV in the lobby was blaring at a bunch of old junkies and elderly people on Social Security that were hunched on fake leather couches, bored and motionless as if suspended in time. A fly buzzed, banging its crunchy body on the glass door. I stepped to the tall fake marble counter and the clerk handed me the phone. The receiver was cold and heavy in my hand as I put it to my ear.

"Well, Alfonso said you can go stay with him in Culiacán," Mama said.

I walked back to my room wondering how my father would react to me. Returning to Mexico strung out was bound to be a little uncomfortable, but I had to do something. Things were actually a matter of life or death. In spite of the imminent difficulty ahead of me, I felt a warm sense of relief that my mother and father were saving me.

I woke the next morning to Mama knocking on the door of my hotel room and relief washed over me. My mother had never really tactically mothered me during the time I had been in San Francisco, although she had always listened to me if I reached out to her. There was still so much unresolved stuff in our family and it hung over us, ambiently destructive. So, when she showed up for me at The Mission Hotel that day, it felt real, like my mother had come to save my life.

Disheveled and dope-sick, I dragged myself through the motions of grabbing things and getting ready to go. Mama came into the room, which was covered in dirty clothes and junk, interspersed with capless syringes and bottle caps used to cook heroin. Undaunted, Mama pulled out a few items that would be helpful to me and shuffled me into her ramshackle blue Toyota with torn seats. I left that shithole with a large bag of dirty clothes and a crack pipe I had squirreled away for emergencies. Somehow, by the time we got to the airport, I realized how stupid it would be to fly into Mexico with a crack pipe and had the presence of mind to ditch it on our way to the gate.

Mama and I talked about hope and her belief in me while we waited from the plane. After the airline folks called out for boarding, I hugged my mother, my large bag thudding against her and nearly pulling me over as

I leaned in. I sensed her fatigue and let her go. Within minutes, I was sitting in my seat on the plane. Exhaustion washed over me and I tilted my head back against the window and fell asleep. I woke a few hours later in Guadalajara and switched to a little prop plane for the final leg to Culiacán.

As I deplaned, the thick humid air hit me and the scent of Culiacán reached out from the past and eased into my bones. It briefly dawned on me that I was going to the home of the Sinaloa Cartel to get clean off of heroin. I emerged from the small airport building to see my dad, Inomar, and my cousin Jaime coming toward me, big smiles on their faces. I eyed them wearily, still drained from the months of my hard drug run. Emaciated, dressed in red and black striped leggings under torn jeans, my hair whipping around my face in the hot desert wind, I must have looked a fright, but Ino put his arms around me anyway, shaking me up and down, almost lifting me off the ground. "Temandía! You are here with us!" I loved and hated that name, depending on the day. Sometimes it made me feel a part of his world and at other times I resented it. He had failed me in so many ways, yet he thought he would teach me to walk in the world? Pffft.

Still, arriving back in Culiacán conjured up memories of the hope I had felt as a girl when I first met my father and Ino in El Remance at the back of Puerto Vallarta and my father's deep voice and strong personality made me feel safe. I knew he would take charge. I no longer had to run my own show and, for the moment, that was a relief.

Ino grabbed my heavy duffle and we all piled into their car and headed toward home. The house on Calle Hidalgo had belonged to my family for generations. We had once owned a great deal of land in Sinaloa, according to family lore, but the revolutionary general, Pancho Villa, had stolen it from us in the Mexican Revolution. What was left was a sizable property that took up a city block in downtown Culiacán. The family had subdivided it into various business spaces they rented out, but a portion had been retained as my father's private residence. When we arrived, I found my old bedroom along the main hall had been turned into a *peluqueria*, or hair salon, run by my father's friend, Alma, so I would be sleeping in Jaime's room down the hall from the kitchen. Alma was a nice woman who wore tons of makeup, nylons under her very tight jeans, and high heels, even in the oppressive heat of Culiacán. Having another woman around was comforting, though Alma always deferred to her boss, my father, so we never had true solidarity.

For the next few weeks I slept and ate and ate and slept. My father had Jaime and Ino wash all my clothes because they stunk of stale cigarette smoke and held who knows what bad vibes from San Francisco. As I got stronger, I started working out in the makeshift gym upstairs and my father began giving me chores and expected me to behave like part of the family. I had lost some of my dignity and good manners during my years doing drugs. My father was having none of it; he had standards.

He caught me eating in bed one day and he said kindly, but firmly, "We don't eat in bed in this house." That was all he needed to say; I didn't do it again.

Another time I set my Marlboro pack on his I Ching and he angrily lectured me about never setting anything atop the I Ching. "And stop carrying your cigarettes from room to room like a security mechanism," he ordered.

Eventually, he forbade me to smoke altogether, tormenting me and making fun of me if I did. He could not abide cigarettes. He said they were selfish because they weren't shared like joints, plus, they wouldn't even get you high. Years later, I would find myself as equally repulsed by cigarettes as he was.

Daddy had saved up a considerable amount of money that he kept in a large safe, which he inherited from his father. He said his intention had been to buy me a whole new wardrobe, but the week before my arrival, the house had been robbed. Men had dropped in through the roof with hoods on and machine guns. They hogtied Ino and Jaime, only sparing my dad because he pretended to be old and feeble. The burglars had somehow known about the safe and insisted Daddy open it and give them all the contents. Then, off they went through the roof like evil reverse Santas. Since his money had been stolen, my dad settled for buying me a few pairs of Mexican jeans with bling on them and told me to never wear my holey clothing again.

He also gave me shit about "being phony" and chatting it up with the customers who came to his shops "as if I were on holiday."

"You burned your life to the ground," he pointed out. "Maybe start being straight with people instead of putting on such a show."

He was ruthless, but I knew he was right. He loved me in his own twisted way and I admired him and loved to hear him say, "You're so much like me," which he did every chance he got. He'd sing to me, *"Te pareces tanto a mi, que no puedes engañarme..."* In a lot of ways, my dad was amazing and bigger than life.

One day, Daddy decided he wanted to go for a swim in the river. The river through Culiacán was muddy and only poor people swam in it. People who had money went to the country club in Chapultepec, but my dad didn't care if people were rich or poor and he wasn't one to put on airs. He knew who he was and he wanted to swim in the river. So, we loaded the car and off we went. We were soon sitting on the grassy edge of the Rio Culiacán surrounded by clouds of gnats. My father went in right away while I stood on the edge and looked at the water, feeling creeped out and scared by what might be in it. There were large groups of lily pads and tall grass along the sides and the bottom was muddy. I didn't want to go in, but I became more afraid of my father's growing irritation, so I slowly lowered myself into the water, feeling the thick cool mud of the riverbed oozing between my toes as I got deeper in the water. Inomar swam with me and we scooted around a bit, doggy paddling with our heads above water. Near the side with the lily pads and tall grass, Ino and I heard a low braying noise.

"Did you hear that?" Ino and I asked each other.

"What was it? A donkey?"

"Um, not really, I don't know. Maybe the donkey is sick."

"Ok, maybe."

We swam around a bit more until I felt my father would be content and then I quickly got out of the river.

A few days later, a 15-foot crocodile was pulled out of the river right where we had been swimming.

That's what life with my dad was like. Whenever I lived with him, I always felt like something big was lurking—and something big always was.

Daddy was still sleeping with all his followers and he had a little group of them that followed him around like penguins. According to my dad, sleeping with him was a spiritual duty and that made everything legit. I didn't care that my dad was bisexual, but the organized way he rotated through his lovers bothered me, so I tried to put the whole sordid business out of my mind until one day my father offered to have sex with me. He thought it would be best if I fell in line like the rest of his "family." I drew back, horrified, the disgust abundantly obvious on my face.

My dad laughed, hearty and deep.

"Ha, ha, my daughter, you've finally found someone more intense than you," he crowed.

I was not amused and quickly called my mom for emergency funds to get me back to San Francisco where people have normal sex lives.

Somehow, the money Mama sent arrived by mistake in Sinaloa de Leyva, which was 180 km north through territory run by the cartels. I didn't care. I refused to stay in Culiacán any longer than I had to, so I insisted Jaime drive me to get my money. Daddy tried to warn me how dangerous my plan was, but I still didn't understand how reckless it was to drive north into the mountains. Sinaloa is home to the infamous Sinaloa cartel and you just never know what you are going to run into. Many a hapless traveler, just passing through, has been found riddled with bullets or burned to a crisp in his vehicle. In fact, years later, my dear cousin Javier would be murdered by hooded men with machine guns in Bachigualato just outside of Culiacán, presumably by cartel guys, for being in the wrong place at the wrong time—a simple birthday dinner with a guy who had somehow been stupid enough to piss them off. But anyway, I insisted, and somehow we made it up there and back alive. Unfortunately, Mama hadn't sent quite enough money to get me all the way to San Francisco. Still determined to get away from my father, I hightailed it on a bus to the border where I hitched a ride from a Desert Storm vet who told me stories of dead bodies and PTSD, then handed me the rest of the money I needed to catch a bus to San Francisco.

***

Back in San Francisco, I went straight to Tony's room at the Sierra Hotel to cop heroin. It was a pathetic, depressing room, but it had two queen beds with the typical hardshell hotel quilts on them, a small bathroom sink in the corner of the room, a TV, and a VCR, so it exemplified what I had come to think of as comfort. There was also a side table on either side of the bed, a small round table, and two armchairs decorated with random cigarette burns—what luxury!

Tony was odious, but he offered me a way to earn some money: I could help him sell drugs. So, I ended up at the Sierra with him. Each room in the Sierra Hotel had been home to horrific crimes, overdoses, various sexual acts with desperate or unwilling participants, and incredible violence. The walls were spotted with blood, and the carpets, furniture, and bedding covered in cigarette burns. I smoked crack endlessly in that hotel—my heroin habit dissipating at the overwhelming insistence of my stronger crack habit. I hadn't intended to quit heroin by using crack, but the intensity of the crack high and the cravings that immediately followed a hit were stronger than my cravings to the shitty black tar heroin I had been doing at that point. I chain-smoked cigarettes, even during the rare showers I took, and never drank water or ate. My body was often overtaken by kidney infections and I would be grateful to succumb to the illness and fall onto the clean white sheets of a hospital bed. On one occasion, my fear and desperation were so bad, I faked acute appendicitis and had my appendix removed just so I could get off the streets and away from the heinous brutality of the Sierra and its inhabitants. I spent many long nights so high I couldn't figure out how to get money and so desperate even the junkies hated me, knocking, knocking on doors, standing on the gray linoleum floor in my torn jeans and holey boots, pathetically hoping for a bump. Occasionally, my attempts to get drugs led me to tweaker houses where burnouts slept in closets and dope houses on Mission Street where people like Courtney Love would suddenly pop in, all harried and important, shooting dope and then hustling back out into the night for a gig. People came and went, lived and died, grey TVs blaring in the background or torn apart on filthy carpets. There was never any food and life was scarce—just ghosts, all of us—hungry ghosts.

Once someone got angry with Tony and slashed all the tires on his ten year old Honda Accord. Tony was incredulous and kept repeating, "You just don't damage someone's possessions." Tony got the idea that Rob had been the originator of his anguish, so we got into Tony's car and started driving around, looking for Rob. Thankfully, we didn't find him. Tony had a penchant for violence. He had once gone outside to stab someone with a dagger and then come back to the room for a blanket, which he covered himself with so he could slide out of the building looking like a homeless person. I believe the victim died, collapsing right there in front of the building as Tony skulked away in the shadows under flashing police lights. On another occasion, Tony mistakenly thought I had stolen from him. I hadn't; in fact I had told a woman who wanted to steal from him I wouldn't do it, but Tony didn't believe me. After grilling me repeatedly about it, he laid me down in his lap and punched me directly in my face while his friend Fernando looked out the window to avoid seeing Tony's cruelty. Somehow, through all of this, I considered Tony and Fernando like family.

***

Tony had sent for Fernando from L.A., where he had recently arrived from Cuautepec de Madero Barrio Bajo in Mexico City. Cuautepec was known for being one of the most dangerous barrios in el Distrito Federal. It was home to murderers, rapists, enablers, and Fernando—a generally good person with faults like the rest of us—as well as lots of good people who lived in a crushing poverty, no matter how hard they worked. Tony told me his friend was coming to work for him and I was to show him the ropes and help him sling dope. Not long after, Fernando appeared at our door looking dazed, very introverted and shy, and pretty much out of his element. I had been hoping he was handsome. He wasn't, but he wasn't ugly either. He was 22, thin, and had long hair with bangs that he teased up tall on his head, Mexican rocker style. He was very quiet, which I interpreted as stupidity, but Fernando demonstrated the kindness that only the not-yet-jaded could exhibit. I quickly took a liking to him. Beholden to Tony and trying to find his way in the new world, poor Fernando spoke not a lick of English and was terrified of every knock on the door. He would anxiously insist I hurry and open the door when someone knocked. His fear annoyed me, but I played along because there was really nothing else to do. It was Fernando's sense of urgency that would one day enable undercover cops to enter our hotel room and catch us in the middle of weighing bags of heroin and cocaine to sell.

At the sound of their knock, I checked the peephole. The undercover narcs looked like Cheech and Chong. One was very tall with long messy hair and the other was a short Hispanic guy with shorter hair. Cheech put his big smiling mouth up to the peephole and I stepped back.

"The cops are here," I said.

Fernando brushed me aside dismissively and flung open the door to find Cheech pointing a gun in his face. Caught red-handed, we all went to jail, were bailed out soon after, and were caught again in the very same circumstances just a month later. Junkies have thick skulls.

We were offered a plea deal where Fernando was able to take one case and I would take the other so neither of us got two felony cases. We were each given a three-year suspended sentence, for which I did a few months in county jail, before being remanded into the custody of a drug program.

I arrived in San Bruno County Jail after a couple of brutal weeks at the San Francisco Jail, or "850" as it is known because it is located at 850 Bryant Street. I was involuntarily kicking dope at 850 and on top of that they had just outlawed cigarette smoking in the jails. Fuck me.

I spent most of my time tossing and turning, sweating

on the plastic mattress atop the steel bed, dragging myself over to the shiny stainless steel toilet now and again to throw up or otherwise relieve myself. A woman in the bunk next to me was even sicker and I felt sorry for her. When I started to feel better, about a week into my kick, I sat on the edge of her bed and massaged her neck, shoulders, arms, and legs, washing her face with a shirt and telling her it was going to pass. Her misery, though somewhat abated when I touched her, remained escalated for about two weeks. When I was about to be transferred to San Bruno, she had just started looking better.

The bus ride to San Bruno was exciting to me because I got to be outside for the first time since I had been incarcerated. We passed a field of buffalo just before we arrived. Inside, there was a TV playing *When Harry Met Sally* at one end of a brightly lit room. I sat on a bench among my fellow inmates and listened to the audio echoing against the walls. Soon, a heavy door opened behind us and a woman came in to take us through to the intake room where we were handed orange pants and sweatshirts, socks, and brown plastic slippers. We stripped and were searched, then dressed and were guided to our bunks in a large dorm. San Bruno County Jail was arranged with the guards' office in the center, overlooking all the dorms, which fanned from the center outward. From their office, the guards could look down at the men's and women's dorms through glass windows.

County was a country club compared to the mundane cell life at 850. We could move around at San Bruno and they had weekly AA meetings and yoga classes led by Maya Angelou's sister—a tall, thin African American woman with high cheekbones and a regal posture. There were also a lot more women to talk to, which was both good and bad. Most people who end up in jail aren't what you'd call emotionally healthy or socially adept, so if you didn't set the record straight when someone was threatening you, you'd be screwed. Eventually, this meant that, even though I was small, I had to fight. One day, some stupid white girl kept bothering me about something while I sat on my bed. She wouldn't leave my area, even though I told her to get away from my bed repeatedly, so I had to clock her a few times to show who was boss. We brawled, briefly tussling on the bed and then the floor, hair falling into our faces and our sweatshirts all sideways. The guards pulled us apart and threw us in solitary confinement, which was a set of glass-ceilinged rooms under the guard station. The guards walked around on top of the solitary confinement room, looking down at me while I paced back and forth, savoring a sense of fulfillment for having stood up for myself for once. When I got out, the women had new respect for me and that's what mattered at San Bruno.

Except for occasional threats from people who had murdered their boyfriends or grown up in gangs and whatnot, life in San Bruno was pretty mellow. I learned how "pruno," a jailhouse liquor, was made using bread and old fruit left to ferment in small applesauce containers with the lids on. Every now and again, someone would let their pruno go too long and the lid would pop off, making a smelly, fermented mess that gave them away. They would lose privileges, have their time in jail extended, or get locked in solitary for a while, but they'd be back at it again soon after. I attempted to make pruno once, but it didn't pan out. Then I realized it opened me up to being snitched out by another prisoner and for once I listened when I told myself I was being stupid. When the lid popped off one evening, I grabbed it quickly and threw it in the garbage, instantly retiring from the pruno manufacturing business.

I was getting stronger and stronger each day. I looked healthier and felt better and safer than I had in years, but naturally, that was all relative.

A filmmaker had been filming Grandma's memoirs for years by that point and he contacted me while I was in San Bruno to ask if he could interview me. I found the idea appealing since it gave me something to do besides read on my bed, so I agreed. The irony was not lost on me that as a girl I had spent so many years alone reading on my bed while living with my grandmother, and now here she was with her movie, inadvertently helping me out of this cave I was in. He came to the jail with my mother and filmed Mama and me talking through the wall of glass in the visiting chamber. I told her how I wanted things to be better and how I was going to change. Words I honestly believed at the time.

At any rate, it wasn't long before my sentence was up. In fact, it was over before I expected. I couldn't believe my ears the day they called my name and told me to "roll it up." Neither could the other women, who murmured "snitch" as I packed my things and walked across the dorm to the exit. I never did find out why they let me out early, but I assume it was for (mostly) good behavior.

I had gone into San Bruno County Jail weighing around 90 pounds, but had gained a lot of weight, so my street clothes no longer fit me. The staff grabbed some random articles of clothing from a big pile in the storage room and I pulled them on. I left the jail in a huge sweatshirt and baggy pants with no belt, a little older, but hardly any wiser. From there I proceeded to a court-ordered drug rehabilitation program. I didn't mind. As always, I was elated to be going to a safe place where someone would help me manage my daily life.

***

For a minute, it seemed like it might work. I had a bed at a sober-living house in the Avenues near the beach and found a job working retail near the Mission. I spent most of my time in the rehab center, going to AA meetings, doing my recovery work, and building connections with my family. Once, my mother even trusted me to take my baby brother, Mischa, out to run an errand with me. I was so proud to walk down the street holding his hand while Mischa chattered happily to me. He was adorable and smart and I loved him dearly, even though he had everything I had ever wanted and never gotten. Mischa had my mother's heart and she took great care of him. He was surrounded by my sisters, who doted on him, and truly the center of his own happy, healthy universe. I took pleasure in watching Mischa thrive and he gave me a new reference point for what family life could be.

I found my boyfriend Fernando one day. He was out of his ever-loving mind on the curb outside the sleazy Star Hotel, nodding off. While I had been in jail, he had picked up a heroin habit. It shook me to see him strung out, because he hadn't used heroin before and had a strong aversion to needles. "Fernando, it's me, Samantha," I said, shaking him repeatedly. His eyes were glassy and his gaunt face sagged. He was so dazed he could barely recognize me.

I left Fernando there that day but was deeply concerned about him. Periodically, I'd go to the Mission to check on him and each time he seemed on the verge of an overdose. I was worried, but worse, I was too new to recovery and I envied his high. One day, I goaded him into sharing his dope with me.

When I came to, I had to beg a friend at the sober living house to piss in an empty aspirin bottle for me so I could fake a UA. Everyone in the house was furious because it was so obvious my eyes were pinned—the pupils were constricted very small—signifying I was high as a kite, but they couldn't prove it. Somehow I had managed to puncture the plastic wrap covering the bottle and spill my friend's urine into the sample cup while a house mother stood in the doorway looking straight at me.

A few days later, I went to my mother's house and explained how scared I was because I was already pulling my bullshit again. I was sure I would either be killed in the Mission by the psychopaths I hung with or end up back in jail.

"Go to Mexico," Mama said, without missing a beat. "Take Fernando with you." She said I could borrow her car to gather my things and find Fernando. At the sober house, the house mother tried to reason with me as I packed, but I knew what I knew: staying in San Francisco was just not reasonable for me. I left the sober house and headed to the Mission to collect Fernando and then went back to my mother's house. She gave me some money to help with bus tickets and soon Fernando and I were on a Greyhound bus headed to Mexico. It never occurred to me until many years later that Mama had saved my life with her unorthodox solution. Everything in society was saying, "Bad girl, do what you're told," and Mama was guided by her soul and her heart when she told me to run. And she was right.

***

My plan was for us to go to Puerto Vallarta, where I knew people and had always been treated well. The trip was torturous for Fernando, who started it badly strung out. He shifted in his seat constantly, sweating profusely, shaking, and vomiting in the toilet at the back of the bus. Everyone could hear him retching through the door. I just tried to look the other way and get some rest. There was nothing I could do for him and we both knew it. He just had to get through it as best he could. At one point on the journey, all the passengers had gotten off to stretch their legs at a bus station. When I returned to the bus, the driver said, "Wow, your friend is pretty bad off, eh?" He knew what was up.

We were broke by the time we got to the Tepic bus station. I went to the bathroom and when I returned, Fernando was in the parking lot with my suitcase wide open, selling my clothes to the highest bidder. I grabbed my red Coca-Cola t-shirt from him, closed the suitcase in a huff, and told the crowd to get away from me. Fernando had made enough money to buy some food, so he was happy while I sulked on the bus.

In Vallarta, I asked a cab driver if he knew Ray Bolivar, my dad's old friend who I had been told was still living there. I knew him as Mahabra, which was Abraham spelled backward.

Mahabra had witnessed how my dad treated Gaby and me in Culiacán years before when we were trying to escape him and he had told us he would help us if we ever needed it. I trusted he would still remember that promise.

Though Vallarta had grown into more of a tourist trap since 1979, it was not unreasonable to reach out to an old cab driver. Most of them knew the old-school people. It turned out the cab driver had bought pot from Mahabra and knew he was living in the jungle south of Vallarta in Boca de Tomatlan.

"Get in, I'll take you there," the cabbie said.

We drove down the winding road out of town as the sun set and were soon walking up a set of moist stone steps through creeping jungle plants to a heavy wooden door. A younger man with a beard answered our knock.

The young man summoned Mahabra, who looked at me quizzically and with a bit of disdain. I explained my predicament and naively told him too much. Then I called for Fernando to come from the cab. Mahabra, who had been appalled listening to my story, took a step back and wrinkled his nose at the sight of Fernando. It was clear to him that Fernando was not from an aristocratic family and Mahabra was shaken at the prospect of having him in his home, but I was Alfonso de la Vega's daughter, so he reluctantly welcomed us into Nadaderos.

Nadaderos was a hillside house that had been built by Nahu, another spiritual leader, artist, and designer who was my dad's equal or nemesis, depending on who you were talking to. But, unlike my father, Nahu had been known for his kindness and gentleness. They were both gay, or "dedicated to the love of men" as my father put it, and each had his own circle of supporters who admired and adored him. Mahabra and Tono had followed Nahu more closely than they did my father and somehow they had inherited Nadaderos after Nahu died.

From Nadaderos, one could look out over the horizon and see storms coming from far off, sheets of darkness tilting down diagonally from the sky. The house had multiple pink stucco rooms with rounded half-walls and stone pathways leading up the hillside from one room to another. The jungle was constantly encroaching and one would often come across a huge nest of writhing ants while simply reaching for a roll of toilet paper. There were *alacranes*—scorpions—in the coolness beneath the couch pillows. Mahabra even told me that on one occasion his 80-year-old mother was resting in her room under a *palapa* roof when a large boa constrictor fell upon her. At the sound of her screams, everybody came running and one of the housemates hacked the thing off her with a machete, a telenovela called *Maria Mercedes* playing in the background all the while.

That night, when Fernando and I were in bed, I felt something plop onto the bed. And then there was another one. And another. They were insects, and they were large. I quickly taught Fernando an old trick Gaby and I had perfected years before: we grabbed the top sheet under our heels and pulled it suddenly taut, sending the critters flying. They soon hit the floor with a large clack.

Fernando and I stayed with Mahabra for about a month, during which time I discovered I was pregnant. Mahabra was sure I should get an abortion, which was illegal in Mexico, and insisted I visit his fancy doctor who would take care of it. I told Mahabra I would do no such thing, but he still took me to the doctor, who was unamused to find out I had no intention of getting an abortion after all. Mahabra escorted me out of the clinic with a stern face, unable to bear the thought of me having a child with Fernando, who was not up to Mahabra's standards. About a week later, at a party at the mayor's house in Vallarta, I shocked everyone by projectile vomiting a large cup of dark red hibiscus tea onto the fancy shoes of the wealthy attendees. Mahabra preferred to tell them I was drunk rather than let them in on the horrible secret of my pregnancy.

Soon after, Fernando developed a hankering for his home in Mexico City and insisted we go. I was kind of relieved. It was obvious Mahabra hated having Fernando around and thought I was making a huge mistake on top of a complete blunder. Staying would eventually become impossible anyway, so we hopped a bus to Mexico City.

FALLING UP FROM THE BOTTOM

CHAPTER 14
AT HOME IN THE BARRIO

We arrived without a peso to our names. Fernando had called ahead to have his brother David pick us up at the bustling station. We had only my suitcase to carry, but the city streets were packed. As we hustled to grab a microbus, I felt the crush of the densely populated Mexican capital upon me.

It took about two hours traveling in a string of small jam-packed buses to reach Cuautepec de Madero Barrio Bajo. I was exhausted and overwhelmed by the chaotic ride and the jumble of concrete houses with tin roofs surrounding us. We disembarked without fanfare, David carrying my suitcase on his shoulder, and started to climb the steep, uneven street to Fernando's family home: a light green cement room in a *vecindad* where two families shared a communal bathroom in the courtyard and the señoras washed clothes in little stone sinks called *piletas*.

Fernando's family had gathered to greet us when we arrived, and surrounded him with hugs and smiles. I sat in a chair that was offered and a bowl of chicken soup was pushed toward me. They laughed and joked and asked me what I had seen in Fernando to make me come so far. Feeling protective of Fernando, I wanted to stand up for him, explain how he had been kinder and more dedicated to me than most of the other people in my life, but how the hell could I explain it all? So I just mumbled something about him being a good person.

A month later, Fernando and I were in Garibaldi—the Mariachi center of Mexico City—at a salsa club. We were having a good time, drinking and dancing, until another man asked me to dance. When I returned to the table, Fernando was drunk and livid with jealousy. We argued. Worried Fernando would get into a fight in the club, I moved us outside. A few young guys hanging around a green VW bug taxi saw what was going on and offered to give me a ride home. I thanked them and took a seat in the back of the cab, but Fernando protested vehemently and begged me to get out.

"These guys aren't going to help you, they are going to hurt you," he insisted. "You are not in the States. You have no idea, Samantha." The guys insisted they were nice as I stepped out of the car.

Years later, in Cuauhtepec, I would overhear local cab drivers bragging to each other about the women they had raped or robbed. One of them—a nemesis of Fernando's—murdered a woman he picked up in his cab. All in a day's work, I guess. But that night, I didn't know about the cab drivers of Cuautepec, I just knew I had an enraged drunk on my hands and I wanted to go home, but something in Fernando's voice got through to me. Finally, I exited the cab, thanking the driver, but declining the ride.

The fight with Fernando picked up where it had left off and he made such a scene it drew the attention of the *judiciales*. Before I knew it, they had Fernando on the ground and were kicking the crap out of him. A jaded Mexican judicial with long painted nails, too much make-up and perfume, and a rum and coke in her hands stood over the scene as the officers kicked Fernando in the head and torso and I shouted at them to stop.

In Mexico, once the *judas* get their eye on you, it's hard to shake them without a *mordida*, or bribe. We didn't have any money, so paying the *mordida* wasn't an option, and they made our lives miserable for the next few hours. They threw us into a police car and drove us around Mexico City in a procession, stopping at various stages to interrogate us. At one point they took Fernando out of the car and a young male officer questioned me. Finally, I mentioned I was pregnant.

"Really?" he said. "Let me see your stomach."

I wasn't showing much yet, but I pushed out my stomach and lifted up my shirt. To my surprise, this seemed to make an impression on him. He went behind the car to talk with the other officers and a few minutes later they let us go.

Once we were free of them, I was furious with Fernando for putting us in so much jeopardy. I called Mahabra the next day and returned to Vallarta, fearful of staying with Fernando in Mexico City.

In time, however, I missed Fernando. The more my pregnancy advanced, the more I wanted to be with him, so eventually I went home to him—such as it was. We had only a small underground room across the patio from his family in the *vecindad*. We slept on a creaky wireframe bed on a mattress that literally folded in half when we laid down on it. I always ended up with Fernando crushing me by morning and would wake to a framed picture of Jesus bleeding under his crown of thorns, eyes cast upward in despair. Still, I was filled with hope because I didn't start the day needing heroin. In my greatest poverty, I was free.

I didn't relate well to Fernando's family, so I mostly stayed in our room. Bored to tears, I slept as much as I could. A color TV standing atop a tall dresser in the rooms of Fernando's family blared cartoons in Spanish across the patio. I had a great distaste for cartoons, with their flashy colors and loud, high-pitched voices, and found it odd that the adults still laughed at them. I had probably never laughed at cartoons, even as a child. Now and again, Fernando's mother, Amelia, would come into the room and grab our dirty clothes, frowning at me, and take them to the cement washboard to launder them. I didn't know how to wash clothes by hand on a *pileta* and I didn't know how to relate to her enough to ask her to teach me. In the face of her disgust, I withdrew more. I was quite often hungry, and once even resorted to eating dried tortillas that had been left on a window sill to dry in the sun for the pigs.

Eventually, we found a place across the street from Fernando's job where we could live on our own. It belonged to a guy named Juan who owned a bunch of spendy machinery for precision work of some sort. He wanted someone to stay in the little tin-roofed cement shack next to the workshop area so they could keep an eye on things. We were a perfect fit and I couldn't wait to get out from under Amelia's critical eye.

It felt good to have my own things, no matter how simple or few of them I had, and I set about making a home. That was no small feat. The walls of the shack were made of porous cement blocks, ill-fitted to each other and drafty on cold nights. The floor was incomplete, so there was a 10' x 2' dirt patch behind the couch that had been given to us by a friend of Fernando's. We didn't care until we heard a scraping sound one night and awoke to find a cat-sized rat dragging our paper garbage back toward the hole he had dug through the dirt patch. There was nothing we could do about it, so we learned to live with it.

The one-room shack had no running water, but there was a spigot on the patio. Fernando set a cement washboard on top of a large rusty metal drum and put some cement blocks on the ground so I could reach the washboard. Then he showed me how to use it. I would fill a five gallon bucket with water, lift it up, and dump it into the sink, then use a cup to grab water and pour it over the dishes or clothes, which sat on the washboard. I had a tape of Right Said Fred I listened to on a cassette player as I washed dishes in the sun: "I'm too sexy for my shirt, too sexy. . ." Sometimes I would lie out on the patio and tan, listening to that tape, feeling so incredibly happy to be alive and have my own place.

My pregnant belly was getting bigger. I started to buy baby clothes on Saturdays at the street market and eventually Fernando was able to afford a simple four-burner gas stove for us. Every week the gas truck would go by shouting "GAAAAAAASSSSSS" and I would go out to the street to signal them to change my tank, which stood on the patio and was connected to the stove through a hole in the wall. We had a five gallon water bottle, too. We placed it on a chair and tilted it to pour drinking water into cups. The water truck would come by the same way the gas guys did, shouting their wares. We had a ten inch black-and-white TV someone had given us, which had no back to it. The TV sat on the kitchen table next to our bed. Reception was terrible, so every show we watched was a lesson in frustration.

***

I was five months pregnant when one night as I lay in bed, I felt a surge of fluid fill my pants. I thought, "It can't be. Has my water broken?"

I reached down to touch the fluid. When I brought my hand out from under the covers, I was astonished to see blood surging out from between my legs and soaking my pants. I got up and showered, but the blood kept surging. Fernando rushed around trying to clean up after me as I moved about our tiny home. He was getting nervous and desperate. Finally, I told him we needed to get to the hospital. He ran to his boss Lupillo's house across the street to call a cab and off we went.

When we arrived at the local hospital, no one knew what to do. They weren't prepared to deal with an emergency of this nature and told me I'd have to go to another hospital across town. Across town in Mexico City means at least an hour's drive. We hustled up a ride as fast as we could. When we arrived at the second hospital, the emergency room was quiet. Only a couple of lights were on, in spite of it being a city hospital in a highly populated area.

They brought me into a back room with no light on and told me to lie on a metal table, which was only half my length. I obliged, head up and feet hanging off the table, as blood continued to escape me. After what felt like an eternity with no word from the nurse who had "gone to get the doctor," I started to get angry. It had now been a few hours since I had started bleeding and I was worried about my baby, when a young nurse walked by the room and I yelled at her to come in. Using all the power I could muster, I channeled my inner Elena Karam.

"Have you any idea who my father is?" I snarled. "If you don't get me a doctor immediately, none of you will have jobs on Monday!"

It worked, and they rushed off to bring a doctor.

Unfortunately, this doctor couldn't do anything for me either and I was forced to transfer to yet another hospital 30 minutes away where they could handle prenatal issues. Arriving at the final hospital, I felt a certain sense of relief when they laid me down on an actual gurney with clean sheets and started to take my blood pressure and do hospital things to me. Soon a nurse came in and started putting foam on my abdomen and crotch.

"What are you doing?" I asked.

She said, "You have to be shaved for surgery so they can remove the baby."

This was the last straw. I sat up on the gurney and said, "GET AWAY FROM ME! You will remove this baby over my cold dead body." My shouts echoed through the stark Mexican hospital, bouncing off oxygen tanks and metal bed pans.

Her childish face froze into a picture of confusion. I was exhausted from blood loss, drained from fear and the cold barren hospital rooms with the stupid faces of nurses and careless doctors. I was done playing nice and I certainly wasn't going to lose my child to these idiots.

Since I refused to abort my baby, they removed me

from the surgery room and sent me upstairs to a two-bed hospital room. My neighbor was loud and her family was louder, but I was drained and fell asleep immediately, holding my stomach and crying quietly to myself. The next morning, I was taken for an ultrasound. As I lay on the table, the nurses chattered about their families and a party, reaching over me carelessly. Their lack of empathy awakened my ire. I sat up on the table and looked at both of them with disgust saying, "Do you have any idea what I'm going through? Can you understand that I almost lost my baby and have no idea why I'm bleeding? I don't care about your gossip and your party. Will you pay attention to what you're doing?"

Blank stares and apologies. They completed the procedure, occasionally reaching down to caress my stomach or thigh and commenting on how soft my skin was.

"Where are you from?" they asked.

"New York City," I said.

"Ah, that's why you're the way you are."

They liked me and I liked them after that. They were young and excited to have a foreigner like me on their table. Ultrasound results showed I had placenta previa and the umbilical cord was wrapped around my baby's neck. If I had a natural birth, the placenta would be delivered before the baby and the baby would be strangled to death. The doctor ordered me on bed rest for the remainder of my pregnancy and said I'd have to have a Cesarean section when it was time.

While I was waiting to be discharged, two young women came to the waiting room, both weeping, bereft. Each had lost her baby because the hospital had removed them early. One of them had been eight months pregnant but the baby had still died. I was silently ecstatic I had had the wherewithal to refuse surgery.

***

There were no more bloody scares, thankfully, even though the prescribed bed rest was impossible. I still had to lift five gallon buckets of water onto the *pileta*, wash clothes by hand, clean the house, and go to market. Then, just two days before I was scheduled to have the Cesarean, I was hit by a car.

I had been sitting in my friend's construction business next door with a girlfriend, learning to knit a sweater for the baby when Fernando arrived home from work. When I saw his truck pull up across the street, I said my goodbyes and started to cross the street to greet him. But by the time I had noticed him and said my goodbyes to my friend, Fernando had crossed to my side of the street and was standing next to our house. I heard him yelling at me and turned back toward the sound of his voice without looking for traffic. The next thing I knew, I was flying through the air, the lights of the houses on the hills spinning around me in the dusk. The impact had hit me in the knees and I landed on the road head first, my legs splayed out awkwardly in different directions. Pain shot through my legs and I reached back to feel my head. It was bleeding.

The car stopped and its occupants got out, but when they tried to move me and I shouted out of fear and shock, they jumped back in their car and sped off. Once I got my legs adjusted, the pain subsided and I didn't look so awkward, so I stayed there in the street, looking up at the faces of the crowd that had gathered as Fernando stood beside me. After a while, an ambulance arrived and I was loaded into the back. Fernando said he would follow us to the hospital in his truck. Unlike ambulances in the States, which have tons of equipment and smell of sanitizer, this one was bare and had a simple metal bed.

"Am I going to die?" I asked the paramedic, who looked like he was my age.

He made a *tsk* sound and said, "No, no, don't say that," and I felt the ambulance start to move.

Hospital doctors determined I was completely uninjured except for a small pebble embedded into my head, but my baby had moved down the birth canal. The date for my Cesarean was moved forward to the next day, a Wednesday. Fernando and I were elated.

At about six p.m. the next day, Fernando and I pulled up in front of the address the doctor had given us. The clinic was housed in a dingy white two-story building. We stepped into a bare hallway with green tiles on the floor where our hushed voices echoed against decrepit walls. The whole place felt lonely. I was ushered up a staircase and into a room where I was told to change into a gown and get comfortable in the bed. Soon the doctor came in and said it was time. I walked into the operating room, which had walls painted a surreal green color. The paint was chipping off in the corners near the ceiling. I climbed onto the table and they closed the doors as they prepped me for surgery.

"I'm going to give you an epidural to numb you from the waist down and then we will tie your arms to a board to ensure your safety during surgery," the doctor explained.

I was soon strapped down looking up at my reflection

in the metal surgical lamp. I looked like a crucifix.

The surgery, which was supposed to take two hours, took about four hours. On occasion, blood squirted above the curtain that was propped up just below my chest.

My beloved Amaranta was born close to midnight. They let me see her quickly and then immediately took her away to be cleaned while the doctor began closing me up. Finally, they removed the curtain. I was astonished by the amount of blood everywhere. They untied my arms from the cross-like structure and I sat up. There was a large puddle of blood on the floor.

"The placenta was such a mess, we had a tough time stemming the bleeding," the doctor explained. "We were actually concerned for a while that you might bleed out."

I slept horribly that night because they gave me no pain meds and I was eager to take my baby home. They had shown her to me briefly and the rest of the time they kept her in another room, too far away for my liking. I asked them several times if she was okay and if I could hold her, but they refused, saying I was in too much pain and the bed was too narrow. Fernando was equally dismayed by the situation but deferred to the doctor and I was too exhausted to fight them all. Now and again throughout the night, Fernando stepped next door to peek at Amaranta and then return, glowing with happiness, to tell me she was doing really well, which provided me enough relief to at least try to rest.

The next day, the doctor came to say she would drive me home and I was helped down the stairs and into her car. Fernando's mother Amelia was with us and offered to hold Amaranta, but I didn't want her to. Because of my obvious inability to perform as she expected, I believed she didn't like me, and anyway, this was my baby. I wanted to hold her. Amelia glared at me, exasperated, and got into the front seat beside the doctor. Fernando and I settled into the back seat. On the way home, Amelia and the doctor chatted with a cloying pseudo-respect that made me angry. Meanwhile, the doctor was banging over speed bumps as if she had not just cut me open the night before. I held Amaranta against my stomach to protect her, holding her tiny head to me and smiling down at her. The joy of having her warm little body in my arms made everything worth it. Nothing else mattered as I fell in love with the beautiful little baby in my arms.

***

Our life in Cuautepec wasn't easy. Once, when riding the bus back from a shopping trip to Carrefour, we saw the corpse of a man. His back was being eaten by street dogs. The river that ran by our house was filthy and filled with garbage, along with the occasional body. Worst of all, the kind owner of the store next door was murdered one night. He had come out of the shower, a towel wrapped around his waist, to find thugs at his door. He refused to open the gate for them, so they shot him in cold blood. They got away with nothing in the attempted robbery except the murder of the father of one of my English students. Fernando heard the shots and had gone running to the security gate to peek at the shooters. I shouted at him to come back inside, fearful they would see him and shoot him, too. He returned claiming he recognized a couple of the shooters, but what happens in Cuautepec stays in Cuautepec unless you want to end up dead yourself.

Hard as Cuauhtepec could be, it felt like a cakewalk compared to my life on drugs in San Francisco. One day my mother called me on the phone at Fernando's boss's house across the street to tell me Uncle Wiley had been found dead and bloated on the floor of his trailer in Florida. Sitting in our little house behind a pile of scrap metal in Mexico City, I pictured Wiley when he was young, before he had been ravaged by speed and life in my grandparents' house. The last time I had seen him he had lost his youthful joy and had little sense of humor left. His house was somewhat barren and smelled stale. I was sure he was accepting a small allowance from Grandma. She had a way of stringing us all along with meager amounts of money—just enough to make us feel like shit for taking it, but never enough to empower us to move forward. It had killed Wiley, who was only in his 30s when he died. I grieved the potential of the Wiley I had known so briefly and couldn't help but think about how I had barely escaped a similar death.

Honestly, I was the happiest I had ever been. I had learned to shop at the marketplace on my own, bartering with the merchants and waiving my finger knowingly at the ones who tried to rip me off. I'd cook local dishes for Fernando and wash our clothes by hand. I felt like a good mother and a good partner to Fernando. I loved my simple life and adored my baby, who had made me a mama once again. The city was rife with dangers, but being just another poor person, I felt safe there with my little family.

Fernando and I lived in the shack for about a year before Juan asked us if we wanted to move into a more "finished" room in the back, right next to the machinery. The room had an actual roof on it and a large window, which was blocked by a pile of rusty scrap metal, but it was a step up. Fernando and I were quite pleased.

I was pregnant again when we moved to the new room and determined my next baby would be born in a true hospital with a capable doctor. Dr. Ruiz was located in La Villa, a half hour away from our home, and I took the bus to see him once a month during my pregnancy. He was a good doctor and his office was in the hospital where Josh would be born, but there was a dark element to Dr. Ruiz that I couldn't immediately figure out. He was obviously judgmental of Fernando and generally wouldn't address him when he talked to me. If Dr. Ruiz did speak to Fernando, he did it as an aside because he had to. I figured it was the usual class prejudice I was picking up on. The separation of classes is still well-defined in Mexico. I was a white woman from a "good" family and Fernando was from humble origins. This wasn't the first time we had noticed disparities in the way we were treated. But there was something else about Dr. Ruiz. It all became clear one day when he offered to buy my baby and find him a "good home." Dr. Ruiz said this with a smile on his face as if he were joking, but he said it on more than one occasion, clearly trying to plant a seed the way one might joke with a police officer about bribing him.

"No, thank you," I always said, feeling dirty because I didn't scream and throw a chair at him, never to return.

I didn't have a lot of options, so I accepted this situation, but I wanted to tell him to fuck off with his stupid smarmy smile.

Maybe Dr. Ruiz didn't understand that people could be happy and well despite impoverished circumstances, but I did. I loved the routine of my life and felt at peace spending my days caring for our home, walking with Amaranta to the marketplace for food each day since we didn't have a refrigerator, and watching the black-and-white TV as I cooked dinner. Fernando and I were generally happy during those years and laughed a lot. Once, when Fernando came home from work, I heard the door to the gate open and snuck out to the machine shop to hide behind a wall and wait for him to walk by. When he came into the shop, I jumped out and startled him. His first reaction was to reach out with his hands curled into catlike claws. We had a small kitten that did this when acting fierce and Fernando had automatically summoned that same response himself. We often played jokes like that, or would just be silly, cracking each other up.

***

My mother and Ayin came to Mexico a week before Joshua was born. They stayed in a hotel in La Villa, but came to visit me at our house in Cuautepec. Mama rolled with it. She had seen a lot in Mexico and the poverty of Cuautepec didn't scare her, not even when Fernando demonstrated how to whack the garbage bag with a stick before opening it, which sent rats leaping out onto the ground. To their credit, my mother and sister watched this spectacle quietly and simply said, "Oh wow." I could feel their compassion, but also their respect for me. They could see I didn't complain because as humble as that home was, it was better than the hell of drug addiction. I didn't fear for my life every day, I had a beautiful baby and another on the way, and my family was able to come visit me. In many ways, I was richer than I had been when I lived in The Dakota or at 800 Park Avenue. But in other ways, I was similarly buried alive.

No one in Mexico City knew anything about my past or my family, except for Fernando, who dismissed my life outside our little home in the machinist's yard anyway. One Saturday morning, when I was sweeping the unfinished cement floor that constantly shed piles of dust, I looked up to see a pair of acrobats on the little black-and-white TV. They had their backs to the camera, but I immediately recognized my sister, Miriam, who lived in France.

"That's my sister Miriam!" I exclaimed.

Fernando looked up, communicating his disbelief with a smirk.

"No, no really, it is!" I insisted.

To my great pleasure, the credits started rolling just then and her name scrolled down the screen: Miriam de Sela. I was happy to see Miriam, but happier to wipe the smug look off Fernando's face.

See, I am here, I thought. I have a life outside of what you think you know of me. A family. A history.

It bothered me that Fernando minimized me and my family. I heard from my mother and siblings regularly and felt their love from far away. Gaby was busily making what seemed like an idyllic life with Nikko in their beautiful Brooklyn brownstone, designing clothes and jewelry, and opening her own store. Sky, Ayin, and Miriam were all performing with Cirque du Soleil (only Ayin performed for a while with Cirque du Soleil, Sky and Mirim performed with other companies, Miriam performed often with Joël, and Sky and Ayin performed eventually in a show directed by Ueli who owned the chateau) and Lhasa was packing the cafes. She told me over the phone people were standing on chairs to see her because the tiny venues where she performed would become crammed with fans. She sent me a cassette tape of her recording, "La Llorona," which I shared with Fernando. He responded with some comment about "her friends clap for her, but it's not real Mexican music."

I understood my family was not as significant to Fernando as it was to me, but his disregard for my family and my life outside him seemed like one more instance of being told to "disappear into the woodwork, darling," as if my very existence outside of him and our little home was pointless. But the longer I was healthy and happy, the more I felt the stirrings of something more trying to rise up in me— some return to myself trying to make itself known, but getting shoved aside time and again.

Fernando drank a lot, leaving me alone with the kids. Lonely, I finally asked him to bring his friends home to drink instead of drinking in the street. After that, we all drank together. Near the end of the five years I spent in Cuautepec, Fernando started bringing home cocaine again. The hangovers, late nights with friends doing drugs at the house, and risk-taking scared me. I didn't want to go back to doing drugs every day and I didn't want to drag my children through loss and destruction.

Once I even traveled to the Basilica in La Villa to swear in front of the Virgen de Guadalupe, side-by-side with a hundred other poor suffering souls, that I wouldn't drink for a year. They shuffled me into an Al-Anon meeting where a woman described how to deal with my alcoholic husband by detaching with love: "If he passes out on the floor and pisses himself, don't clean it up. You can put a blanket over him, but let him lie in it until he wakes. Give him the dignity of the consequences of his actions."

I wasn't so sure Fernando would be impressed by the consequences of his actions, but I was determined to stand by him because I told myself he had stood by me when I was at my worst. The truth was he had failed me on a number of occasions, like that time Tony was punching me in the face and Fernando literally looked the other way. Still, I felt a deep sense of loyalty to him. He had problems growing up in the tough life of Cuautepec and I understood what could happen to people who had the soul crushed out of them young.

In the Mirador Restaurant in Mexico City, I threw the I Ching over the phone with my mother. It had given me Chapter 21—Biting Through, which I took as a clear signal to go. I had always loved biting through things because taking action made me feel empowered. Fernando must have felt a sense of loyalty to me as well, because he agreed to return to the States with me.

***

In the spring of 1997, Fernando and I gave away all our things, sold the Ford F350 my grandmother had bought us, and jumped on a northbound train with a few suitcases of clothing and our children in tow. A few days later, we stepped off the train into the heat of Juarez, one of the world's most dangerous cities. Our luggage weighed heavily in our arms and the kids clung to our clothes as we shuffled through the train station to the street. We needed to find the coyote who would help Fernando cross the Rio Grande while I took the kids and our luggage across the border in a taxi. At a payphone, Fernando pulled a wrinkled paper out of his pocket and dialed the number.

Me, Amaranta, and Ayin in La Villa, a part of Mexico City

(Photo: Alexandra Karam)

He was given an address and a cab took us to the meeting place, a small green cement building. Inside, it was cool and dark. After my eyes adjusted, I saw there were a few guys in their twenties hanging around the periphery and one guy sitting in an old chair near the back wall. He stood up and shook Fernando's hand. They discussed the plan and then it was time for me to go. Worried, I reached out and touched the old man's arm. "Please bring him across safely. Watch out for him." I had heard plenty of stories of coyotes taking people's money and killing them. I wanted to assure he would arrive on the other side, although I knew if he was to be killed there was nothing I could say that would melt their hearts. They would have already made up their minds.

As planned, I crossed into the US in a cab. The border agents only briefly checked the trunk to see my luggage and waved us through. We proceeded to the gas station in El Paso that was to be our rendezvous spot. About 25 minutes later, Fernando showed up with wet hair but a dry shirt and pants. He had crossed the river naked, holding his clothes above his head.

From there, we hoofed it to the Greyhound station and boarded a bus for Portland, Oregon, which was just north enough from San Francisco to keep us out of trouble. . . or so we thought. At a checkpoint, we realized Fernando's fake ID was obvious: the visage faced the wrong direction. The border patrol agents must have noticed, but seemed to ignore this detail. We turned away from each other so as not to draw attention to our awareness of our good fortune.

The bus ride was long, but I was glad for the time to relax after the fearful trip from Mexico. We traded off holding Amaranta and Joshua on our laps. At times when the bus wasn't too full, the kids would cross the aisle to empty seats and I would doze off to the rumble of the bus's engine. Entering the Columbia River Gorge, I felt like we were far away from everything, but soon we approached the urban boundary of Portland and traffic picked up. I felt the weight of the next step approach and wondered how long our money would last. We had about $1,000 left and the burden of supporting our family would fall on me since Fernando still didn't speak English and was in the country illegally. Frankly, we hadn't really thought through how we were going to survive, we had just been keenly aware we had to leave Mexico. On that bleak, rainy day in the Greyhound bus, fleeing a rapid decline into drug use and headed toward the unknown, the weight of the world seemed to press in on me.

The bus lurched to a stop in downtown Portland and we hustled the children off into the cool night air, grabbing our things from under the bus, and standing there looking around as it drizzled lightly. Fernando was like a deer in headlights. Exhausted and frustrated with his powerlessness, I found some hotel ads on the bus station walls, decided on TravelLodge and moved outside with the kids to flag a cab. Fernando pulled our bags behind him. At the TravelLodge, a tired looking woman from India peered over her glasses at me as I rested a suitcase on my leg and questioned her about rooms and prices. She sat beneath a yellow light and the room smelled of boredom, and my sense of despair escalated. Had I been able to fall apart in someone's arms at that moment, I would have sobbed and leaned in, aching for comfort, but that feeling was old and familiar and I didn't fall apart. I heard my voice taking care of business, extended my hand outward to exchange cash for a room key, and guided my family out into the night and up cement stairs to our room on the second floor. The kids were tired and hungry, so we settled them into the room and I went to a nearby restaurant called The Galaxy to order some Chinese-American food. On the second night, I asked the owner of that restaurant for a job and he said yes. It was a start.

FALLING UP FROM THE BOTTOM

CHAPTER 15
SAVING SAMMY

Over the next year, I grabbed at every opportunity I could find, trying to stay one step ahead of the sense of imminent homelessness that seemed to hang in the air around me at all times. To my surprise, I found I was good at waiting tables, but our shitty apartment up the street from The Galaxy was creepy no matter what we did to it and amplified my feelings of dread. During the earlier hours of the evening, it was populated by a slow-moving overweight crowd of cigarette smokers, and after the bars would close, the hipster crowd would file in to order cokes and fries. When I started taking shots at the back table with the cooler customers at The Galaxy, I realized we needed to get out of there. I reached out to a friend of my father's, whom my dad had renamed Masodan back in the Oaxaca days, and asked him to give me a job writing for his newsletter. Then I moved my family to Alsea, Oregon to live and work in a beautiful little house that stood on a rocky section of land overlooking Fall Creek. Masodan's lover Peter sold me my first car on payments, which he insisted we needed, living so far out in the country. It seemed idyllic for a moment. Fernando and I even got married there, on the deck above Fall Creek on a warm day with bees buzzing around us and the kids looking on sweetly, Amaranta holding a bouquet with flowers in her hair. That bouquet would kick around our houses for years, even after I had divorced Fernando, but right then it looked sweet and delicate and fresh in her tiny hands. We had been living there for just four months or so when Fernando started to get restless. He didn't like doing odd jobs for Masodan and ended up going back to Portland where he found a job at a roofing company through his friend, Flaco.

While Fernando was working in Portland during the week, life was peaceful in the little house in Alsea. I worked from home in a cute little room that looked out over the creek and was able to look after my children. I loved the safety and security of that cottage and enjoyed being able to fill the fridge with groceries after trips to town. We had a good life on the weekdays. Then Fernando would come home and get drunk and make a scene or punch me in the jaw. I stayed with him for years more, thinking I needed him or that I couldn't bear to be alone. I had the kids, I was new to living a healthy life and in my mind, Fernando was the strong one. I still saw him as the man who had saved me from heroin and stayed with me despite everything. I was beginning to get inklings that my beliefs about my husband were wrong-headed, but they were still just whispers that floated past me once in a while. Even when he hit me, which was rare, I had no thought of leaving him. I saw it as a fleeting mistake. He yelled and swaggered and sometimes hit because that was the way things were. It's what he knew and it didn't seem too terrible. After all, I thought he was generally a good man.

Before long, Fernando started pestering me to join him in Portland. Although the kids and I were doing well in our country home, I felt uncomfortable being so dependent on Masodan, so I finally agreed to return to Portland at the end of November 1997. I borrowed some money from an old friend to get us into an apartment and found work at a collection agency where I began to thrive in the structured environment of corporate America.

The corporate world had rules people generally seemed to follow. Professionalism offered a format for respectful dialogue and provided a structure I could safely

Fernando circa 2000 Portland, OR
The father of three of my children; I still love him dearly

operate within. In my corporate job, demonstrating my skills and competence was rewarded rather than censured. It was as if I had walked through the door of that company into the normal world and, for the first time in my memory, I could see how to make a normal life work.

I had spent years berating myself for not knowing how to behave, watching others do it, whatever it was, and being baffled by what others saw as simple tasks. People around me probably assumed I was just willfully lazy or stupid, but actually, I had been stunted by lack of exposure to how daily tasks got handled. I was 14 years old before I held a dollar bill in my hand and walked into a store alone to purchase something. I was a married woman before I learned how to cook a meal and wash clothes. Jim and Mrs. Collins had managed the everyday necessities of life in my grandparents' homes and I barely had been let out of the house except to go to school. After I was taken from Debbie, there hadn't even been any training about basic things like bedtime routines where you brush your teeth and change into your pajamas instead of sleeping in your clothes.

For people who have been taught to function, it must seem like a simple thing to walk in the world, but when I lived with my grandmother, the world seemed distant and alien to me. Riding a bus without Mrs. Collins or going to a movie with friends was incomprehensible and even nerve-wracking, yet I craved it, believing that all I had to do was step out into life and take my place in it. Simple as that, I would be free and happy. I couldn't see that I didn't have the skills required to handle the most basic elements of adult life. When I had lived in Boston so many years ago, I'd ride the train and sweat, staring at all the people in their hats and coats, talking to each other or reading books, carrying umbrellas, their shoes shining, and I'd wonder how they did it. All that normalcy baffled me. How could the mundane be so alien?

Oddly, the corporate world became the stable, mentoring parent I had always needed and I began to flourish there. I worked hard and started to shed my past shame like a scratchy wool coat. Within a few months I was promoted from my entry-level position on the phones to a nearby desk to handle written complaints. I was elated. I'd walk in the door to find a stack of letters on my desk, some handwritten, some typed, always telling stories of difficulty and asking for mercy. I'd take the wrinkled pages in my hands and read them one by one, slowly but surely working my way through the pile. I'd call people and talk to them and sometimes they'd cry. Sometimes they'd yell and say things like "Hold on there, hero," or they'd hold the phone while they urinated, then audibly flush the toilet. But everyone had a story and a reason, and I felt for them.

On one call, a woman told me she was eating dog food because she was so broke, so I wiped away all her debt and told her I'd call local services to try to get her some help. Social Services in her area thought I was a saint and it felt good to bring some peace in a world full of debtors and drunkards. I'd reach out to the internal Compliance Department on more risky legal issues, and over time I built a relationship with them. I was effective and thorough, and they liked that. Eventually, I was offered a job in Compliance, handling escalated complaints. At each step of my success, the knowledge I was gaining was freeing me from the impossibility of life. Bit by bit, I was learning how to do this thing called life. At times, it felt like I would burst from the pleasure of discovering that I too had some competence and personal power. At the same time, I experienced moments of tremendous cognitive dissonance and grief as I realized the extent of my childhood neglect and the terrible consequences that it had caused—consequences I still paid at home.

Fernando was working at the roofing company and was always tired. I came home from work exhausted too, but he couldn't understand why. He would mock me, pretending to type, his hands suspended in the air, his fingers playing on an imaginary keyboard, and saying, "Oh yeah, I'm so tired," as if my work took no effort at all. I knew it was hard for him to labor outside in the elements through all the seasons, but it still angered me. Meanwhile, on top of my job, I was the one that managed the daily business of our family, making sure bills got paid and taking the children to their doctor visits. Fernando went to work, brought his paycheck home, and partied. Any respect I earned from him for my successes ended up getting pissed away on the weekends.

Fernando drank a lot and still brought home drugs, just when we were doing really well. Because I still hadn't dealt with the true origins of my addiction, I'd fall back into that pit every time. Fernando could handle that lifestyle better. For some reason he never seemed to get hungover. I would be the one suffering in bed the next day, so he'd cook for the children and watch movies with them or take them to the park. Such a saint. In his mind, this proved what he'd thought all along: I wasn't such hot shit after all.

In the spring of 2001, Mama called to tell me about an issue with Grandma's health.

"That's not good," I said, sensing my grandmother was about to die. "I'm coming down."

Grandma had been suffering from dementia for some time. My mother had moved her to San Francisco, admitted her to a modest, but very good care facility, and visited her nearly every day. Grandma's dementia had caused her to fire her lawyers multiple times over the years because she was paranoid they were stealing from her, so Mama also had to take charge of Grandma's money. The Duchess had fallen. It felt significant to me that she was no longer in New York living at the Dakota, no longer a woman in her power, not even able to be the grand lady anymore. I felt stripped of familiarity seeing her there fumbling with her sloppy pants and a bathrobe, putting her feet up on a table in the dining room and saying things like, "Alexandra, have the attorneys draw up the papers. I'd like to buy this place."

Fernando and I made it to San Francisco on the last day of Grandma's life. Grandma had been agitated and had terrible fits. She once told me she wasn't afraid of dying, she was afraid of the idea that she wouldn't be anywhere on the earth. In the end, her eyelids sagged till the bright red flesh inside them showed like the droopy eyes of a Basset Hound, and she kept repeating, "Please God, in God's name."

Fernando was very sweet, gentle, and kind to her, which was beautiful to see. Still, she was in a panic until death finally brought her peace in the wee hours of the morning. Mama received the call around 2 a.m. and she woke me up. We bundled up Joshua, who was still small, and we piled in Mama's bizarre little Toyota Corolla, which had been stolen a number of times by gang-bangers in the Mission. A young guy named Jimmy whom she had befriended from the projects had done her "a favor" and painted it with bright green house paint so no one would want to steal it again. My mother hadn't signed off on that little effort, and you can imagine her surprise when she went out to her car one day and it was bright green with clumpy house paint! But the car ran, so we drove in it to the care facility, too late to comfort Grandma anymore. She looked so peaceful in her bed, like the truest version of herself, and I saw so clearly how death brings final peace from this mortal coil. I was relieved, and felt sharp awareness that this was the end of an era. The tiles of the floor were cold and the air was cool in Grandma's room. She didn't move. It was heavy, but the calm on her face and the lack of tension in her body elicited a deep sense of relief in me. She looked so peaceful and finally free of the strains and stresses of life. She was no longer afraid. I wondered if all strong women were truly afraid.

I received a small amount of family money and when I went home to Portland, Fernando and I moved to a cute little house in the Brooklyn district. I bought a used Subaru and enrolled the kids in the Portland Waldorf School. There, I met a group of loving, caring parents that gave me a sense of community I had never had, though I still felt like I was on the outside looking in because I continued to drink until I started to feel nauseous and began to have headaches.

The doctor suggested a pregnancy test after I described my symptoms. I scoffed, but went ahead with it. A little while later, she walked into the room with a silly smile and raised eyebrows to tell me I was pregnant.

Unprepared for this news but also wildly elated, I said,

"Oh boy, oh boy, what do I do?!" From the steps of the doctor's office, I called Fernando at work and we celebrated over the phone. Overjoyed, I stopped drinking and focused on being healthy for the rest of my pregnancy.

One of the parents from the Waldorf School was a Realtor named Phiamma. She advised me I should be able to buy a house despite having no credit history, and took me to a mortgage lender who was willing to review hard copies of all my bills, which I had paid religiously. And boom! Before I knew it, Phiamma was joyfully showing Fernando, the kids, and me our own little home in the Lents neighborhood. We were ecstatic. We moved in just a week after my daughter Carmen was born and Fernando put plastic up around my bedroom so I could nurse our baby without breathing in the fumes and dust from his renovations.

Carmen was a happy baby and Amaranta and Josh would fight over who got to hold her. Amaranta, who was a very loving older sister to Josh, often won because she was older. Then we'd let Josh hold Carmen with our arms wrapped around him to support them both.

I kept telling myself life was good and we would put our troubles behind us in the end, but I didn't believe myself. I still felt insecure and different, possessed of a deep, dark secret and pursued by random terrors. We were often on the financial edge and a couple of times I had to borrow from Gaby or Mama to pay the mortgage. At work, it seemed like everyone else was doing fine and sailing through life on a wave of Starbucks and competence. I couldn't understand how they did it.

Unhappy at home, I slipped back into drinking and using, and believed this would always be my lot in life. I couldn't imagine myself living any differently.

I wept at my therapist and told her, "They ruined me—all the 'theys' that had fucked me up and abused me and didn't parent me. I will never be ok."

I don't even know why I was going to therapy because I didn't think there was any hope for me. No one did. My husband thought I was kind of a loser and my children lived in constant fear someone at Waldorf School would ask them how they were doing and they would end up admitting how bad things were in our home.

At the time, I believed putting my kids in private school would save them. I told myself they would get good support at Waldorf school, the kind of support I hadn't received and couldn't seem to give them. They would be safe there and know I loved them because I sent them to such a safe, nice place. Still mired in my addictions and sick thinking, I didn't recognize I was repeating an old family pattern. Like Grandma stepping out of the car looking a mess that long-ago day at Hewitt School, I simply couldn't pull my shit together for the sake of my children. They longed for me to wake up sober and take them to school every day, just as I had longed for a family member to drop me off and pick me up from school when I was little. Like Grandma, I thought if I made sure they were fed and slept safely next to me, I was doing all right by them. I didn't realize they needed lots of loving attention, daily routines, and regular trips to the park. And even if I had understood all that, I was still drinking too much to show up for my kids the way they needed me to.

Fernando's lifestyle hadn't changed at all. His boss distributed payroll at the Space Room Lounge, a local bar that made strong drinks and still smelled of the old days. It drew a mixed crowd of cool young hipsters and old school alcoholics who liked to lurk in the dark. Fernando came home drunk every payday, but he'd place his paycheck's worth of money on the table. He had a strong work ethic and took pride in being on the job on time every day and working harder than anyone else. He was eventually promoted to foreman and largely managed the day-to-day processes at the company, but his past dogged his steps as surely as his "work hard, play hard" philosophy did.

Fernando and I had both gotten into trouble with the law during our days in San Francisco. I was able to go back and clean up my problems with the help of two good lawyers hired by Grandma, but Fernando didn't have access to a wealthy relative. His criminal record prohibited him from becoming a U.S. citizen, despite our legal marriage and American children. Fernando felt the unfairness of that for many years. Once in a while, he'd put his finger in my face and call me a piece of shit in Spanish and I would sense his resentment. He always seemed to bring home drugs just when we were doing better and there were times when I wondered if that was, at least in part, to keep me down so I wouldn't leave him.

But one day, Fernando threw my keys at my face and said, "You're going to be shit without me, you'll see," and stormed out to stay with a friend. That was the day I was finally sick and tired of being sick and tired.

***

On February 15, 2003, I walked into my therapist's office and said to her, "I think I am an alcoholic." I had been seeing her for five years and I can assure you that, although I thought I had it under wraps, she was well aware of my alcoholism. She jumped up from her chair, grabbed a phone book, and said, "Great, let's call AA and find a meeting!" Within an hour, I was sitting in a circle in one of the dorms at Reed College listening to people saying things out loud I had only dared think to myself. They talked about being defeated, how awful it was to be trapped in their addiction, how badly they wanted to heal, and what healing felt like. Tears streamed down my face.

In AA, I could admit my deep, dark secrets and nobody judged me. In that room, I felt like an anvil had been lifted off me. The people in the room were like me and I told myself if they could heal, I could heal too. They gave me an example of what healing looked like and mentored me in how to start.

I gave Fernando a year to get into therapy or recovery, but he just crossed his arms and said, "Nope." He loved us and was good about helping around the house and being a dad to his kids, but he refused to think about how his drinking affected them. It wasn't good for them to see their dad shit-faced drunk all the time and it didn't occur to Fernando that he shouldn't be coming home with cocaine and needles because that was going to hurt his children and wife. Sober, I didn't see him as the strong one or my savior. Literally a year to the day after I told Fernando to see a therapist or join AA, I handed him divorce papers.

Finally, finally, I was not shut away from the world by anyone else or my own addiction. One day at a time, I began to recover.

CHAPTER 16
NEW LIFE

I cleaned up real good. Once I stopped digging the hole I was in, I found myself healing quickly. I thrived in the structure of my corporate job now, and found joy in going to work. When I had been drinking heavily, I'd go into work at the office after being up late at night and then waking up hungover, and I'd hope as I made the long walk to my desk past a series of grey cubicles that no one would say hello to me. I'd make it to my desk, sweat building up on my lip and on the back of my neck, and I'd sit down, tired and depressed, dreading the day ahead. I'd hear people talking about their weekends in the cubicles next to me, drinking their Starbucks and laughing, and I'd think, "How are they happy?" I genuinely couldn't imagine what it would be like to be relaxed and joyful on a Monday morning.

When I got sober, I was immediately transformed into one of those happy people, and my whole outlook changed. On occasion, I'd wake up in the morning before work, and for a moment I'd be sure I was hungover, then I'd realize I wasn't and I'd jump gleefully out of bed and get dressed, amazed at my luck. I had a new chance at life, and this time I had the support of other sober folks in recovery. I had assumed that if I quit drinking, I'd be bored to tears and craving the relief of alcohol and other substances all the time, but it was the opposite. I started feeling hopeful, and I started doing things with others that I had merely dreamed of before.

I met a guy who was an avid rock climber, mountaineer, and cyclist, and we started dating. Soon, I found myself buying a Specialized road bike, and doing 25-mile daily rides around Portland, then riding centuries on weekends with my boyfriend. I learned to rock climb in the summer, and did my first climb on the Beckey Route on Liberty Bell in the North Cascades, my boyfriend teaching me to belay—that is, hold the rope attached to the climber to keep a degree of tension on it in case he falls—on the fly. And speaking of flies, the flies made a tasty meal of me as I belayed my boyfriend while he roped up and led the route, then waited for me to climb up to him. The flies disappeared after a while, as we climbed higher and the air cooled. It was amazing to be out in the mountains, scaring the shit out of myself on a stellar rock route, then topping out and surveying the surrounding forest and mountains. And when winter came, I started mountaineering, making Mt. Hood my first summit. I didn't have the proper gear, but I had the basics. I drove out to the mountain with my boyfriend, and we got an alpine start from Timberline, starting to climb around 2 a.m. He had a mountaineering setup called a *randonnee*, which consisted of a set of skis with bindings that could be adjusted to allow the heel to be higher, facilitating climbing while wearing them. A pair of "skins" attached to the bottoms of the skis enabled him to climb on them with a lot less effort than I, who had only my mountaineering boots to hike in, while I carried my snowboard on my back. The terrain on the Palmer Snowfield was icy, and the dark sky and wind were a challenge to my spirit. My boyfriend climbed faster than me and had an attitude of "either you're going to be tough and handle your business or I won't climb with you," even though he never outright said that. So I kept my thoughts to myself, and doubled down. Lowering my head to the wind, I fought my way up the icy climb, as my snowboard acted as a sail and tried to drag me back down the mountain with the steady winds. We made it to the top of the Palmer and climbed to the Silcox Hut, stopping for a snack as the sun started to rise. I was tired and a bit cold, but really proud of myself. I felt strong and inspired as I looked back down the mountain. We summitted that morning by way of the Pearly Gates, a steep and icy but short entry to the summit. It was June of 2005 when I first stood atop Mt. Hood, and there have been numerous other climbs since then, but I'll never forget the feeling of that first summit.

As the years went by, I found many opportunities to do climbs in the Pacific Northwest and beyond, and my mental and physical strength grew as I challenged myself. I prided myself on being a strong team member, even if I wasn't always as fast as everyone. And frankly, though speed is cool, enjoying time on my feet in some of the most beautiful terrain in the country was what it was all about for me. I was smart about my preparation, taking responsibility for my own gear and continued learning, poring over mountaineering books and studying climbing routes carefully. I knew that any team is only as strong as its weakest climber, so I learned everything I could and trained hard to be a strong partner. And it served me well on a particular climb of the Hotlum Bolam route on Mt. Shasta during which my boyfriend got altitude sickness and I had to take charge to get us both down.

Because my boyfriend was an avid, long-time climber, I got to climb many mountains and rock and ice routes that many new climbers wouldn't get exposed to. He was safe and strong and I knew we'd be okay, but that was it. He didn't baby me, and I really had to hold my own when I went on adventures with him. In some ways, he could have been more supportive, but there's a certain ethos in the Pacific Northwest that I've seen on many an adventure that makes people tough and hardy because people refuse to carry the mental loads of their adventure buddies. You just have to hold your own or go find another sport.

And so it is that I climbed mountains all over Oregon and California, climbed splitter cracks on the smooth red rock of Indian Creek with the likes of Jim Donini, who was at one time the President of the American Alpine Club, and the hilarious and sweet Mica Dash, who later died in an avalanche whilst pushing the limits on a mountain in China. I played on ice routes in the Box Canyon in Ouray, Colorado, in addition to many more amazing adventures. And once, when planning a trip to climb Mt. Shasta, my boyfriend and I decided at the last minute to climb Rainier instead. This proved to be a somewhat risky effort, being that Rainier, though similar in height, was twice the size of Shasta and quite heavily glaciated. But, after climbing long and steadily, passing over the crackling Ingraham Glacier and watching massive seracs—large pieces of ice—calving off in the distance, we managed to top out in the frigid morning air. I had spent a good portion of the climb with serious stomach issues, finally vomiting red Gatorade onto the white snow after a long traverse above a giant gaping crevasse at 12,000 feet. The sense of achievement and awe was huge as we looked out from the summit onto the world below. And when my boyfriend decided to go spend a month climbing a high peak called Pumori in the Himalayas, I decided I had to focus on a project myself. Thus was born my foray into triathlons, which later culminated in a strong effort at the Coeur d'Alene Ironman.

I sailed through Ironman training quite well, sticking to all of my training and following the advice of a friend who had finished Ironman ten times. I would work my office job during the day, then go do my brick training, which consisted of back-to-back swim then bike workouts or bike then run workouts. I made all kinds of rookie mistakes, but I was consistent, and it paid off.

I competed in Ironman Coeur d'Alene in June of 2011, but was cut from the race just a few miles before the finish because my run was too slow. I had a strong swim in that freezing cold lake that many elite competitors had dropped out of, their freezing hands slowing their performances so much that it didn't make sense to continue. And I had completed the 112-mile bike in decent time. But my legs were like lead when I got off the bike, and I shuffled for 19 miles before I could barely move. The driver of the race crew vehicle who pulled me from the course sounded sorry when he broke the news to me, but I was elated and so glad to be done. There are no marching bands for the folks who get out there and do it and stop short just before the finish, but I'll tell you what: YOU DID IT! I had the experience of training, showing up in the cool morning air, stomach sick from the jitters I got in that frigid water, which had been unusually cold and choppy that year, and I gave it my best.

There were other big efforts with similar ends. Once, I signed up for a 10k swim at Applegate Lake—a deep, clear lake in Oregon—and the week before, just to see if I was ready, I swam 9k in a local 24-Hour Fitness pool. Big mistake! I learned the hard way that you don't train for long stuff by doing other events of virtually the same distance. I made it almost all the way through the 10k swim the following week, but my right shoulder froze up near the finish and I was pulled out of the water by a safety boat. I was disappointed not to get the finish but I've always been super proud of those efforts. After all, life is in the experience.

It was after my Ironman effort that I decided to run trail ultramarathons. I figured if I could get strong at ultras, I could come back and slay Ironman. And so it was that I launched into a seven-year period of racing and running ultra distances. During my first year or so of running trails, I raced almost monthly, most of them ultra distance races of 50k, or 40 miles. In my second year, I started running 50-milers and was super stoked to finish the Miwok 100k in California, put on by a lovely woman who had walked it in with me from about 12 miles out when we were both deciding to drop from the Cascade Crest 100-miler on my first attempt of that race. We had talked during that 12 miles about life and self-love and injuries and effort as we walked through an old dark and wet railway tunnel with little mice scurrying around. She had been kind while I was suffering from severe chafing and stomach issues.

Ultrarunning fed my soul because it was in nature,

it was tough, and people were bonded through fire in those things. There's nothing like finding yourself on a remote course in pretty bad pain, as you work through your demons, then stumbling upon another runner going through the same thing. There's no phoniness or charade of propriety. It's raw and real out there and it takes grit and determination to show up for the experience and gut it out. Powerful moments are had on the trails.

Sometime around 2008, my little sister Lhasa was diagnosed with breast cancer. I received a phone call from my mother while I was sitting in bed one morning.

"Sammy, we just found out...Lhasa has been diagnosed with breast cancer, but it's a small tumor and they're looking at options for treatment and possibly surgery. I'll let you know as things evolve."

My mother's voice on the phone sounded calm and I didn't get overly freaked out, having had no prior experience of cancer except when my grandmother apparently breezed through treatments years earlier when I was just a girl. But as time went on, the news worsened. I started traveling to Montreal, where Lhasa lived in the Mile End district, to help take care of her. My siblings and my stepdad and their spouses and kids came periodically from the various corners of the earth, and my mother stayed with Lhasa around the clock as all of us came and went repeatedly. Lhasa started off quite hopeful, then as the test results became more dire, she became sicker and started to let go of commitments that she had once looked forward to. For a period she rallied and even started a new tour, her first stop in Reykjavík, Iceland, but she soon developed splitting headaches and vertigo and had to cancel her tour and return to Montreal. The cancer had traveled to her brain. She gave up being the creative director of a large Parisian festival, and little by little, her world became smaller and quieter as her health declined. The house was silent as we accompanied her in her final months, talking in hushed voices so as not to disturb her. Life felt too big, and we protected her from it. We slept with her in our arms, or sat on the chair in her room watching her sleep. Sometimes she would sit bolt upright in bed then immediately try to stand, as if she had somewhere very important to be. Her hallucinations were strong and she would see vines wrapping around people, or a woman sitting in the sun in a field. We learned to pay attention so she wouldn't fall and hurt herself. And when she asked if the hallucinations were real, we would say, "No, Lhasa, they're not," and she would nod in acceptance. We paid special care not to patronize her, but to honor her in her journey. She was so courageous, even when afraid and even in the face of her own mortality. My mother was tireless in her efforts. It was exhausting and sad and yet also powerful and beautiful. On occasion, my mothers and sisters and I would go for a walk to the health food store or to get coffee at the Club Social down the street, and Lhasa would wave to us from the couch and say, "Don't forget to let down your hair, put some lipstick on, and flirt a little." The winter felt colder that year, and it snowed for four straight days after she died on January 1, 2010.

The night she died, I was meditating at home, holding a wooden statue of the Weeping Buddha that a friend had given me, tears rolling down my face as they had for so long now. Suddenly Lhasa appeared to me, smiling as she spoke: "I'm okay. I'm really okay." Her voice was soft and full of ease and it comforted me.

Once in her kitchen, she and I had spoken of music and determination and passion. I had sung to her a few songs I had written, and she had told me to never, ever let anyone discourage me.

"Do what you have to do, and don't let anyone stop you with their lack of belief," she had said.

Years later during the Covid pandemic, I would start taking voice lessons and playing the banjo, and I'd give myself permission to fill up a room with my soul, unapologetically. Every time I'd sing, I'd feel Lhasa in my bones, and would recall a time when she told me, "Sammy, when I have to be strong to go on stage, I channel you." And now I channel her.

FALLING UP FROM THE BOTTOM

CHAPTER 17
ONE LAST HAUL

At the start of 2020, I had 16 years of sobriety. Putting one foot in front of the other, doing the next right thing, falling down and getting up, laughing and weeping, feeling defeated and refusing to give up, I somehow managed to build a balanced, sane life surrounded by friends and family who loved and supported me.

Professionally, I was thriving within the structured environment of corporate life. My career in business made me something of an outlier in my family of entertainers and creatives but it served me very well, giving me the ability to create the safe, stable home I had long craved.

Athletically, I pushed my boundaries as a cyclist, climber, swimmer, and ultra-distance trail runner. Extreme sports provided me with adventure and made me feel alive and free.

Personally, I managed to deepen the bonds with my family. In time and with recovery, I built relationships with my mother and siblings and I was deeply engaged in mentoring my children to work through the emotional scars left from their own childhoods.

Truly, I was living a life beyond my wildest dreams, yet something restless still churned within me, subtle but persistent. I could feel myself seeking, but I could not name what I was looking for. Was I just too intense? Why couldn't I simply be where my feet were and be content? Before I could figure that out, Covid-19 arrived.

I had been training hard and was planning to fly to the Grand Canyon to run a double crossing known as Rim-to-Rim-to-Rim (R2R2R) with a couple of friends. The R2R2R is run over 40 miles on difficult terrain with more than 10,000 vertical feet of gain and loss. It is not for amateurs, and people who have run it say it will change your life. I had been looking forward to seeing my friends and communing with them on what promised to be an awe-inspiring run, but as the day of my trip drew nearer, news of Covid-19 was increasingly grim and warnings from the medical community were weighing heavily on me.

Finally, just days before the trip, I wrote to my friends and told them I didn't feel safe flying on a plane or being far from my kids at a time with so many unknowns hanging in the air. All around the world, people were asked to go home and shut the door on the novel coronavirus to prevent hospitals from being overwhelmed by the number of sick and dying. Reports of the number of deaths in Italy were mind-boggling, yet the U.S. government was sending conflicting messages. The death count skyrocketed in New York City where my sister and her family lived. My company put all staff on remote work, so I went home to live alone with my dogs and cats for an indeterminate amount of time.

The forced isolation of the Covid pandemic triggered old traumas, remnants of the solitude of my childhood, and I was deeply dissociative for a couple of months, which made everything around me appear to be behind a veil again. But, as I did all those years ago when I learned Greek during the long, lonely nights at the house in New Milford, I cast about for something to occupy my mind. This time, I found a banjo I had purchased shortly before the pandemic started.

I had always wanted to play the banjo and every time I heard one, I yearned for it. And suddenly there I was with a banjo and time on my hands. I asked around and found a banjo teacher. Music lessons gave me something to focus on that had nothing to do with the world's problems.

As I played, I remembered the part of me who wasn't terrified, the girl who danced and rode horses, the one who swam in the muddy Rio Cuale in the heat of the Mexican rainforest. She had stories to tell about our journey—stories interwoven with the music that had always been in me and was now spilling out with no one there to stop it. Before Lhasa died, we stood in her kitchen in Montreal one day. I sang her a couple of songs I had written and she told me to never let anyone stop me from singing my songs and telling my stories. I started to refine short stories from my book to prepare for a book tour once this memoir was complete, and I talked aloud around the house, telling my stories to my cats and the dog as I cooked dinner or whispering them to myself on long runs. I recorded them and listened to them, refining them, changing my tone, deepening my understanding of myself and what I projected to the world. The project became a part of my bones, almost standing on its own. I would decidedly not disappear into the woodwork anymore. It was clear to me that I had to tell the story, even if it were just to the dogs. I was speaking myself into existence. And that knowledge, that absolute conviction that I would, indeed, go forward with my own story and my own songs, began to fill the empty, disconnected spaces between me and the world. In time, it would bring me home to myself, and how the world responded was no longer the point.

I recalled a story I once heard from a scholar who said that the Buddha had reached Nirvana when he realized he could be aware of two vastly opposing truths and accept that they both existed. I felt life closing in on me and at the same time it was expanding within me. I found meaning in my solitude, and in spite of the harshness of it, I found solace in it too.

I didn't know at the time about the wave of pain that was coming my way, but when it came, I was able to handle it because the creativity of the moment filled the gaps. Like leaping from one pillar to another in a sea of fire.

CHAPTER 18
CARMEN'S STORY

On a cool sunny morning in June of 2020, I was preparing to head out to run 18 miles on Table Mountain with a friend when I got a call from a woman who spoke in a slow, purposeful tone, as if trying to soothe me.

"Is this Samantha? Samantha de la Vega?"

"Yes, who's calling?"

"This is Doctor So-and-So from Legacy Peace Health Hospital in Vancouver. Your daughter has been in an accident."

My mind raced. Which daughter?

"Carmen is ok, but we had to amputate her thumb."

CARMEN? Amputate? WHAT?!

"Oh god, nooooo!" I wailed into the phone. "What?! Why? What? Her thumb? WHAT HAPPENED? Oh my God…"

"Can you get to the hospital?"

"Yes, oh my God, yes. I'll be there. I'm coming. She's ok? She's ok, right?"

"Yes, she's going to be ok. She's pretty banged up, but she's ok."

I hung up the phone and dialed my friend to cancel the run.

I rushed around gathering my things—wallet, bag, car keys, jacket—and was out the door and in my truck in a few minutes. I raced to the hospital and was met with a tumultuous scene in the ED. Carmen was medicated and lying on a gurney, her bloody hand wrapped and propped up on a pillow. Her hair was caked with blood, part of her head was shaved, and her macerated forehead was stitched in a chaotic profusion of what looked like black fishing wire. The hospital room was surprisingly messy, with clumps of cotton and gauze saturated with blood scattered on the floor, and there were machines that beeped around her. The doctors bustled, and a drunk woman on the other side of the room behind a curtain repeatedly screamed in the gutteral voice of too many years of cigarettes and gambling, "I wanna get the fuck outta here!"

I looked at the doctors.

"Is she ok? Can I wake her up? How long has she been out?"

They told me she had been out since surgery, but they indicated it'd be okay to wake her and take her home, so I slowly leaned onto the gurney and moved her shoulder with my hand. She barely moved, heavy under the sedation. I felt heavy myself. I shook her again and she groaned and started to open her eyes. "I wanna get the fuck outta here!" the woman croaked again, and things banged and shuffled around behind the curtain. The Fellini movie around me continued, surreal and disjointed.

"Carmen, it's Mama. Wake up, sweetie. I'm going to

take you home," I said, doing my best to be strong and not let my emotions get the best of me.

Carmen opened her glazed eyes. She looked confused, as if she had been on a long journey walking toward a white light and suddenly here I was and here we were, and the light was bright in the room and the air was too cold, and…

"Mama, they cut off my thumb," she said, looking at me through the fog.

"I know, baby. I know. It's going to be okay. You're alive, that's what matters. You're okay. It's going to be okay. I'm here. I'm going to take you home."

The police had found Carmen and her boyfriend after they had rolled his SUV on a windy road in Washington. They were under the influence and had blacked out. The car went about 50 yards on the grass alongside the road, then flipped a few times and landed across the road in a ditch. The police later would send me pictures of the accident, and it was so terrifying that I had to look away. The car landed on the roof, which was crushed down to the bottom of the windows. Carmen's hand had been outside the window and her thumb was crushed as the car rolled. But the one thing they had done right that night was to put on their seatbelts, and that's what saved their lives. Carmen would tell me a year later that at that time she and her boyfriend only intermittently wore their seat belts. This time they must've put them on reflexively while they were blacked out.

I finished talking to the doctors as I picked up Carmen's bloody possessions from the gurney and helped her to sit up. She was a mess, dazed from the head injury, drugged and in pain, and baffled by the immensity of the situation. I vacillated between the reality of the situation and seeing her as a foolish little girl who had no idea what she had just done, no idea how the choices she had made for months prior had led up to this moment. The permanence of the damage weighed on me. Now was not the time for me to fall apart. I knew that how she handled this now, how we handled it together, would determine how she processed the situation and how well she would do both physically and emotionally. After a while, Carmen felt good enough to be moved to a wheelchair and I slowly wheeled her out to the lobby, the automatic doors opening with a whir as I rolled her out into the cool morning air. It was a sunny day, and I flashed back to my escape from Whitey in the Mission in San Francisco.

Carmen slept for a few days through the weekend, and I kept her pretty well medicated to avoid the pain. What was left of her thumb was wrapped in gauze, and we'd rinse it and change the bandages daily so they wouldn't stick to the raw flesh. The doctors had removed the large part of the tissue that had been crushed and was dead, but a jagged bone protruded out of the thumb and there was a little tissue left down near the first joint where the thumb connected to her hand. The rest was raw skinless flesh. They had left it like that so the plastic surgeon could have something to work with when trying to rebuild the thumb. Carmen slept in my bed and I slept beside her, waking up to get medications and such. We made it through the weekend, and Monday morning Carmen had surgery to complete the amputation and rebuild the thumb with a skin graft. The doctor moved one of the nerves in her forefinger to the thumb along with skin grafts from the forefinger and her forearm, and managed to make it look like she still had half a thumb left, in spite of the loss of the two top joints. Carmen came home with a cool dark purple plastic shell over her hand and a bunch of pain meds. She was bouncing back quickly. She sat on the edge of the bed and smiled and talked. She was getting stronger by the minute.

She still rested a lot for about a week more, slowly weaning off the meds, and then she turned her focus to her boyfriend, Ray, who had been kept briefly in jail by the police, but was released soon after due to Covid protocols. I was furious with him and blamed him completely for the accident. He was the one who was driving and had almost killed my girl. I did everything in my power to convince Carmen not to go back to him, but when she healed, all she wanted to do was to see him. The police had sent forms to her stating she and Jorge couldn't see each other until he went to court, but nothing could keep them apart, and I was out of my mind, feeling powerless and miserable. I paced the house back and forth the day Carmen went back to him.

The next few months involved a series of additional poor decisions on Carmen's part, including two accidental overdoses. Carmen was partying heavily, and in her naiveté she would take Molly—a psychedelic amphetamine—mixed with Xanax and weed and alcohol, or some other variation on the theme. The pills were made in the street and most likely had fentanyl in them, a very strong chemical opioid. She was tiny, weighing just over 100 pounds, and she had accidentally overdosed twice. It was a nightmare. On the first occasion, I was at home when her housemates called me to tell me, "You'd better come get your girl, she's not waking up!"

"WHAT? What's going on? What have you done to

help her? Is she breathing? Call an ambulance. Call 911. Do you know CPR? She needs air. Hurry! I'm on my way!"

I raced to my truck in the middle of my workday, telling my boss I needed to take the rest of the day off. When I arrived, an ambulance was just leaving. I ran to the door and knocked firmly. Ray's grandmother Karla opened the door, a cigarette in hand, and a herd of little dogs yapping loudly at her feet. She yelled at them to shut the fuck up.

"What happened? Where's Carmen? Did they take her?"

"No, she's upstairs with Ray," she croaked.

"WAIT, WHAT? WHY? Why didn't she go? Is she ok?"

"I don't know. She ain't listenin' to nobody." Cough, cough.

I pushed past Karla and ran up the stairs in the shitty little apartment, and threw open the bedroom door. There was Carmen, on the bed with her eyes closed with Ray leaning over her chastising her in a low voice.

"WHAT'S GOING ON HERE?" I yelled? "What's happening? Why didn't she go with the ambulance?"

"I don't know. She won't go."

"Carmen, what's happening? Carmen, WAKE UP!"

I stepped to the bed and pulled the covers off her, and was shocked to see that Carmen's thighs were bruised and black from her knees to her crotch.

"NO! WHAT THE HELL IS THIS?" I yelled, looking at Ray like I was about to light him on fire.

"I dunno. She fell down the stairs," he muttered.

"SHE DIDN'T FALL DOWN THE FUCKING STAIRS! WHAT THE FUCK DID YOU DO TO HER? WHAT HAVE YOU DONE?"

By this time, my yelling had startled Carmen, who sat up groggily, hair disheveled and going in all directions, makeup smeared black down her face.

"Carmen, you're coming with me. Now." I said in a firm voice. "Let's GO!"

But instead of getting up, Carmen refused. She dug in.

"WHAT HAPPENED TO YOUR LEGS? WHAT'S GOING ON? IS HE HITTING YOU?"

I glared at Ray. "WHAT HAVE YOU DONE? WHAT HAPPENED TO HER? WHAT'S GOING ON HERE?"

"I dunno, she was talking to some guys in a van outside. I looked everywhere for her and found her there. She had all these bruises."

"WHAT? WAS SHE RAPED? WHY DID THEY BEAT HER? WHO ARE THEY?"

Ray clearly wasn't telling me something. His stories went in circles and morphed into something else the more I questioned him. I was out for blood, but Carmen wasn't cooperating. She simply refused to come with me. Finally, utterly desperate and realizing the impossibility of the situation, I said, "Carmen, I'm leaving. If you don't come home, I'm calling the police and reporting this." She just shrugged and laid back down on the bed, pulling the sheets up over her legs.

I knew I had to leave. I couldn't stand there all day pleading with her. I couldn't help her if she wouldn't cooperate. I wanted to wring Ray's neck, but didn't want to make a worse drama out of the situation. I drove home furious and desperate to protect my daughter, and on top of it, utterly confused. Why was she staying? Why wouldn't she tell me what had happened? What the fuck had happened? What was going on?

When I reached home, I called the police and filed a report, asking for a wellness check. I was determined to get her out of Ray's house and I was sure that if the cops went there, they'd file a report or take him in or find some drugs on them and put a stop to the mess, but they called me a short time later to say she had refused the wellness check.

"You can refuse a wellness check?" I asked, completely stymied.

"Yes, ma'am. I'm sorry. I know this is hard."

The cop sounded like he had said this many times before. I hung up the phone and wailed into the emptiness of my house. I paced back and forth and cried and wrung my hands and cried some more. The dogs stayed close to me, Rumi by my feet, and Boo Boo under the covers if I was in bed. For days, I was out of my mind with concern, but I had to work, so I'd wake up and sit at my computer, hold meetings, be professional, then cry on lunch breaks, unable to be on video during calls. I got through somehow. My boss asked me how things were and I told her too much.

"We've got you," she would say, but it would later come back to bite me.

Carmen and I didn't talk for a while after that, because every time I'd call, I couldn't help but grill her. I was intense. I couldn't stop myself. I couldn't accept that she had been hurt and that no one was telling me what had happened. Not even her. Who was she protecting and why?

And then I got another call. Almost a month later. This time Carmen had taken a bunch of drugs again, but the OD was much more serious and they had called the ambulance.

I threw on some shoes and raced to the hospital. This was getting to be a habit.

When I arrived at the hospital, Carmen wasn't there, and I queried the tired looking woman at the intake counter. She looked at me with a blank expression as I told her that I had raced over when I was told my daughter was in the ambulance, and that I couldn't understand why my daughter wasn't here yet.

"Ma'am, we don't bring dead people to the ED," she said.

I was astonished and immediately felt like I was going to completely lose my mind. The room seemed too bright, as I looked at her, searching for words.

"I'm sorry, what did you say? My daughter was on her way in an ambulance. She should be here."

"If she's on her way, then she hasn't arrived yet."

Her cryptic responses were getting to be too much for me.

"I left my house after the ambulance took her from her house…right when they called me. She should be here. Did I get here first? Is everything okay? How is it that she's not here?"

I tried not to raise my voice. The Covid fatigue was showing on her face and I could tell she was ready to project "crazy lady" onto me.

"Ma'am, I need to know what's happening. My daughter, is she okay? Are they coming?"

She repeated her first statement but with a little more detail: "I already explained to you, we don't bring dead people to the ED, so if she's on her way, then she's still alive."

I wanted to scream at her, "ARE YOU FUCKING

KIDDING ME?! DO YOU HAVE ANY IDEA WHAT WE'VE BEEN THROUGH THIS YEAR? HOW CAN YOU BE SO COLD?"

"Okay, thank you," I said, turning to walk back outside to the truck where Joshua was waiting with a blank look of subdued gloom on his face.

"She's alive. She's still on her way, I guess."

After a while, I went inside again, and the woman told me that Carmen had, in fact, arrived in the ambulance and they had managed to save her life, after resuscitating her a few times on the way. She showed me into a curtained room where Carmen lied on a gurney, disheveled hair a matted halo above her puffy face on the pillow. I put my hand on her shoulder and was relieved to feel the warm softness of her body. I had long ago touched the dead body of my grandmother after she had been at the morgue for a few days, and the electric coolness of it had sent a shock through me. I leaned into Carmen, shaking her.

"Carmen, it's Mama, honey. Carmen."

Eventually, after a few attempts to wake her, her heavy eyelids opened slightly and she looked at me with glazed eyes, murmuring, "Mama? What happened?"

"You overdosed, sweetie. You took too many drugs. What did you take?"

"I don't know, I don't know," she said, closing her eyes again, her head becoming heavy on the pillow as she dropped into a deep sleep beneath the weight of the drugs coursing through her body.

It was about an hour before I tried to wake her up again, this time saying, "Come on, sweetie, you need to wake up so I can take you home. Can you wake up?"

"Where's Ray?" she asked, still slurring her speech.

"Ray? He's at your house. I'm taking you home with me, to my house."

"No, Mama, I want to go home. I want to be with Ray."

By this time, the ED nurse had come in and she stood by the bed as I looked incredulously at Carmen. When I looked up, I realized it was a friend of mine from my ultrarunning crowd, and I felt exposed for a moment. The juxtaposition of the two worlds collided momentarily, but I didn't have enough energy or emotional bandwidth to resist. I looked at her almost pleadingly and said, "Oh Syd, if she won't come home with me, I'm not taking her home. I'm going to leave. I can't do this anymore."

"It's okay, Sam. I understand. You go home. I'll take good care of her. She'll be okay."

I didn't waste any time haggling with Carmen this time, trying to convince her that if she kept hanging out with Ray doing what she was doing, that she was going to die. I spared myself the sickening emotional upheaval and grabbed my bag and almost ran out of the ED, flummoxed and exhausted. I drove home, feeling heavy, my heart aching and feeling the darkness of the world surrounding me, crushing in on me like an ocean. I was atmospheres deep beneath the surface of the heavy waters, in the depths with strange sea creatures, their sharp teeth growing out of transparent cartilaginous jaws, eyes bulging, moving slowly toward me, then fading into the depths with a slow, purposeful swish of their tails. I envied them that they belonged here and were in no rush to get anywhere. They were beyond death.

When I got home, I wailed into the emptiness of my house. I set things down and walked to the kitchen, leaning on the white counter. Its whiteness hurt, so I turned and walked to my office, sitting down at my desk, and stared at my computer screen. I had been working on that computer earlier that day, and I suddenly felt a pang of anxiety like a razor through my body. A feeling of exposure like agoraphobia hit me.

"How can I keep a lid on this?" I wondered? "I can't. I can't do it."

I didn't talk to Carmen for days after that incident. I didn't call her number, didn't try to find out…I couldn't. And she didn't call me. Depression shrouded me like a cloak. I sunk into its depths, and wrapped it around me.

It took me many months to realize that both Carmen and Ray had made a series of decisions and lifestyle changes that led up to that accident and her overdoses, and that, ultimately, Carmen would be okay without her thumb and would survive her tomfoolery with drugs. But it seemed, in spite of surviving the madness of almost losing her a few times that year, there was more to come with Amaranta and Josh, my two other kids.

SAMANTHA DE LA VEGA

FALLING UP FROM THE BOTTOM

Photo of painting I commissioned as a prayer to the Virgen de Guadalupe to take care of my kids, with me in the background releasing my motherly wisdom to the universe, represented by an owl

(Artist: David Joaquin, www.theartofdavidjoaquin.com)

CHAPTER 19
MAKE IT STOP

One night in October of 2020, I got a call from Joshua. It was 10 o'clock and I was in bed watching a movie when the phone rang. Josh had been upstairs in his room earlier, and now he was on the phone, so I was confused.

"Ma, can you pick me up?" he asked.

Josh wasn't one to ask for favors much and I sensed it was one of those times when you don't ask, you just say yes.

"Where are you?" I asked, as I slid out from under the warm covers, putting on my slippers.

He told me where he was and we agreed to meet at a place nearby on the southeast side of the river, where it would be easier for me to park. I pulled on some pants and a sweater and stepped out into the cool night air, and hoofed it toward the shape of my truck.

I drove toward inner Southeast Portland, calling him as I neared, and he told me what corner he was on. Within minutes I saw him standing on the side of the road. I pulled over and unlocked the passenger side of the truck, wondering what was going on. Josh opened the door and I felt the blood drained out of my face as icicles of adrenaline coursed through my body. There were clumps of blood on the side of his head and his sweatshirt and head were covered in blood. I looked at him incredulously, my voice raising with slight panic.

"What happened, Josh? Who did this to you?"

It looked as if his ear had been chopped off or his head smashed in on one side. He looked dazed. My initial plan had been to bring him home, but as I drove, I realized he needed to go to the hospital.

Josh told me the story as we went. He had gotten drunk and bumped into a homeless guy in a tent who became infuriated with him. The man attacked Josh with a maglight flashlight—the kind of large heavy flashlights police officers use—hitting him over the head repeatedly, as his friends continued to push Josh toward him whenever he tried to back away or escape.

My heart ached as I drove home, but I slipped easily into practical mode. I was always good in emergencies. Life was one big emergency.

We arrived at the hospital near our house and the nurses and doctors rushed him into a room and started cleaning him up. It was a few hours before he was ready to come home with 17 staples in his head and a bad concussion that would take him weeks to recover from.

After Josh's injury, he laid low for a while, and things seemed to calm down for a few months. Carmen had recovered from her OD's and I figured the worst was over.

***

A few months passed with relative calm, when in April of 2021 my daughter Amaranta was shot sitting in a car at Rocky Butte with her boyfriend, just days after her 28th birthday. The attackers' car had pulled up as if to park next to them, but instead hung back a few feet so the front end reached just behind the midpoint of their car. The engine idled, interrupting the quiet coolness of the morning. Amaranta and her boyfriend were lying back with their seats fully reclined, watching a movie on his cell phone, tilted sideways and down so that the backlight shone on their faces, creating shadowy reflections. Amaranta thought it seemed strange that the car held back some, the lights still on, and the engine running. She and her boyfriend commented to each other how odd it was, but kept watching their movie. But Amaranta felt something was off and briefly sat up on her left elbow, glancing over the back of the seat out the rear passenger window in time to see three people with Covid face coverings and dark sunglasses exiting the other car simultaneously, each of them holding a gun. It was surreal, like watching *The Terminator*, but here and now, real time, oh-shit-not-this time. Like this-is-it time. That distant moment is here now, the I-wonder-how-I'll-die time was happening, and all too fast.

She screamed to the boyfriend next to her in the car and, as if in slow motion, he sat up in his fully reclined driver's seat, grabbing the wheel with his left hand and shifting into reverse with the right, yelling, "What the fuck?! What the FUCK?!" as he hit the gas. In the few seconds it took them to recognize the shit was going down, the assailants had sped into high gear as they strode intentionally toward their targets. Cutting corners, they zipped into position, shooting as they walked. One stood in the misty headlights of the car and shot into the windshield, hitting the boyfriend in the chest. At the same time, one walked around to Amaranta's side of the car, shooting through the passenger window and hitting her in the wrist, the 9 millimeter bullet traveling down her arm and getting stuck in her elbow. And the other, shooting through the driver's side window, but hitting nothing but the car in spite of his proximity. Thankfully, they were only unskilled idiots with chips on their shoulders, because in the hailstorm of bullets, only one hit each of their targets.

***

Amaranta had been a sweet little girl. She was loving and kind to her little brother, even though he tormented her and pulled at her hair from his rolling walker, and took her toys when she was playing. Amaranta loved Josh and wanted him to feel safe, so she mothered him like a little girl playing house, her arm always around his shoulder in new situations. She would bend over and whisper to him, "It's ok, Joshie. It's ok," and he would believe her.

In spite of my love for her, there was no magic pill for my imperfections, and I had hurt Amaranta, breaking her little heart, moment by moment, time after time, until it was crushed and impossibly folded and bent like a little butterfly's wing that couldn't be repaired.

I ached over the years when I realized what I had done. I had not been mothered or cared for, and I wanted my kids to feel the incredible love and protection I had to offer, but there were steps missing and I didn't know how to do it. It had something to do with schedules, and food, and nutrients, and sometimes doctors—which I did figure out—and holding her, lots of holding her, and teaching her little things like how to wash a table and how to save money. It had something more to do with those little things than it did the Montessori School I sent her to in La Villa in Mexico City, and there was something more to it than cute clothes and baths in little pink plastic baby tubs. There was more to it, but I didn't guess that until it was way too late for her.

So I broke her heart, little by little, until I stopped breaking it and she picked up the tools of the war on her soul and beat herself with them. I yelled at her so harshly once that she flew back as if I had punched her. I felt the thrust of that invisible beating and I knew there was an unintended cruelty in it. I felt the tear in the walls of her heart, and felt her soul break under the weight of that cruelty, and there was no *I'm sorry* or *I didn't know* or *I don't know how to do this* that would repair it. Her little legs held her up, but she needed to fall, to throw herself on the ground and yell and cry and say, "You scared me, you hurt me." But it was too late for any of that, because to do that you have to feel safe and loved, and Amaranta was already too hurt. All the nights I held her in my arms, all the food I cooked and the shopping trips I took her on with Josh in the giant double stroller, and the stories I read them and the songs I sang them—none of that could take away the hurt of the hurts, like a thousand tiny cuts that make a person bleed out until there's just no more blood.

And ultimately, it was my own childhood lack of love that crushed her little soul—reaching into the ethers of the now and breaking her heart. It was many years later before I could see how deeply the damage had burned her aching little heart, and then it was too late. Maybe if I had gone looking for her in apartments, pulled her out of parties, yelled at her to come home, insisted she eat dinner, taught her how to save money and to get a job, to talk about her feelings and told her that they were welcomed… maybe then she wouldn't have chosen the boyfriend and the drugs and the dark corners of the city at night. Maybe then she wouldn't have been in a city park at odd hours. Maybe she wouldn't have been shot. But it was too late.

***

When I saw her, the blood dripped from the wound and her hand hung down limply from the wrist. She could barely move her fingers.

"The pain feels like burning and pressure," she said, looking worn.

She cried sometimes like a little girl, like my little girl, the one buried so far down I rarely got to see her, but mostly she was a tough, angry young woman, railing at the world, pissed off and somehow. . . petty. She made jokes that were inappropriate. Poorly-timed jokes that landed wrong and seemed redundant, even though they were new today. She grimaced and screeched when the EMTs transferred her to the new gurney to transport her to the hospital, yelping out like she was hurt, then saying she was kidding. She was in pain at times. And then she was just high on the fentanyl they were giving her every half hour. Her eyes were crusted with old mascara, tears ran down her face and then dried. I wanted to wipe them because they looked uncomfortable. I wanted a cool wet washcloth to wash her face, and to hold her, but the nurse was in the way, so I stood back. It wasn't my place.

I came home and sat on my bed. Then I sat at the kitchen table. I looked at the sunlight on the plants and the warm yellow wood of the table I had sanded. I looked at my hands and then at the cat. I forgot what to do. I ate. I knew I had to eat, so I ate. I talked to my therapist. People in crisis need to do first things first. Eat, drink water, shower, rest. I stared out the back door for a while. *I'll clean the garage,* I thought. So, I tidied up for a bit. I hung the shovels that were out of place from the contractors who had been working on the back deck. I had the deck built so the house would be nice. To help us enjoy our lives. To spend time with friends and family. To sing and eat and to lie in the sun. To lounge with the dogs. The deck was for us to have fun on.

But I built a deck for my family, I thought.

The incongruence felt hard. Like a bullet lodged in my elbow. It wouldn't go away. I was stuck, wanting to rewind. I walked back and forth a bit. Picked things up and put them down. Forgot where I put them. Found them and didn't need them. I sat on the bed. The cat tapped me with his paw, and I pet him. The dreadlocks behind his ears needed to be clipped. I pictured using Josh's clippers to shave him. I'd probably do it wrong.

I should take him to the groomers, I thought.

The dog nudged me on the other side, his ball in his mouth. I loved on him a bit, hugging him and petting him. He raised his paw, happily absorbing the affection. I felt loved by my sweet little animals. They were with me all through the isolation of Covid. They were with me when my renters were mean and when Carmen lost her thumb in the car accident. I saw that thumb when the doctor took off the wrappings.

"Don't look," I had told her.

I felt sick, but I looked at it as if I were looking at a book in someone's hand. No effect. I was strong for Carmen and I was proud of that. Even if no one knew it. The doctor had told me to be firm with her. Not mean, but firm. He said kids can get more emotional if you hover too much. Gotta be firm. So I was firm but kind. I stayed by her side for days. And when she woke up one morning looking really depressed, I said, "Carmen, you have to choose now how you're going to process this. You can go down the dark path or feel your feelings, accept it, and move through it with gratitude that you didn't die." She heard me. She chose the latter.

Amaranta was shot, and the nurses treated me with disdain. That's how they treat the mother of a young person who is addicted to drugs. I had to remind them that this addict has a family who loves her and that we are all traumatized by this incident. I had to remind them my daughter is loved and she is in there somewhere, even though I didn't say quite those words. I had to remind them about respect. I told the doctors. Those nurses don't know what we were going through.

I looked at my daughter as the darkening blood crusted on her arm, the wound clogged with sticky blood and the bullet lodged in her elbow, protruding. Her hand hung limply from her wrist. She cried now and again, and I could see my little girl. And then she swore and winced at the pain as they took her away.

And then I was home wondering what to do. I counted. Five times in the last year. I got five calls for five different incidents like this one with different details. Carmen's rollover accident. Carmen's overdose. Carmen's second overdose. Josh's beating. Amaranta's gunshot. I opened the front door, grabbed the hoe, and walked out to weed the garden. I swept the back steps, stared out the window some more, and then slept for a while.

I thought, "Maybe now I'll mow the lawn," but instead, I just stared at something else.

FALLING UP FROM THE BOTTOM

CHAPTER 20
KEEP GOING

In spite of all the torment and worry with my kids, I kept running throughout. There were brief periods where I couldn't bear to move and I sat on my back deck with the dogs, but for the most part, training kept me feeling more balanced. And in late 2020, I committed once again to making an attempt at an ultra distance trail race that had given me a run for my money twice before: the Cascade Crest 100. I called a local female coach named Dana and found her knowledge and attitude refreshing. She really seemed to understand my particular set of challenges, and had a great outlook that focused on finding joy in training and racing, and not overdoing it like so many do. In ultrarunning, it's often more, bigger, faster, but she focused on quality. And so it was that I trained with Dana and got stronger and stronger, and then pulled the trigger and signed up for Cascade Crest for one last go at it.

Cascade Crest is a tough technical race on a remote mountain course, with about 23,000 feet of climbing, but

FALLING UP FROM THE BOTTOM

I knew the course well, as I had run it in stages multiple times and attempted to race it twice before. Every time I ran that course, it was like a tectonic-plate-shifting spiritual rolfing. I knew I could finish it if I trained smart, but I knew it would take everything I had; not just physically, but mentally. I was actually scared of the course because I had run it a couple of times either in stages or partially, during my race attempts. It had some dark sections through the night that were mentally daunting. The trees looked like bears in the dark, and the silence of what I referred to as the "witching hour," when the birds stopped chirping and the mountain lions started prowling, made my hair stand on end. I had once run the course in one of the worst storms in the history of the race: a sub-latitudinal typhoon, whatever that is. The rain drenched me, starting early in the day, and my crew had forgotten to give me a new windbreaker at the 35-mile aid station. I went into the dark forest with rain coming down sideways and was so caught up in making relentless forward progress that I didn't realize I was cold until I was a couple of miles away. And that's when I had gotten that blister under my left big toenail, which had already been loose from so much running prior to the race. With each soggy step, I felt a stabbing pain in the nerves under the nail. I contemplated sitting down, but knew I had to keep moving. It was painful and dark and I felt depressed, but it was those times that I felt the presence of an incredible life force: the human will. I also felt alive, brave, and strong. They say you are who you are when no one is looking. I loved those moments that required grit. Where it would be so easy to give up and find immediate relief, but I kept on going. And all the others in the race were continuing on too, so there was a sort of kinship born out of the fire. We always came out of these events like new people.

***

I felt super strong and was just about to run my first race of the season leading up to Cascade Crest, when I rolled my ankle hard on a descent during hill repeats in Forest Park in Portland. I could tell this one was bad and I rolled around in pain for a few minutes, my head reeling and feeling like I was going to vomit. When I finally got a grip and was able to slow my breathing, there were two men nearby who helped find me some walking sticks in the woods off the side of the trail, and I held onto the sticks and hobbled the mile or so back to my truck. As I headed home, I figured I'd just go home and ice it and everything would be okay. I had sprained my ankles many times on the trails and would often just tape them up and go run the next day, but as I drove on, the adrenalin started to wear off and I could tell this one might be a break. I drove myself to a nearby hospital and hobbled into the ER to get X-rays. As it turned out, I had an avulsion fracture, which meant that when I rolled my ankle, I had rolled it so hard that it had torn off a fragment of bone. It took me a few weeks of trying to rehab it before I realized I wasn't going to be running the Cascade Crest.

My son Josh eyed me in the first few days after the break, then as the weeks went on he mentioned a few times that I should try Jiu Jitsu. He had been doing it for a while now and thought I'd really like it. So when my ankle healed enough that I could walk around without pain, I went to a local gym that was recommended by my friend

Boston Mike. It turned out that the gym I chose was a super solid outfit with a number of fighters and coaches who fought in the UFC (Ultimate Fighting Championship for MMA fighters). As I walked up the door of the gym, there was a fighter going in, and I looked for a patronizing hello from him, but instead he warmly greeted me with a sincere kindness as he walked in the door.

I was 56 years old when I started Brazilian Jiu Jitsu (BJJ), and was pleasantly surprised to find that the professors and coaches took me seriously. It was clear that I was physically fit, and I think that helped, but I had put on weight due to a thyroid problem, and it would have been easy for them to assume I wasn't going to do well. But they didn't seem to judge me at all, and welcomed me with open arms. I was super sore the first few weeks of training, and it took me a while to figure out my schedule. I was used to training anywhere from 10 to 15 hours a week for ultras, so I figured I could do the same with BJJ. That was not the case. But I quickly learned what would work and settled in at around six to eight hours of BJJ a week, with a few boxing and Muay Thai classes thrown in to boot.

There've been some tough times since I started BJJ, but it's been a great way to stay focused, feel strong and healthy, and show myself that I can get past my own mental pitfalls of pride, grief, sadness, fear, etc.

***

A few months after starting BJJ, I awoke to the vibration of my phone ringing on my bedside table. How many times had my tiny grandmother stepped on that table that looked like a set of mahogany steps, climbing down from her grand Chinese bed so many years ago? But now the phone was ringing on that same table, and I answered it in the dark, squinting into the backlight of the phone. It was Amaranta calling me to say she had almost died from an overdose of fentanyl. The words swirled through my head, banging into the shadowy figures of my dreams.

"What? Overdose? You overdosed? On what? How'd they find you? Are you okay? Yes, yes, I'll come get you. Where are you?"

I'd go pick her up, nurture her for two days, and she would escape into the mean streets again without a word. Days later, my son Josh would nod off at the wheel, probably on fentanyl too, and crash his car. The one I had gotten him to show him that I loved him, to say, "I believe in you, it's going to be all good. You can do this." Whatever this was. And after a while, I realized that the story had to change. That I could choose to live in constant reaction to my children's woes, or I could wake up to the life inside me that was happening, and I could choose that.

Two weeks later, I flew with Carmen to Mexico to see her dad at my step parents' house in San Jose del Cabo. And instead of joy, I spent seven days in the same bed with Carmen as she kicked a horrific fentanyl habit I knew nothing about, her aching body thrashing against me for days and nights. She would vomit all over me and the bed, and the warm Mexican air would whisper, "Let go. Let go. Let go," as Rancheras played off in the distance and a tuba belched intermittently.

There were birds in the overhead lamp, and they chirped when they shouldn't chirp, like when I was trying to call the States and my phone refused to work, like that nightmare I had over and over. . . the phone wouldn't work and I was dying, and it had to work, but it wouldn't. . . and these birds were chirping, chirping. How is it that something so precious as delicate new life can be such a burden in just the wrong moment?

CHAPTER 21
AND FINALLY

"Adversity is the path to truth." ~ *Lord Byron*

Life has a way of fooling you, and just when you think it can't get any worse, it straightens out. My mother has often talked about those who are "poor in poverty," meaning they who have not suffered are missing the contrast of pain and gratitude. How can one truly know gratitude without having suffered? And yet, don't we all suffer at some point?

Sometimes I have to get to that state of complete incomprehensible demoralization before I can grow beyond the hurt. I may have to curl up in the fetal position or loaf around sullenly on the couch for a little while, but I'll get there. Though I'm not prone to sulking, as I don't even suffer my own foolishness for very long. My childhood Snoopy is replaced by my little dog BooBoo who snooches down under my covers and sleeps between my feet, though every now and again she snooches into my pajama bottoms by mistake! And of course there's big giant Rumi, my Rottweiler and defender of the realm, who can't understand why he's not a lap dog too. And the millions of cats my grandmother "saved" are now replaced by two cool cats who side-eye me when I sit beside them, purring and wondering why I haven't yet bestowed great treasures upon them.

The key is not to quit before the miracle happens. Once when Lhasa was dying and I was fed up and furious with whatever created this blasted universe, a friend of mine asked, "Is there anything that might make you think that whatever created this universe, in all its complexity, is benevolent?" She waved her hand at the summer beauty around us, as birds chirped happily in the fluffy green trees and the warmth of the sun bathed our faces. I looked at her and softened, and tears ran down my face as I said, "Yes, I suppose you're right."

Lhasa herself even said one day when she was very sick, "I guess I have to say yes to whatever comes, even if it's my own death." After that, I would do my daily meditation, and at the end, I would stand up, open my arms to the sky, and say, "YES."

I picture my grandparents' lighthouse on Narragansett Bay, high above the stormy seas crashing on the rocky shores, the beacon of light shining across the waters, illuminating the way for the weary. The quiet loneliness of those walls didn't take away the purpose of the edifice. It still guided folks into home, to the warm embrace of loved ones.

My life is informed by both hardship and beauty, strength and wisdom, suffering and joy, lack and abundance. I once thought the Hewett School girls with their matching knee socks and penny loafers, fabulous hair, and doting parents had it all, but then it turned out that their gilded cages were often just cages. Glamor doesn't cover up for scanty inner resources. It can often make what's lacking in character protrude all the more like garish makeup on a miserable wretch who's trying too hard. And I see this over and over. Success, wealth, talent, skill—the world is full of more, bigger, better faster. But do you move people? Do you draw them to you with kindness and heart? Does your soul call out to them and warm them?

***

Now and again, people ask me about the scar on my face, or they're baffled by my intensity or my breadth of experience, and even at times they say, "You know, that's the kind of thing people lie about?"

When I swam in the frigid waters of Lake Coeur D'Alene during my Ironman attempt, and wondered if I had it in me, it wasn't that I knew I could do the whole thing; it was that I knew I could do the next stroke. And then that stroke informed the next one, and so on. And when I stepped on the mat for my first class of Jiu Jitsu feeling like a bug under glass, I knew I had a right to be there, to exist, to show up. I had lived for years with my grandmother telling me to disappear into the woodwork, and survived the soul-crushing juggernaut of neglect as a child. When I do hard things, I ask myself, "Why on earth would I not be able to survive this now?"

I wonder how you will receive this story, dear friends. You and I who are so alike and so different simultaneously.

FALLING UP FROM THE BOTTOM

I suppose you may both revile me and know me as you know yourself because I am I and we are we. Are we humans all together, just in different times, layer upon layer of life, wrinkles in time, floating above and into each other? We both know each other and are foreign. And the signs repeat themselves until all the lessons are learned a million times over and the pain and the joy become one and life explodes into the stars and we are reborn into another galaxy at another time, and then we are just one small atom in a sea of atoms and nothing means anything and it all means everything. Cartels and candy stores, kings and paupers, whores and lovers, me and you.

Climbing Prusik Peak in the Enchantments, Leavenworth, WA

SAMANTHA DE LA VEGA

A visit with my mother at the Towners house

Me in Bangor, ME circa 1973

My grandfather, John Wiley Hill (far right)

SAMANTHA DE LA VEGA

Ayin on tight wire

(Photo by Marie Clauzade)

FALLING UP FROM THE BOTTOM

Amaranta and Ayin, West Sand Lake, NY, 1998

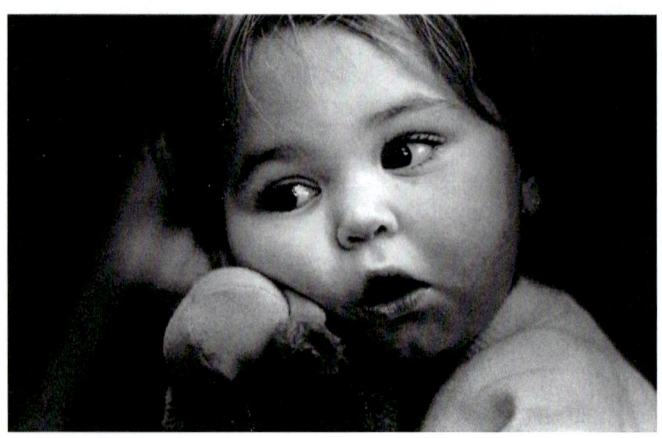

Simika

(Photo by Dale Dani)

SAMANTHA DE LA VEGA

Beloved Jim with a bunny made for me by my mother

FALLING UP FROM THE BOTTOM

Sky (Ibou) and Paco 2015

(Photo by Matthiew Hagene)

Grandma and Mama circa 1944

SAMANTHA DE LA VEGA

Grandma in America America

Ayin and me, Geneva, Switzerland, 1998

(Photo by Sotho Houle)

DEDICATION

I tell you my story to give voice to what happened, but also to let you know that no matter how dark things are, love wins. Courage, friends.

I dedicate this book to the all light givers in my life who have served as beacons when the dark was too dark. Biggest love to my mother for always bringing the original thought, standing for what is meaningful and true, and for ultimately saving my life. Love to my sister Gabriela who reminded me of who I was when I had forgotten; to my sisters Ayin, Sky, Lhasa, and Miriam for their wisdom, creativity, and courage; and to Mischa for always getting it, being inappropriate, and making me laugh. Love to Fernando for being there always. And love to my children for being the most wondrous, maddening, and beloved beings to come through me and explode into the world.

Special thanks to Lura Frazey for helping me get the book off the ground when I had tried so many times before, and for her wonderful research skills. And special thanks to Nick Jaina who gently supported me through the process of knowing just what I wanted to say and how I wanted to say it, and for his masterful work on the layout and cover for this book.